Canadian Fiction:
An Annotated Bibliography

Canadian Fiction

AN ANNOTATED BIBLIOGRAPHY

Margery Fee   Ruth Cawker

Peter Martin Associates Limited

The research for this project was funded by Opportunities for Youth, a Canada Council Explorations Grant and the Ontario Arts Council.

Canadian Cataloguing in Publication Data

Fee, Margery, 1948–
    Canadian fiction

ISBN 0-88778-134-9 bd. ISBN 0-88778-140-3 pa.
Includes indexes.

1. Canadian fiction (English) — Bibliography.*
I. Cawker, Ruth, 1953– II. Donald, Gail, 1941–
III. Title.

Z1377.F4F44   016.813   C76-017050-9

Design: Tim Wynne-Jones

PETER MARTIN ASSOCIATES LIMITED
35 BRITAIN STREET, TORONTO, CANADA M5A 1R7

United Kingdom: Books Canada, 1 Bedford Road, London N2, England.
United States: Books Canada, 33 East Tupper St., Buffalo, N.Y. 14203.

Acknowledgements

Marie Amyot, Peter Birdsall, Delores Broten, Maria del Junco, Anna Harvey, Brian Henderson, William Marsden and Amanda Stovell wrote annotations for the bibliography. Ben Shek of the University of Toronto and Jeannette Urbas of Glendon College, York University kindly provided comments on the translations from French. Thanks are due to Pierre Fortier, Richard Handscombe, Grace Jolley, Ann Mandel, and Michael Ondaatje of Glendon College, York University and to Eli Mandel of York University and Bill Mitchell of the Ontario Ministry of Education for their advice and encouragement. Dr. A. Tucker, former principal of Glendon College, York University kindly provided us with office space and encouragement. The members of CANLIT— Peter Birdsall, Delores Broten, Bart Higgins, and Sandra Stewart— gave generously of their time and energy in assisting us with the project. Gail Donald deserves special mention for editorial help. Finally we are indebted to all those Canadian scholars whose initial work in compiling Canadian bibliographies provided us with much basic information.

Contents

Introduction

We began this bibliography in a mood of incredulity. A friend who was surveying the teaching of Canadian literature in secondary schools assured us that there were no bibliographical guides designed specifically for teachers.[1] Since few of them had studied Canadian literature, they found it difficult to organize courses or find reference material, especially in isolated places. We couldn't believe that such bibliographies did not exist. After two weeks of hunting, several bibliographies were uncovered (they are annotated in the Secondary Sources section) but none were of much help to teachers in the selection of books. *Canadian Fiction* is designed to provide that help, although we hope it will also prove useful for librarians, students and those who simply read Canadian literature for pleasure. The bibliography makes no claim to be exhaustive. Despite the excellence of our source—the combined collections of the Toronto Public Library and the libraries of the University of Toronto, York University and the University of Alberta (Edmonton)—some books were impossible to locate. Apart from the limitations thus imposed upon us, there were several principles on which we based our selection of books to be included.

At least three major problems of definition face the compiler of a bibliography of Canadian adult fiction. The first has attracted the attention of many competent critics: who is a Canadian author and what is a Canadian novel?[2] The large core of works about which there is no doubt is surrounded by a hazy aureole where lurk expatriates, landed immigrants, tourists and natives who write novels indistinguishable from any produced in New York or London. No hard and fast rules have emerged from the controversy and it is to be confessed that this bibliography undoubtedly includes authors claimed by other countries for their own (e.g., Malcolm Lowry and Brian Moore). We sincerely hope that we have erred on the side of over-eager assimilation and have excluded few authors who have a genuine claim to be considered Canadian.

1. Sandra Stewart, *Course countdown: a quantitative study of Canadian literature in the nation's secondary schools* (Toronto: CANLIT, 1974).

2. Most of the works which discuss this question are listed in the Secondary Sources section. See Frye's *Bush Garden* (Toronto, 1971), Atwood's *Survival* (Toronto, 1972), Jones's *Butterfly on rock* (Toronto, 1970), Moss's *Patterns of isolation* (Toronto, 1974), and the introductions to Mandel's *Contexts of Canadian criticism* (Toronto, 1971) and Davey's *From there to here: a guide to English-Canadian literature since 1960: our nature/our voices*, volume II (Erin, Ont., 1974). Ronald Sutherland considers the issue in a comparative light in *Second image* (Toronto, 1971) and in an article, "The Mainstream", in *Canadian literature* 53 (Summer 1972), pp. 30-41.

The second problem concerns the title of the bibliography, since many works are included which are not, strictly speaking, fiction. Perhaps a better title would have been *Canadian literary prose*, if that didn't seem both confusing and pretentious. Northrop Frye, in his *Anatomy of criticism* (New York, 1957) argues that the words "fiction" and "novel" should be redefined or replaced, and suggests more accurate terms. Until such terms become general usage, however, this kind of prefatorial explanation must suffice. The simplest justification for the inclusion of "non-fiction" in this bibliography is that such works by Susanna Moodie, Emily Carr, Farley Mowat and John Glassco (among others) are frequently discussed in literature classes. These works often seem to deal with their subject and evoke responses in much the same manner as do works of fiction. The kinds of non-fiction included here most often are autobiography and fictionalized history.

It is also difficult to find a clear line of demarcation between adult and children's fiction. Nineteenth- and early twentieth-century authors rarely wrote anything that would offend Dickens's Podsnappian "young person" and were and are popular with all ages. The bibliography includes some works for children, especially those written before or around the turn of the century and those which appeal to a wider audience. Interestingly, the animal stories of Grey Owl, Seton, Roberts and, latterly, Burnford, Bodsworth and Mowat, all seem to have this ageless appeal.

The limited length of the annotations prevents a coherent justification for a critical judgement. Although the annotations are not intended to be purely objective, and vary in length and warmth according to the reviewer's interest, the sweeping one-sentence evaluation has been avoided in favour of description. We have tried to provide enough information to allow the user to decide which books will most likely suit his needs and tastes. Clearly, complex major works such as Leonard Cohen's *Beautiful losers,* Marie-Claire Blais's *A Season in the life of Emmanuel* and Malcolm Lowry's *Under the volcano* are served badly by short descriptive annotations. The bibliography should be seen for what it is—not an end, but a means to one. The end we hope it will serve is the wider reading and study of Canadian literature.

Although we have tried to organize the bibliography as sensibly as possible, a certain amount of preliminary clarification is necessary. Only authors who had at least one work in print during 1973 or 1974 are listed. (Occasionally these works have since gone out of print; we have retained those we thought valuable or likely to be soon reprinted.) Apart from the afore-mentioned exception, only in-print works are annotated. Bibliographical information for all out-of-print fiction works is listed, however, normally for the first edition.[3] The list of authors was compiled mainly from those included in *Canadian books in print 1973* and was subsequently brought up to date by the annotation of any further works appearing in *Canadian books in print 1974*. No fiction with a copyright date later than 1974 is listed or annotated, but an attempt has been made to list and annotate critical works issued in 1975 and 1976.

Bibliographical Format

The authors are listed alphabetically according to the author's last name. The items in each entry are listed in the following order:

1. Author's name. If an author has used a pseudonym for all works, his entry appears under the pseudonym.
2. Dates of author's birth and death, if available.
3. Title and sub-title. If the work is a translation from French, the English title is given first and is separated from the French title by a slash.
4. Date of first publication.
5. Series name or abbreviation (e.g., NCL—New Canadian Library), if applicable.
6. Names of translators or editors.
7. Place of publication, followed by the publisher's name. The place names in our entries are those used in the publishers' address list in *Canadian books in print*.
8. Date of the edition. Since the dates given in the British and American catalogues used (Whitaker's *British books in print* and Bowker's *Books in print*) are often those of the most recent printing rather than true dates of publication, we have not listed dates for British and American editions.
9. Binding—cloth (cl) and/or paper (pb)—and price (for books in print only). Price and binding are not given for American editions if there is a Canadian edition available. British bindings and prices are not given. Prices are subject to change and should always be checked with the publisher.
10. International standard book number. ISBNs are given for Canadian editions only, where available, and are enclosed in square brackets. They are useful for ordering purposes since they identify a particular edition and binding. (The Standard Book Numbering Agency, R.R.

---

3. Most of our information for out-of-print titles up to 1960 came from R.D. Watter's monumental *Check list of Canadian literature and background materials 1628-1960* (Toronto, 1972). Michael Gnarowski's *Concise bibliography of English-Canadian literature* (Toronto, 1973), and the annual lists of *Canadian literature* were helpful, up to 1970. Then we relied on the bibliographies in the *Journal of Canadian fiction*, and finally when all else failed, the catalogue of the University of Toronto libraries and the printed catalogues of the Library of Congress and the British Museum.

Bowker Company, 1180 Avenue of the Americas, New York 10036, provides information concerning the function, history and use of these numbers.)

11. Out-of-print books are designated o/p. If a book is in print but was unobtainable, it is marked "not seen".

12. Annotation. If several books are annotated collectively, asterisks are attached to the annotation and the relevant titles.

13. Critical books, biographies and collections of letters. If in print, critical books and biographies are annotated.

14. Multi-media materials.

15. Abbreviations of relevant secondary source titles. If one of the following secondary sources contains an entry for an author, the abbreviation of its title (see abbreviations, p.xiii) is the final item to appear in our entry: Michael Gnarowski's *Concise bibliography of English-Canadian literature,* Brita Mickleburgh's *Canadian literature, Canadian writers,* edited by Guy Sylvestre, Carl Klinck and Brandon Conron, J. Raymon Brazeau's *Contemporary French-Canadian literature,* Clara Thomas's *Our nature/our voices: a guidebook to English-Canadian literature,* volume I, Frank Davey's *From there to here: a guide to English-Canadian literature since 1960: our nature/ our voices,* volume II, Norah Story's *Oxford companion to Canadian history and literature* and the *Supplement* to the latter work edited by William Toye. All give useful bibliographical, biographical or critical information and are themselves annotated in the Secondary Sources section.

Abbreviations

ABCS	*A Book of Canadian stories*
Abr.	Abridged
BCP	*The Book of Canadian prose* vol. 1
CB	*A Concise bibliography of English-Canadian literature*, Michael Gnarowski
CBL	Canadian best-seller library (McClelland & Stewart)
CFS	Canadian favourites series (McClelland & Stewart)
CL	*Canadian literature: two centuries in prose.* Brita Mickleburgh
cl	cloth
CSS	*Canadian short stories*
CSS2	*Canadian short stories*, 2nd series
CSS(K)	*The Canadian short story*
CV	*Contemporary voices: the short story in Canada*
CVCW	Critical views on Canadian writers (McGraw-Hill Ryerson)
CW	*Canadian Writers/Ecrivains canadiens*, Sylvestre, Carl Klinck and Brandon Conron, eds.
CWS	Canadian writers series (McClelland & Stewart
CWT	*Canadian winter's tales*
CWW	Canadian writers and their work series (Forum House)
dist.	distributor
FC	*Contemporary French Canadian literature*, J. Raymond Brazeau
FSH	*Fourteen stories high: best Canadian stories of 1971*
FWCS	French writers of Canada series (Harvest House)
GCSS	*Great Canadian short stories*
ISBN	International standard book number
K	*Kaleidescope*
KI	*Klanak Islands: eight short stories*
LL	Laurentian library (Macmillan)
MCS	*Modern Canadian stories*
NCL	New Canadian library (McClelland & Stewart)
NV	*The Narrative voice: short stories and reflections by Canadian authors*
ON	*Our nature-our voices: A guidebook to English-Canadian literature*, Clara Thomas
ON2	*From here to there: Our nature our voices volume 2: a guide to English-Canadian literature since 1960.* Frank Davey
o/p	out of print
OX	*The Oxford companion to Canadian history and literature*, Norah Story
OX2	*Supplement to the Oxford companion to Canadian history and literature*, William Toye, ed.
pb	paper bound
pseud.	pseudonym
SBT	*Sixteen by twelve*
SCL	Studies in Canadian literature series (Copp Clark)
72 NCS	*72: New Canadian stories*
73 NCS	*73: New Canadian stories*
74 NCS	*74: New Canadian stories*
SFAC	*Stories from Atlantic Canada*
SFO	*Stories from Ontario*
SFPAC	*Stories from Pacific and Arctic Canada*
SFQ	*Stories from Quebec*
SFWC	*Stories from Western Canada*
SHC	Social history of Canada (University of Toronto Press)
SMC	Saint Martin's Classics (Macmillan)
TCE	*The Canadian experience*
TSSF	*The Story so far*
TSSF2	*The Story so far 2*
TSSF3	*The Story so far 3*
TS	*Tigers of the snow*
WS	*Winnipeg Stories*

Secondary Sources

This section annotates works which are useful in the teaching and study of fiction and fiction writers. It includes collections of critical articles concerning several authors, literary histories, bibliographies, biographical dictionaries, literary periodicals, general critical works and works about multi-media materials.

I. Bibliographic Sources

Bell, Inglis F., and Gallup, Jennifer. **A Reference guide to English, American and Canadian literature: an annotated checklist of bibliographical and other reference materials.** Vancouver: University of British Columbia Press, 1971. cl $7.00 [0-7748-0002-X] ; pb $3.50 [0-7748-0003-8].

Although this is a useful guide for an undergraduate student of English, most of the Canadian sources listed are easily found elsewhere.

Canadiana. The National Library. Ottawa: Queen's Printer, 1950—

This catalogue lists those publications of Canadian origin and interest received by the National Library. Its organization has undergone several changes since its origin in 1950. Now appearing monthly, it separates federal and provincial government documents from each other, as well as from the many categories of trade publications. Other categories are monographs, theses, periodicals, brochures, sound recordings, and films. Entries are in English or French, depending on the language of any given publication. The listings are of current publications; each annual index cumulates the new publications issued during its respective year. Literature entries indicate genre, along with other bibliograpical information.

Cotnam, Jacques. **Contemporary Quebec: an analytical bibliography.** Toronto: McClelland & Stewart, 1973. pb $2.95 [0-7710-2249-2].

Although this bibliography includes works about all aspects of contemporary Quebec, its section on literature is quite comprehensive. It has these headings: "Theatre", "Criticism", "Poetry", "Fiction", "Bibliographies", "Present state of research", "Histories and surveys" and "Books on various aspects of Quebec literature and its different genres". It also lists English translations of literary works.

Fulford, Robert; Godfrey, David; and Rotstein, Abraham, eds. **Read Canadian: a book about Canadian books.** Toronto: James, Lewis and Samuel, 1972. cl $7.00 [0-88862-018-7] ; pb $1.95 [0-88862-019-5].

This book is a guide for the serious non-academic reader in Canadian literature, art, history, economics, politics, sociology and publishing. The editors have solicited experts in these various fields to write articles which serve as introductions, suggest a variety of approaches to the subject and include a bibliography of relevant Canadian books.

Gnarowski, Michael. **A Concise bibliography of English-Canadian literature.** Toronto: McClelland & Stewart, 1973. cl $5.95 [0-7710-3361-3] ; pb $3.95 [0-7710-3360-5].

This bibliography is very selective since it attempts to include every notable Canadian writer of each genre from the eighteenth century to the 1970s. Basically, a straightforward list of authors, with their works and selected criticism (reviews, articles and books), it includes many early authors who are out of print and lists their first editions. This is a useful general bibliography for the high school teacher or undergraduate, as well as for those engaged in more detailed bibliographical work.

Gnarowski, Michael. **Theses and dissertations in Canadian literature (English): a preliminary check list.** Ottawa: Golden Dog, 1975. pb $3.50 [0-919614-12-4]. Not seen.

Lochhead, Douglas. **Bibliography of Canadian bibliographies.** 2nd ed. rev. & enl. Toronto: University of Toronto Press, 1972. cl $20.00 [0-8020-1865-3].

This is a recent revision of Raymond Tanghe's earlier work. Listed alphabetically by name of compiler or institution, both English and French bibliographies are included. An index gives subject headings, compilers and information on location. This is a useful source for regional bibliographies.

Moyles, R.G., and Siemens, Catharine. **English-Canadian literature: a student guide and annotated bibliography.** Edmonton: Athabascan Publishing Co., 1972. pb $1.50.

This hard to find but invaluable booklet attempts to provide "a systematic and comprehensive guide to locating both *primary* (creative works) and *secondary* (critical) materials" in English-Canadian literature. Chapter I presents a selective list of titles and sources for reading. Chapter II deals with secondary sources of information including biography, literary history and encyclopedic sources, and a selected list of studies in related fields such as linguistics and folklore.

Newman, Maureen and Stratford, Philip. **Bibliography of Canadian books in translation: French to English and English to French / Bibliographie de livres canadiens traduits de l'anglais au français et du français à l'anglais.** Ottawa: Humanities Research Council of Canada, 1975. pb free.

This bibliography, the most comprehensive of its kind, includes titles in literature, the arts and the humanities. The titles are divided into generic categories, e.g., fiction, essays, bibliographies, etc. Translators and authors are indexed. Translations in progress are listed, and the compilers intend to update the bibliography periodically.

Pluscauscas, Martha, ed. **Canadian books in print.** Toronto: University of Toronto Press, annual, 1967–. cl $25.00 1976 [0-8020-4521-9].

Owned by most Canadian libraries and bookstores, *Canadian books in print* attempts to list all the in-print titles produced by Canadian-based publishers. It excludes books by Canadian authors published outside Canada. (See: *Canadiana, Books in print, Paper bound books in print,* and *British books in print.*) It includes French titles only if they are produced by publishers who produce mainly English language titles. (For French titles, see *Répertoire de l'édition au Québec.*) It has author, title and publisher indexes and for each title gives the author, publisher, date of publication, binding, price and International Standard Book Number.

Pluscauskas, Martha, ed. **Subject guide to Canadian books in print.** Toronto: University of Toronto Press, annual. 1974–. cl $35.00. 1976 [0-8020-4520-0].

This companion subject guide to *Canadian books in print* is produced annually. All books listed in *Canadian books in print* are listed under subject headings based on the Library of Congress *List of subject heads* and the supplementary Canadian list produced by the Canadian Library Association. It is particularly useful to teachers of Canadian literature as it lists Canadian literature separately by genre, eg., "Literature—Canadian—Drama"; "Literature—Canadian—Drama Collections". Under the heading "Literature—Notes and Questions", teaching and learning guides are listed. There is a separate section on children's literature. Occasionally titles are listed under the wrong heading.

Rome, David. **Jews in Canadian literature: a bibliography.** Rev. ed. Montreal: Canadian Jewish Congress and Jewish Public Library, 1964. 2 vols. o/p.

Rome, David. **Recent Canadian Jewish authors and la langue française.** Montreal: The Bronfman Collection of Jewish Canadiana at the Jewish Public Library, 1970. pb $5.00.(Supplementary to Rome, David, **Jews in Canadian literature.**)

This bibliography extensively annotates publications by Jewish Canadian authors whose work has come into prominence since 1964 when Rome's *Jews in Canadian literature,* now out of print, appeared. Rome also annotates publications by French-Canadian authors whose work deals with Jewish themes.

Tougas, Gerard. **A Check list of printed materials relating to French-Canadian literature.** 2nd ed. rev. & enl. Vancouver: U.B.C. Library, 1973. cl $9.50 [0-7748-0007-0].

A check list of all University of British Columbia holdings in French Canadian literature, this bilingual collection includes all literary forms and related materials such as folklore, travellers' chronicles, and parliamentary speeches.

Urbas, Jeannette. **Thirty acres to modern times: an introduction to French-Canadian literature.** Scarborough, Ont.: McGraw-Hill Ryerson, 1976. pb $4.95 [0-07-82323-5].

This critical work is intended to give the reader a unified view of French-Canadian literature in translation. Concentrating mainly on the novel, Urbas traces the parallels between the novel and society in their development in focus from fidelity to the land to revolution. Authors discussed are: Louis Hémon, Félix Antoine, Ringuet, Germaine Guèvremont, Roger Lemelin, Gabrielle Roy, Robert Elie, Yves Thériault, Gérard Bessette, Claire Martin, Anne Hébert, Marie-Claire Blais, Réjean Ducharme, Jacques Ferron, Jacques Godbout, Hubert Aquin, Claude Jasmin and Roch Carrier.

Watters, R.E. **A Check list of Canadian literature and background materials 1628-1960.** Rev. ed. Toronto: University of Toronto Press, 1972. cl $30.00 [0-8020-1866-1]

This check list is the best source of complete bibliographic material up to 1960. Part I records all titles of poetry, fiction, and drama. Part II contains a selective list of books by Canadians useful to students of Canadian literature or culture. This section includes material such as biography, literary criticism, scholarship, local history, and religion. Entries are coded for their library availability in Canada.

Watters, R.E., and Bell, I.F. **On Canadian literature 1806-1960.** Toronto: University of Toronto Press, 1966. cl $8.50 [0-8020-5166-9].

The title page identifies this as a "check list of articles, books, and theses on English-Canadian literature, its authors and language". Part I contains bibliographies, and background materials on literature in generic categories that include songs, folklore, and journalism, as well as poetry, fiction, and drama. Part II contains works on individual authors.

II. Historical and Biographical Sources:

Creative Canada: a biographical dictionary of twentieth century creative and performing artists. Comp. by the Reference Division, McPherson Library, University of Victoria, B.C. Toronto: University of Toronto Press, 1971; 1972— 2 vols. cl $15.00. Vol. I [0-8020-3262-1]; Vol. II [0-8020-3285-0].

Each volume contains a selective list of Canadians involved in various areas of the arts. Writers make up about 28 percent of the first two volumes. The entries are arranged alphabetically and include biographic and bibliographic details. Although the method of selection is fairly arbitrary it allows for the development of comprehensive coverage in each category as compilation continues, and the cumulative index should make it easy to locate individual artists. The third volume is forthcoming.

Dictionary of Canadian biography / Dictionnaire biographique du Canada. Toronto: University of Toronto Press, 1966—.

This detailed and scholarly reference book is intended, when finished, to be of the same standard as the British *Dictionary of national biography* and the *Dictionary of American biography*. It is arranged chronologically. To date, the following volumes have been issued:

I. 1000-1700. Brown, G. and Trudel, Marcel, eds. 1966. cl $20.00 [0-8020-3142-0].
II. 1701-1740. Hayne, David and Vachon, André, eds. 1969. cl $20.00 [0-8020-3240-0].
X. 1871-1880. La Terreur, Marc, ed. 1972. cl $20.00 [0-8020-3287-7].
III. 1741-1770. Halpenny, Frances S.G., ed. 1975. cl $20.00 [0-8020-3314-8].

The remaining volumes will be issued in order by year. The date of death of the subject determines in which volume he will be listed. A list of courses is given after each entry. Each volume ends with a general indexed bibliography including locations of sources.

Encyclopedia Canadiana. 1957. Toronto: Grolier, 1972. 10 vols. cl $139.50 [0-7172-1601-2].

First produced in 1957, the *Encyclopedia Canadiana* is owned by most high school and public libraries. Unfortunately it is very out-of-date—especially the photographs. Some articles have been updated to 1971, including "Literary awards", "Literature—English language, French language, and other than English". Most recent authors are not mentioned. This encyclopedia is of little value to the student of Canadian literature as most of its information can be found elsewhere.

Klinck, Carl F., gen. ed. **Literary history of Canada: Canadian literature in English.** University of Toronto Press, 1965. cl $25.00 [0-8020-5147-2].

This comprehensive and pioneer history although occasionally pedantic contains information impossible to find elsewhere. It is a compilation of several hands, covering literature and related writing. Also included are essays on the development of Canadian language and the state of Canadian publishing. The book is divided into four sections chronologically, beginning with an interesting section on Old World conceptions of Canada in literature from the Elizabethans to the early 1800s. The second section deals with the writing during settlement and development of nationhood. The final period, from 1920-1960, is dealt with in terms of individual authors. There is a brief, highly selective bibliography.

Mickleburgh, Brita, ed. **Canadian literature: two centuries in prose.** Fwd., Malcolm Ross. Toronto: McClelland & Stewart, 1973. pb $3.95

This useful collection of prose fiction excerpts is arranged in chronological order beginning with the work of Frances Brooke and ending with that of Margaret Laurence. Included with the excerpts are biographical and in most cases critical introductions. There is also a brief bibliography at the end of each piece. The book is particularly valuable as a means of examining potential teaching material.

Story, Norah. **The Oxford companion to Canadian history and literature.** Toronto: Oxford University Press, 1967. cl $22.50 [0-19-540115-8].

This invaluable work contains biographical sketches of both English and French Canadian writers of fiction up to 1966. Its supplement (See Toye, William, gen. ed., *Supplement to the Oxford companion to Canadian history and literature*) includes books published to 1972. Each article offers brief comments on the themes of the writer's books, and often includes plot summaries. No critical observations are given. It contains an article on Canadian literature (short stories included) which provides a rough chronological list of books published throughout the history of Canadian literature, and comments in a very broad sense on their historical importance. Its scope is very wide and it is a good source of obscure biographical and bibliographical information.

Sylvestre, Guy; Conron, Brandon; and Klinck, Carl F., eds. **Canadian writers / Ecrivains canadiens.** 2nd ed. rev. & enl. Toronto: Ryerson, 1966. o/p.

This is a biographical dictionary of French and English Canadian critics, poets, novelists and short story writers. Contained in each entry are brief descriptions of the author's works, including plot and theme summaries. The book offers a short bibliography of poetry and short story anthologies, critical material and reference books. It also supplies an index of titles and a chronological table of publications ranging from 1608 to 1960. Articles on French language authors are in French. Although *Canadian writers* includes authors not discussed elsewhere, it is somewhat out-of-date.

Sylvestre, Guy, ed. **Manitoba authors / Ecrivains du Manitoba.** Ottawa: National Library, 1970. Free.

Written in both French and English, this slim volume contains short annotations on history, fiction and poetry by authors who lived in Manitoba. It also annotates, though very scantily, any translations of these books into English, French or German. In addition it offers short notes on the locations of manuscripts and unpublished works. Catalogue #SN 3-1170. Free on application to National Library, 395 Wellington St., Ottawa K1A ON4; Attention: Public Relations Office.

Thomas, Clara. **Our nature/our voices: a guide book to English-Canadian literature.** Vol. I. Toronto: New Press, 1972. pb $3.75 [0-88770-619-3].

This guide is divided into three sections: "The Settlement to 1867", "Canada and the empire: Confederation to World War I" and "The Modern period 1918-1970". Under each author's name is a biographical sketch and a description of his or her works. The entries include brief bibliographies and are often illustrated, usually with photographs of the author. A useful guide for the high school student or teacher. (See Davey, Frank, ON2, vol.II, p.6.)

Tougas, Gérard. **History of French-Canadian literature.** 2nd ed. Tr., Alta Lind Cook. Toronto: Ryerson, 1966. o/p.

This detailed literary history is somewhat out-of-date now, but it is the only work of its scope in English about French-Canadian literature. It covers the early periods well, and contains a chapter on the relationship between French-Canadian literature and French literature and culture.

Toye, William, gen. ed. **Supplement to the Oxford companion to Canadian history and literature.** 1967-1972. Toronto: Oxford University Press, 1973. cl $9.50 [0-19-54020-7].

The *Oxford companion* was published in 1967; the *Supplement* covers the years from 1967 to 1972. It includes articles of new or newly-prominent authors and revised or additional articles on authors included in the *Companion* who are still publishing.

Waterston, Elizabeth. **Survey: a short history of Canadian literature.** Methuen Canadian Literature Series. Toronto: Methuen, 1973. cl $8.50 [0-458-9050-5]; pb $4.75 [0-458-90930-0].

This is a series of short, interlocked essays, arranged chronologically, on the sources, developments and themes of Canadian writing. Each of the eight chapters ends with a bibliography under topic headings for further study, including information on mixed-media resources. A survey chart gives across-the-page readings of historical and literary events in Canada, and literary events abroad. An elegantly-produced book, which gives an impressionistic view of the development of Canadian literature, this would serve as a good introduction and source book for the whole field.

III. General Critical Works:

Atwood, Margaret. **Survival: a thematic guide to Canadian literature.** Toronto: Anansi, 1972. cl $8.50 [0-88784-713-7] ; pb $3.25 [0-88784-613-0].

Survival has been criticized from both extremes of the academic spectrum—conservative and left-wing—for the same thing: over-simplification. Atwood does not claim to cover all of Canadian literature, but somehow the impression is left that all worthwhile Canadian literature fits into her thesis. Nevertheless, *Survival* provides a good stimulus for discussion. The bibliographies and appendices are very useful.

Brazeau, J. Raymond. **An Outline of contemporary French-Canadian literature.** Toronto: Forum House, 1972. pb $1.50 [no ISBN].

Despite its brevity, this book reveals a broad knowledge of French-Canadian literature. Brazeau studies ten authors: Léo Paul Desrosiers, Gabrielle Roy, Yves Thériault, Gerard Bessette, Claire Martin, Anne Hébert, Hubert Aquin, Claude Jasmin, Marie-Claire Blais and Gilles Vigneault. A bibliography of works by and about each author is provided, as well as a brief biography. Brazeau examines each author's works in the light of a particular viewpoint or theme to prevent the discussion from becoming diffuse. In his introduction he gives a history of French-Canadian literature and a bibliography of relevant critical works in French.

Cameron, Donald. **Conversations with Canadian novelists.** Toronto: Macmillan, 1973. cl $11.95 [0-7705-0890-1] ; pb vol. I $3.95 [0-7705-0942-8] ; pb vol. II $3.95 [0-7705-1008-6].

In these interviews, Cameron focuses on what he feels to be the important aspects of an author's work, be it regionalism or surrealism. The result is some very interesting conversations. Although this book and Graeme Gibson's *Eleven Canadian novelists* overlap occasionally, the interviews cover different ground. A photograph, biographical note and list of works accompanies each interview. Novelists interviewed in volume I: Ernest Buckler, Roch Carrier, Robertson Davies, Timothy Findley, Harold Horwood, Robert Kroetsch, Margaret Laurence, Jack Ludwig, Hugh MacLennan, David Lewis Stein. Novelists interviewed in volume II: George Bowering, Morley Callaghan, Dave Godfrey, W.O. Mitchell, Brian Moore, Martin Myers, Mordecai Richler, Gabrielle Roy, Rudy Wiebe.

Davey, Frank. **From there to here: a guide to English-Canadian literature since 1960: our nature/our voices.** Vol. II. Erin, Ont.: Press Porcépic, 1974. cl $13.95 [0-88878-036-2] ; pb $4.95 [0-88878-037-0].

Rather than sharing volume I's historical orientation, volume II of *Our nature/ our voices* is arranged like a dictionary, alphabetically by author, and is concerned with evaluative-descriptive criticism. The writers included are English-Canadian "post-moderns", those whose work has been important or influential since 1960. Photographs and bibliographies supplement each entry. An appendix gives a helpful bibliography of contemporary anthologies. The introduction offers critical alternatives to the thematic approaches which have dominated Canadian criticism. Davey proceeds to discuss the work of previously neglected writers like Bissett, Coleman, McFadden and Nichol with respect and critical acuteness. Though idiosyncratic in some judgments, Davey has assembled vast amounts of material in a highly accessible format. (See Thomas, Clara, *ON*, vol. I, p.5.)

Dorsinville, Max. **Caliban without Prospero: an essay on Quebec and Black literature.** Erin, Ont.: Press Porcepic, 1974. cl $13.95 [0-88878-034-6] ; pb $6.95 [0-88878-035-4].

Dorsinville uses the relationship between the "barbaric" Caliban and the cosmopolitan Prospero in Shakespeare's *The Tempest* as a metaphor to explain the relationship between "minor" ("post-European" in Dorsinville's terms) cultures and literature and the "mainstream". His emphasis is on the parallels in the development of Black American and Quebec literature and culture, illuminated by examples from the Third World. He discusses the possibility of discovering a common distinctive set of qualities shared by literatures written outside the dominant European and American traditions.

Egoff, Sheila. **The Republic of childhood: a critical guide to Canadian children's literature.** Toronto: Oxford University Press, 1967. pb $3.50 [0-19-540150-6]; rev. ed. 1975 (not seen).

Egoff describes books suitable for children aged ten to twelve, written by Canadian authors or by long-term residents. Sample chapter headings are: "Indian legends"; "Fantasy and folk and fairy tales"; "Stories: outdoor, adventure, mystery, city life, career, sports". Each chapter contains a critical discussion of the material followed by an annotated list of titles. There are also chapters on illustration and design and early Canadian children's books, a bibliography of children's literature in general, and a list of winners of the Book of the Year Award. In her final chapter, Egoff compares Canadian children's literature with British and American children's literature and briefly outlines its history.

Frye, Northrop. **The Bush garden: essays on the Canadian imagination.** Toronto: Anansi, 1971. cl $7.50 [0-88784-707-2]; pb $3.50 [0-88784-620-3].

Northrop Frye's ability as a critic has meant that even a collection including many reviews written for the *University of Toronto quarterly* between 1950 and 1959 has had an enormous impact on subsequent Canadian criticism. Much of Frye's concern in the short theoretical sections of the work is with culture and geography and their effect on literature. His idea of the "garrison mentality" has been expanded on by several later writers as has his idea of the pastoral as the central Canadian poetic myth. An essential work for any student of Canadian criticism, and an interesting one for the student of poets of the fifties.

Gibson, Graeme. **Eleven Canadian novelists.** Toronto: Anansi, 1972. cl $10.50 [0-88784-712-9]; pb $4.50 [0-88784-714-5].

This series of interviews gives readable outlines of the ideas of several English-Canadian authors concerning their lives and works. Questions such as "What is the role of the novelist in society?" are asked of: Margaret Atwood, Austin Clarke, Matt Cohen, Marian Engel, Timothy Findley, Dave Godfrey, Margaret Laurence, Jack Ludwig, Alice Munro, Mordecai Richler, and Scott Symons.

Jones, D.G. **Butterfly on rock: a study of themes and images in Canadian literature.** Toronto: University of Toronto Press, 1970. cl $10.00 [0-8020-6189-9]; pb $3.50 [0-8020-5230-4].

This work is a thematic study of primarily English-Canadian literature with emphasis on the poetry since 1880. Taking a "cultural and psychological" approach, as opposed to the "purely aesthetic or literary", Jones follows in Frye's footsteps, enlarging the Frygian idea of the "garrison mentality" in Canadian literature. He traces the theme of rational Western man against chaotic nature and looks at the possibilities, expressed in the literature, of overcoming this conflict by going into and accepting the wilderness. According to Jones, the result is wholeness of vision and the ability to make the wilderness vocal. Though this book offers interesting insights into much Canadian poetry and fiction, the general argument is obscured by the author's tendency to rely on idiosyncratic associations rather than on clearly defined terms as a basis for discussion.

Mandel, Eli, ed. **Contexts of Canadian criticism.** Toronto: University of Toronto Press, 1971. cl $11.75 [0-8020-1779-7]; pb $3.45 [0-8020-1780-0].

Represented in this solid collection of criticism is a wide range of outlook and style, from E.K. Brown to Marshall McLuhan. Mandel attempts to cover three main approaches to Canadian literature: the socio-historical, the formal and theoretical, and the developmental. In reality the contexts are "all those . . . within which discussion of literature takes place". Mandel's introduction gives a history of Canadian criticism and asks the questions which need to be answered by future critics and literary theorists. There is a useful bibliography. *Contexts* is an essential work for the serious student of Canadian criticism.

McCourt, Edward A. **The Canadian west in fiction.** Rev. ed. Toronto: McGraw-Hill Ryerson, 1970. pb $3.25 [0-7700-6037-4].

McCourt takes an historical approach to western fiction, dealing at length with Ralph Connor, Frederick Niven, Frederick Philip Grove, Nellie McClung, Arthur Stringer, Robert Stead, Sinclair Ross, W.O. Mitchell, Margaret Laurence, and to a lesser extent with Laura Goodman Salverson, Edmund Collins, Vera Lysenko, Rudy Wiebe, and Adele Wiseman. McCourt closes his short, highly readable book with a provocative hypothesis about the future of art and the possibility of myth in Prairie society.

MacCulloch, Clare. **The Neglected genre: the short story in Canada.** Guelph: Alive Press, 1973. pb $2.95 [0-919568-14-9].

Although the title accurately defines the state of short-story criticism in this country, MacCulloch's book makes only a little headway in a vast area. With reference to nine short stories, eight brief chapters establish chronological stages in the development of the genre in Canadian literary history. The state of modern criticism is glanced at, and suggestions are made for the establishment of a programme of teaching. Many interesting points are raised, though discussion is too sketchy to be very useful.

Moss, John. **Patterns of isolation in English Canadian fiction.** Toronto: McClelland & Stewart, 1974. pb $4.95 [0-7710-6568-X].

Moss expands Frye's term "garrison mentality" and integrates it into a series of "exiles" which he feels are central themes of Canadian literature: garrison, frontier, colonial, and immigrant. He devotes chapters to the theme of the Indian lover, the bastard and the fool saint in Canadian literature as well as examining the "geophysical" imagination in such authors as Thomas Raddall, Ethel Wilson, Sinclair Ross, Sheila Watson, and Charles Bruce. He examines irony in Grove, Garner, MacLennan, Buckler, Richler and Laurence. Moss's thesis seems weaker than his insight into individual novels. His "patterns of isolation" seem a feasible but not inevitable way of organizing Canadian literature.

New, William H. **Articulating west: essays on purpose and form in modern Canadian literature.** Toronto: New Press, 1972. cl $7.50 [0-88770-704-1].

A collection of essays, written over a period of five years, on Canadian fiction and poetry, *Articulating west* uses the terms "east" and "west" to represent settled static order and imaginative "mythic potential" respectively. The central weakness of the book is that the introduction sets out a thesis which is only superficially carried through in the remainder of the work. New devotes chapters to Frederick Niven, Carol Cassidy, E.J. Pratt, W.O. Mitchell, Sinclair Ross, Ethel Wilson, Hugh MacLennan, Mordecai Richler, Robert Kroetsch, Malcolm Lowry, Margaret Laurence, Margaret Avison, Earle Birney, and groups of other poets and novelists.

Pacey, Desmond. **Creative writing in Canada: a short history of English-Canadian literature.** 2nd ed. rev. & enl. Toronto: Ryerson, 1968. pb $3.75 [0-770-6023-4].

Although the author states that he is essentially interested in considering the quality of Canadian writing, he makes little or no attempt at evaluation. The book is thus mainly descriptive, detailing the history of Canadian literature since 1750. It is useful in specific areas and as a general introduction to Canadian fiction. Clearly marked historical and regional divisions are made which contain useful biographical and literary information.

Pacey, Desmond. **Essays in Canadian criticism 1938-1968.** Rev. ed. Toronto: Ryerson, 1969. cl $7.95 [0-7700-0289-7].

This collection of Pacey's essays on Canadian literature, written between 1938 and 1969, includes articles on Frederick Philip Grove, Stephen Leacock, Charles G.D. Roberts and Leonard Cohen. Other articles concentrate on the novel, literary criticism in Canada, and Canadian literature in the fifties, concluding with a short piece speculating on the future of Canadian literature. The essays are primarily descriptive, with few serious attempts to evaluate the works discussed.

Ricou, Laurence. **Vertical man/horizontal world: man and landscape in Canadian Prairie fiction.** Vancouver: University of British Columbia Press, 1973. cl $8.00 [0-7748-0022-4]; pb $4.50 [0-7748-0023-2].

In his study of Prairie fiction, Ricou sees the relationship between Western man and his environment as the central unifying factor. He concentrates on the works of Robert Stead, F.P. Grove, Martha Ostenso, Sinclair Ross, and W.O. Mitchell. Although the book's style is readable, Ricou tends to see all Prairie fiction as somehow fitting into his thesis. In some cases the connection is weak. The book does provide a generally useful study of the Prairie writer. There is a bibliography of Prairie fiction and of miscellaneous books and articles dealing with regionalism in literature.

Shek, Ben-Zion. **Social realism in the French-Canadian novel. 1944-1969.** Montreal: Harvest House, 1976. cl $12.50 [0-88772-150-8]. Not seen.

Smith, A.J.M. **Masks of fiction: Canadian critics on Canadian prose.** NCL. Toronto: McClelland & Stewart, 1961. pb $2.25 [0-7710-9502-3].

Although somewhat out-of-date, this collection of critical essays provides a solid and useful background to some of Canadian fiction's mainstream writers. Thomas Haliburton, Susanna Moodie, Stephen Leacock, Morley Callaghan, Malcolm Lowry, A.M. Klein, and Robertson Davies are discussed by well-known critics. Semi-autobiographical essays are provided by Frederick Philip Grove, Ethel Wilson and Hugh MacLennan. Also included is E.K. Brown's classic article on the problems of Canadian identity and Canadian literature.

Smith, A.J.M. **Towards a view of Canadian letters: selected critical essays, 1928-1971.** Vancouver: University of British Columbia Press, 1973. cl $9.00 [0-7748-0019-4]; pb $5.50 [0-7748-0020-8].

This selection, which contains both essays and some of the many introductions Smith has written to anthologies, is historically interesting and critically useful. Individual poets such as E.J. Pratt, F.R. Scott, Earle Birney, Anne Wilkinson, Margaret Avison and P.K. Page are discussed. The various "polemics" give a sense of the movement of Canadian literature out of obscurity.

Stevens, Donald G., ed. **Writers of the Prairies.** Canadian Literature Series. Vancouver: University of British Columbia Press, 1973. pb $5.50 [0-7748-0021-6].

A collection of essays on Prairie fiction, this book offers criticism on major writers as well as biographical articles on some authors and autobiographical pieces by Margaret Laurence and Rudy Wiebe. The essays provide a good introduction to the major critics of Prairie fiction, although some of the articles are very academic in tone. The authors discussed are Ralph Connor, Robert J.C. Stead, Martha Ostenso, F.P. Grove, Adele Wiseman, W.O. Mitchell, Robert Kroetsch, Gabrielle Roy, Margaret Laurence and Sinclair Ross.

Sutherland, Ronald. **Second image: comparative studies in Quebec/Canadian literature.** Toronto: New Press, 1971. cl $7.50 [0-88770-047-0] ; pb $3.95 [0-88770-048-9].

Sutherland's basic thesis is that there are as many similarities as differences in French- and English-Canadian literature. He feels part of this is due to shared geographical and economic circumstances and also to equally repressive religions— Protestant Calvinism and Catholic Jansenism. He also discusses race, separatism, child narrators and attitudes to changing morality in both literatures, examining many important authors en route. There is a short chapter on translation and a bibliography which includes translated novels. This is a useful beginning in comparative Canadian literature.

Warwick, Jack. **The Long journey: literary themes of French Canada.** Toronto: University of Toronto Press, 1968. cl $10.00 [0-8020-5198-7].

The role of *"le nord"* or the equally ambiguous *"pays en haut"* in French-Canadian literature is studied in this work through early historical documents, its geography in reality and the imagination, and in terms of literary responses to it. Conflicting visions of the north as, on the one hand, a place of freedom, even licence, and on the other as the locale for conversion and settlement make this book an interesting one for both the historian and the critic. Warwick relates the many journeys to the north in French-Canadian literature to the ideals of cultural stability and survival and the opposed ones of individual freedom and revolt.

Wilson, Edmund. **O Canada: an American's notes on Canadian culture.** New York: Farrar, Straus & Giroux, Noonday, 1965. cl $4.95 [0-374-22352-1].

This well-known American critic examines both English- and French-Canadian writers. Morley Callaghan, Hugh MacLennan, John Buell, Jean Paul Desbiens, Anne Hébert, Jean Le Moyne, Jean Charles Harvey, Louis Hémon, Marie-Claire Blais, Gabrielle Roy, Roger Lemelin, and André Langevin are the novelists discussed. Wilson also looks at forces and events which he feels have affected the Canadian consciousness, such as the relationship with the United States, immigrants, the Duplessis era, the FLQ bombings and the separatist movement. Occasionally oversimplified, the literary and social approach Wilson uses nevertheless raises some important questions.

Woodcock, George, ed. **The Canadian novel in the twentieth century.** NCL. Toronto: McClelland & Stewart, 1975. pb $3.95 [0-7710-9215-6].

Woodcock has chosen twenty-seven articles from *Canadian literature* which concern the fiction writers he considers to have been most central to the emergent Canadian tradition. The authors discussed are Stephen Leacock, Frederick John Niven, Frederick Philip Grove, Robert Stead, Mazo de la Roche, Ethel Wilson, Morley Callaghan, Malcolm Lowry, Hugh MacLennan, Sinclair Ross, Ernest Buckler, Robertson Davies, W.O. Mitchell, Shiela Watson, Mavis Gallant, Brian Moore, Margaret Laurence, Hugh Hood, Mordecai Richler, Howard O'Hagan, Robert Kroetsch, Leonard Cohen, Margaret Atwood and Gwendolyn MacEwen. The articles are arranged chronologically and there are a few brief pieces by authors on their own work. Since some of the articles were written as much as fifteen years ago, not all of the authors' most recent works have been discussed. Nonetheless, this is an extremely useful work.

Woodcock, George, ed. **A Choice of critics.** Toronto: Oxford University Press, 1966. o/p.

This collection of essays taken from *Canadian literature* covers the period from the twenties to the mid sixties. A general section attempts to define a Canadian cultural identity through thematic and imagistic examples from the literature. The fiction writers examined are MacLennan, Davies, Roy, Callaghan and Klein. Woodcock has aimed at choosing essays with a "permanent critical value", and has represented many creative writers whose views don't always coincide with his own, resulting in an interesting and varied approach to the criticism of Canadian literature.

Woodcock, George. **Odysseus ever returning: essays on Canadian writers and writing.** NCL. Toronto: McClelland & Stewart, 1970. pb $2.50 [0-7710-9171-0].

George Woodcock, as editor of the periodical *Canadian literature,* is in an excellent position to gather together the threads of Canadian literary opinion and taste. His articles on the development of Canadian literature and criticism indicate that he has taken advantage of this. He writes good evaluative essays on such authors as Hugh MacLennan, Morley Callaghan, Brian Moore, Malcolm Lowry, Irving Layton, Leonard Cohen, A.J.M. Smith and Earle Birney. Throughout Woodcock's writing there is the sensible and scholarly tone of a man who has thought about his subject and knows it thoroughly.

Woodcock, George, ed. **The Sixties: writers and writing of the decade.** Vancouver: UBC Publications Centre, 1969. cl $3.50 [0-919494-63-3].

Published to mark the tenth anniversary of the periodical *Canadian literature,* this collection includes essays by writers discussing their own work, and by critics assessing the achievements of the decade. Three poems are included, a reprint of a CBC documentary, and a paper by A.J.M. Smith on the achievements of *Canadian literature.* An interesting collection which through example and discussion conveys the flavour of Canadian literature in the sixties.

IV. Periodicals & Indexes:

Books in Canada. Ed., Douglas Marshall. Toronto: Canadian Review of Books, 1972—. Free from book stores; $9.95 per year. This monthly is solely devoted to reviewing new books.

The Canadian fiction magazine. Ed., R.W. Stedingh. Vancouver, Winter 1971—. $2.00 per issue; $7.00 per year.

This impressive quarterly review of "fiction, manifestoes, reviews, graphics, photos and interviews" contains mostly short stories.

Canadian literature. Ed., George Woodcock. Vancouver: University of British Columbia Press, 1959—. $5.50 per year.

This quarterly publishes scholarly critical articles on Canadian literature. From 1959 to 1970, it printed annual checklists of books and articles on language, literary history and criticism, as well as listing books of fiction, poetry and drama by Canadians (continued in *Journal of Canadian fiction* and *Journal of Commonwealth literature*). Besides the English- and French-Canadian literature bibliographies, lists of theses on Canadian studies were printed for the period 1959-1968; a list of theses on Canadian literature was printed for the period 1969-1970 (continued in *Journal of Canadian fiction*). An index of authors and subjects for numbers 1-54 was published in 1973.

Canadian periodical index. Ottawa: Canadian Library Association, 1966—.

Now published monthly, this author and subject index dates back to 1938. Included are the authors and subjects of articles from over eighty Canadian periodicals. Though there are two separate sections, one listing book reviews and the other poems and short stories, individual entries can be found under the names of authors as well. The index also lists reproductions of paintings, sculptures, and other works of art under the names of artists.

Canadian essay and literature index 1973. Eds., Andrew Armitage and Nancy Tudor. Toronto: University of Toronto Press, 1975—. cl $27.50 [0-8020-4518-9].

This index supplements the *Canadian periodical index*, indexing essays, book reviews, poems, plays and short stories published in ninety-one anthologies and thirty-eight magazines in Canada during 1973. Items can be found under author, title or subject. It will be published annually.

Essays on Canadian writing. Ed., Jack David. Toronto: Coach House Press, 1974—. Tri-annual.
This new journal contains essays on all periods and genres of Canadian writing. Interviews of such writers as Eli Mandel, Michael Darling and George Bowering have appeared, as well as bibliographies of such contemporary writers as b p Nichol.

Journal of Canadian fiction. Ed., John G. Moss. Montreal & Fredericton: Bellrock Press, 1972—. $2.50 per issue; $9.00 per year; $6.00 per year for students.
This quarterly publishes short stories, articles, reviews and interviews in French and English. Less scholarly than *Canadian literature*, more conventional than *Open letter*, and more critically oriented than the *Canadian fiction magazine*, the *Journal of Canadian fiction* offers a provocative selection of writing by and about Canadians. Occasionally it includes bibliographical information on Canadian fiction and criticism. One issue per year is devoted to regional groups. It publishes an annual bibliography of Canadian literature and a list of Canadian theses on Canadian literature; this is a continuation of *Canadian literature*'s check lists, which were discontinued in 1970.

Journal of Commonwealth literature. Ed., Arthur Ravenscourt. London, Eng.: Heinemann Educational Books & The University of Leeds, 1965—. $6.50 per year.
This scholarly journal contains reviews and critical articles about the literature in English and Commonwealth countries other than Britain. Each issue has a regional emphasis. Published semi-annually since 1967, it will be published tri-annually from 1974, with the third issue devoted to the "Annual bibliography", which includes Canadian writing.

"Letters in Canada". July issue. **University of Toronto quarterly.** Ed., W.F. Blissett. Toronto: University of Toronto Press, 1937—. $8.00 per year.
When "Letters in Canada" first appeared in 1937, the idea of an annual synopsis of books of fiction, poetry, drama, and of religious and social studies may have seemed reasonable. Though this section of criticism has expanded in response to the growth of Canadian literary production, it has failed to keep pace with it. The consequent discussions of selections of books is unfortunately far from objective.

Open letter. 2nd Series. Ed., Frank Davey. Toronto: Coach House Press, Winter 71/72—. $7.25 per year.
Open letter, 1st Series, was both edited and printed by Frank Davey in Victoria between 1965 and April 1969. The nine issues were mainly devoted to poetry, and included poets' letters to other poets. Its format (photo offset, 18-32 pages) varied from issue to issue. On the whole, the magazine's orientation was less criti-

SECONDARY SOURCES / 13

cal than its Toronto-based sequel's has been. Though numbers 4 to 7 inclusive are out of print, numbers 1, 2, 8 and 9 can be obtained at a cost of $2.00 per issue, by writing to Frank Davey, c/o Coach House Press.

The quarterly *Open letter*, 2nd Series, claiming to be a review of "writing and sources", contains reviews, pictures and prose pieces about a great variety of subjects, including Canadian literature. With its searching experimental outlook, *Open letter* represents the avant-garde of Canadian writing.

Three Media Resource Books:

Beattie, Eleanor. **The Handbook of Canadian film.** 2nd ed. Toronto: Peter Martin, 1976. cl $12.00 [0-88778-130-6]; pb $5.95 [0-88778-131-4].

This book is useful mainly because it provides sources with addresses for films and other multi-media material. The section on filmmakers also lists films that could be used in conjunction with Canadian literature.

Maynard, Richard A. **The Celluloid curriculum.** New York: Hayden Book Co., 1971. cl $9.15 [0-8104-5893-4]; pb $6.85 [0-8104-5892-6].

Although this book is written to provide ideas for film courses and is oriented to American teachers, it is of some value for its annotations on films that would be useful to the teacher of English. A few Canadian-made films and films based on Canadian works are suggested.

Whattan, W. Victor, *et. al.* **The Uses of film in the teaching of English.** Toronto: The Ontario Institute for Studies in Education, 1971. cl $4.95 [no ISBN].

This book accomplishes its aim to "assist the teacher of English who wishes to incorporate films into his program". It is the only Canadian book available that concentrates on teaching methods rather than on the technical aspects of film in the classroom. The essay on *The Drylanders* and *Settlers of the marsh* is particularly useful.

This section includes only novelists who have works in print. All novels are listed (except untranslated French works) and those in print annotated. Also included are biographies, autobiographies and critical books concerning individual authors, as well as some relevant multi-media materials. (For a more detailed explanation of the format, see the Introduction.)

Following the annotation section is an Index to annotated titles, and a Subject Guide which provides a selected list of titles under a few important headings. Elizabeth Waterston's Survey *and* Read Canadian, *edited by Robert Fulford, David Godfrey and Abraham Rotstein (both annotated in the Secondary Sources section), provide lists of useful non-fiction reading concerning many of these subjects.*

Novel Annotations

ADAMS, Ian

—**The Trudeau papers.** Toronto: McClelland & Stewart, 1971. cl $5.95 [0-7710-0052-9]

Setting: Canada

Due to a series of blunders, the Prairies are wiped out by nuclear explosions, and Ontario is converted into an American-run police state. The narrator, an ex-journalist, plays an important role in the ensuing resistance movement. Told in a documentary style, this science fantasy tackles several topical issues.

ALLEN, Ralph 1913—1966

—**Home made banners.** Don Mills, Ont.: Longman, 1946. o/p

—**The Chartered libertine.** Toronto: Macmillan, 1954. o/p

—**Peace River country.** London, Eng.: Hodder, 1958. o/p

—**Ask the name of the lion.** 1962. New York: Popular Library, 1968. pb 60¢

Setting: Belgian Congo

Six people, including a young Canadian doctor, an African government official, and a U.N. "trouble-shooter" and Spanish Civil War veteran, attempt to flee drunken soldiers in the Belgian Congo. Allen uses the tensions of personality and situation to illustrate the themes of exile and survival in modern civilization.

—**The High white forest.** Garden City, N.Y.: Doubleday, 1964. o/p

CW OX

ANGERS, Marie-Louise-Félicité see Laure Conan

AQUIN, Hubert 1929—

—**Prochain episode / Prochain épisode.** 1965. NCL. Tr., Penny Williams. Toronto: McClelland & Stewart, 1972. pb $1.95 [0-7710-9184-2]

Setting: Montreal, California, Switzerland

A young separatist awaits trial in the psychiatric ward of a Montreal prison. He

writes an espionage novel, complete with secret codes, thrilling chases, and a beautiful blonde, in which is traceable the disguised account of the events which led to his arrest. One can also find symbolic parallels between his fictional creation and real life—for example, that between his love affair with the beautiful "K" and his political relationship with Quebec. The acceptable violence of the spy story convention is a suitable medium for somewhat less widely accepted ideas concerning anarchistic violence. *Prochain episode* is a protest against the Québécois' fear of changing the situation that is oppressing them, and a plea for Quebec intellectuals to fulfill their social duty. The translation distorts significant portions of the novel.

—**Blackout / Trou de mémoire.** 1968. Tr., Alan Brown. Toronto: Anansi, 1974. cl $8.50 [0-88784-434-0]; pb $3.50 [0-88784-332-8]

Setting: Montreal, London, West Africa, Switzerland

Aquin uses a tortured, fragmented, hallucinatory style to create a symbolic picture of Quebec's political situation as a colony. Pierre X. Magnant, murderer and revolutionary, chemist and addict, has a strange relationship with two sisters. His agonized, loving, violent behaviour towards them and their reactions toward him can be seen as analogical to political relationships, emotions and behaviour. The life of Magnant's black *doppelgänger*, Olympe Ghezzo-Quenum, slowly meshes with that of the Québécois. The story unfolds in their diaries, prepared for publication by a mysterious editor.

—**The Antiphonary / L'Antiphonaire.** 1969. Tr., Alan Brown. Toronto: Anansi, 1973. cl $7.95 [0-88784-426-X]

Setting: California, Montreal, Magog, Switzerland

Violent, even pathological emotion fills the diary of a medical doctor. She is writing her Ph.D. thesis on sixteenth-century medicine, and the account of her life alternates with her description of the life of a Renaissance medical historian. Crimes of passion, violent scenes between lovers, and suicides are some of the events in this com-

15

plex double novel. Aquin, as is his custom, comments through the narrator on his style and structure as he writes.

CW FC OX2

ARDIES, Tom

—**Their man in the White House.*** Toronto: McClelland & Stewart, 1971. cl $4.95. [0-7710-0949-6] ; Paper Jacks. Don Mills, Ont.: General Publishing, 1974. pb $1.50 [0-7737-7061-5] ; London, Eng.: Macmillan; Panther. St. Albans, Eng.: Granada
—**This suitcase is going to explode.*** Toronto: McClelland & Stewart, 1972. cl $5.95. [0-7710-0948-8] ; Paper Jacks. Don Mills, Ont.: General Publishing, 1974. pb $1.50 [0-7737-7062-3] ; London, Eng.: Macmillan
—**Pandemic.*** Toronto & Garden City, N.Y.: Doubleday, 1973. cl $5.95 [0-385-01521-6] ; Paper Jacks. Don Mills, Ont.: General Publishing, 1974. [0-7737-7066-6]

*These books form a trilogy about Charlie Sparrow, a journalist turned spy for an American counter-espionage agency. *Their man in the White House* concerns a plot by the Russians to assassinate an American presidential candidate. The second is about a bomb scare initiated by a fanatical group in the American military in order to provoke the president into bombing Russia. And in *Pandemic*, a fabulously wealthy man has plans to wipe out the human race and begin again. In all three of these fast-paced and entertaining spy mysteries, Sparrow uses his wits, muscles and lady-killer good looks to battle the forces of evil.

—**Kosygin is coming.** Toronto & Garden City, N.Y.: Doubleday, 1974. cl $6.95 [0-385-08426-9]
Setting: Vancouver
Timothy Shaver, a corporal in the RCMP, has been suspended for striking a superior. A chance to redeem himself appears in the form of an assignment from Special Branch — to kidnap a man suspected by the Russian secret police of wanting to assassinate Kosygin on his visit to Canada. As it turns out, both Shaver and the suspect are dupes of an intricate plot by the Russians to kill their own leader.

ASPLER, Tony 1939—

—**Streets of Askelon.** New York: M. Evans, 1972. cl $5.95; London, Eng.: Secker & Warburg
Setting: Montreal
An iconoclastic and alcoholic Irish poet,

Bart Shea, arouses the ire of Montrealers by giving a scurrilous television interview and by inciting a group of students to invade McGill University in support of free speech. The link between the poet's art and his childish rebelliousness is examined. The satire, mainly directed at the Canadian cultural philistine, hits home, despite occasional stereotyping of the characters.

—**One of my marionettes.** London, Eng.: Secker & Warburg, 1973
Setting: London, England, and Ireland
The mystery of Diana Grierman's death obsesses the narrator/author, whose love for her was strong but unfulfilled. He transforms her life into a novel and tries to unburden himself of his guilt and sorrow by reading it to her father. A surprise revelation brings him to the realization that he did not understand her, or her life, at all.

ATWOOD, Margaret E. 1939—

—**The Edible woman.** Toronto: McClelland & Stewart, 1969. cl $6.95 [0-7710-0060-X] ; NCL. Toronto: McClelland & Stewart, 1973. pb $2.75 [0-7710-9193-1] ; London, Eng.: Deutsch
Setting: Toronto
Marian McAlpine, although well-intentioned enough, gradually finds herself unable to fill the roles society expects of her. After her engagement to an ambitious law student, she finds herself identifying with the things she eats. Almost consumed herself, she cannot consume—but manages to escape (at least partially) with the help of a scruffy and neurotic graduate student. This pre-women's liberation novel examines Marian's predicament with a good deal of prophetic humour, but also with the underlying seriousness which is cannibalism's due.

—**Surfacing.** Toronto: McClelland & Stewart, 1972. cl $6.95 [-07710-0822-8] ; Paper Jacks. Don Mills, Ont.: General Publishing, 1973. pb $1.95 [0-7737-7049-6] ; New York: Simon & Schuster; London, Eng.: Deutsch; London, Eng.: Wildwood House
Setting: Northern Quebec
In some ways, *Surfacing* is an illustration of the thesis presented in *Survival*, Atwood's critical work on Canadian literature. At the news of her father's disappearance, a rather cold, distant woman returns with her lover and another couple to the isolated cabin where she spent her childhood. In her search for him she slowly comes to terms

with the ways in which her personality has been distorted by society. The process is a painful one, in which she must immerse herself in her natural surroundings before she can return to society in any role other than that of victim.

CB 0N2 0X2

AUBERT DE GASPÉ, Phillippe (Père) 1786-1871

—The Canadians of old / Les anciens Canadiens. 1863. NCL. Tr., Sir Charles G.D. Roberts. Toronto: McClelland & Stewart, 1974. pb $2.95 [0-7710-9206-7]
Setting: Quebec City, St. Jean-Port-Joli
Forces of history come between two friends, one Scottish and one French, and separate potential lovers forever, during the aftermath of the British conquest in 1960. The story is often interrupted by anecdotes of everyday life at the time, legends, songs and customs of the French in early Canada. The translation is satisfactory.

CW OX

AUBRY, Claude 1914—
—The Magic fiddler and other legends of French Canada / Le violon magique et autres légendes du Canada français. Tr., Alice E. Kane. Toronto: Peter Martin, 1968. cl $17.50 [0-8878-022-9]
Sometimes moralistic, sometimes historical or biblical, these legends can be read not only for pleasure, but also for the picture they give of French-Canadian society during the French Regime ca. 1700. Aubry's commentary is helpful, although sometimes ironic, and does not destroy the mysterious and somewhat supernatural atmosphere of these legends. Aubry's primary sources were Philippe Aubert de Gaspé and Louis Frechette, both of whom collected versions of these legends.

BACQUE, James 1929—
—The Lonely ones. Toronto: McClelland & Stewart, 1969. cl $6.95 [0-7710-1001-X]. Republished under title: Big lonely. Don Mills, Ont.: New Press, 1971. pb $1.50 [0-88780-041-1]; London, Eng.: Macmillan
Setting: Montreal and Toronto
When a young painter finds that the world does not live up to his ideals, he falls into despondency. He becomes submerged in self-doubt as an artist, a lover, and as a human being. Eventually, because of his loneliness, he is lured into a political group in which he does not believe.

—A Man of talent. Don Mills, Ont.: New Press, 1972. cl $6.95 [0-88780-154-X]
Setting: Toronto
The "man of talent" is a brilliant and wealthy young man, who, at the age of thirty, is an accomplished university professor and dean of arts. His naiveté and self-righteousness bring him into conflict with student radicals and the university administration, as well as a few Canadian Indians. The climax is his rejection by all three and his subsequent downfall.

0X2

BAILEY, Don
—If you hum a few bars I might remember the tune. Ottawa: Oberon Press, 1973. cl $6.95 [0-88750-083-8]; pb $3.50 [0-88750-084-6]
Setting: Toronto
Don Bailey's fictional writing seems to be largely autobiographical; in this collection of stories, the central character Gus is probably an expression of the author's own personality. The trivial events in Gus's life described in these stories are not really essential: it is the thoughts and observations of his tortured mind that count. The book evokes the depressing lifestyle of people who feel they are failures at life. Gus himself is obsessed with failure and the lack of communication between himself and those around him. Nevertheless, he emerges as an intensely likable, even strong character.

—In the belly of the whale. Ottawa: Oberon Press, 1974. cl $6.95 [0-88750-103-6]; pb $3.50 [0-88750-104-4]
Setting: Toronto
When Don Bailey was twenty-three, he robbed his first bank; he later spent five years in prison, "in the belly of the whale". This novel is about that experience, and in particular, the events that led up to his prison term. As in his earlier collection of stories, the writing here is tortured and perceptive; the style spare and bleak, but relieved at times by passages of lyricism and poignancy.

BAIRD, Irene
—John. Philadelphia: Lippincott, 1937. o/p
—Waste heritage. 1939. LL. Toronto: Macmillan, 1974. pb $3.95 [0-7705-1107-4]
Setting: British Columbia
One of the strongest Canadian novels of social protest to emerge from the Depres-

sion, *Waste heritage* is centred on the emotional and intellectual growth of Matt Striker, a young man who joins the Communist-organized march of the unemployed from Vancouver to Victoria in 1938. Though somewhat dated by its didactic style, the novel remains a valuable and unusual social document because of its historical accuracy.

—He rides the sky. Toronto: Macmillan, 1941. o/p

—The Climate of power. Toronto: Macmillan, 1971. o/p

Setting: Ottawa and the Arctic

An elderly "mandarin" from the federal civil service is upset when he is bypassed for promotion because of a new political emphasis on youth. Surrounded by ambitious men, his resentment results in murder during a government inspection tour of the Arctic. This is a readable exploration of the hidden mechanics of power.

OX

BALLEM, John

—The Devil's lighter. Don Mills, Ont.: General Publishing, 1973. cl $7.95 [0-7736-0025-6] ; Paper Jacks. Don Mills, Ont.: General Publishing, 1974. pb $1.75 [0-7737-7067-4]

Setting: Calgary, Vancouver, and the MacKenzie Valley

Rivalry between a consortium of oil developers and a small western drilling company involves sabotage, murder, and psychological drama. Sabotage is disrupted by personal loyalties.

—The Dirty scenario. Don Mills, Ont.: General Publishing, 1974. cl $7.95 [0-7736-0035-3]

Setting: Ottawa, Toronto, N.W.T., and Washington

This novel explores U.S.—Canadian power politics during an international energy crisis. Ballem uses his considerable knowledge of international energy politics to describe conflicts between personal and national interest.

BARBEAU, (Charles) Marius 1883—

—The Downfall of Temlaham. 1928. 2nd ed. Canadiana Reprint Series. Edmonton: Hurtig, 1973. cl $9.95 [0-88830-070-0]

Setting: the upper Skeena River, B.C.

Barbeau has based this novel on his wide knowledge of the native people of British Columbia. Using oral accounts, ethnographic notes and ritual songs, he tells the story of an Indian tribe fighting for its survival. The story centres on the breakup of the marriage of Kamalmuk and Hanamuk who disagree about how to react to the incursions of the white man into their territory. The events are loosely based on the Skeena River rebellion of 1886-7.

CW OX

BARR, Robert 1850-1912

—In a steamer chair & other shipboard stories. 1892. Short Story Index Reprint Series. Plainview, N.Y.: Books for Libraries. cl $10.50. Not seen

—In the midst of alarms. London, Eng.: 1894. o/p

—The Measure of the rule. 1907. Intro., L.K. Mackenzie. Literature of Canada: Poetry and Prose in Reprint. Toronto: University of Toronto Press, 1973. cl $15.00 [0-8020-2072-0]; pb $4.95 [0-8020-6197-4]

Setting: Toronto

Set in Toronto towards the end of the nineteenth century, this fascinating novel is full of authentic details of the culture, morals and architecture of that time. The hero, Tom Prentiss, is a somewhat naïve young man from the country who comes to Toronto to further his education. He ends up attending the Normal School (teacher's college), which the author at times satirizes and condemns for its rigid and ridiculous rules and moral strictures. On the whole, the style of the novel is thoroughly enjoyable: old-fashioned, yet always humorous and urbane.

OX

BEATTIE, Jessie Louise 1896—

—Hill top: a tale of Ontario rural life. Toronto: Macmillan, 1935. o/p

—Three measures. Toronto: Macmillan, 1938. o/p

—Blaze of noon. Toronto: Ryerson Press, 1950. o/p

—The Split in the sky. Toronto: Ryerson Press, 1960. o/p

—Strength for the bridge. Toronto: McClelland & Stewart, 1966. o/p

—A Season past: reminiscences of a rural Canadian childhood. Toronto: McClelland & Stewart, 1968. cl $6.50 [0-7710-1169-5]

Setting: rural southern Ontario

These recollections of the author's childhood offer a clear and nostalgic picture of her life.

BEAULIEU, Victor-Lévy 1945—

—The Grandfathers / Les grand-pères. FWCS. Tr., Marc Plourde. Montreal: Harvest House, 1975. pb $2.50 [0-88772-160-5].

Setting: St. Jean-de-Dieu, Lower St. Lawrence

A senile old man obsessed with his past watches his hated second wife die, incapable, either physically or emotionally, of helping her. Beaulieu goes deeply into the old man's thoughts and feelings and records them in unorthodox and poetic prose—sometimes sexual, sometimes violent.

OX2

BELANEY, Archibald Stansfeld see Grey Owl

BELL, Don

—Saturday night at the bagel factory and other Montreal stories. Toronto: McClelland & Stewart, 1972. cl $6.95 [0-7710-1188-1] ; Markham, Ont.: Simon & Schuster, 1974. pb $1.25 [0-671-78416-1]

Setting: Montreal

All of the stories in this collection were previously published in *Weekend Magazine*. They are humorous sketches of individuals and places in and around Montreal.•

BENOIT, Jacques 1941—

—Jos Carbone / Jos Carbone. 1967. FWCS. Tr., Sheila Fischman. Montreal: Harvest House, 1974. pb $2.50 [0-88772-157-5]

Setting: a fictional village

The characters in *Jos Carbone* seem ruled by their worst instincts, which perhaps explains the strange events in the novel. Two couples, each living in isolation, unite against the intrusion of a violent and mysterious psychopath. After much violence and suspense, one couple is again alone. The style mirrors the action, sometimes violent, sometimes reflective.

BERESFORD-HOWE, Constance Elizabeth 1922—

—The Unreasoning heart. 1946. New York: Popular Library, 1968. pb 60¢. Not seen.

—Of this day's journey. New York: Dodd Mead, 1947. o/p

—The Invisible gate. New York: Dodd Mead, 1949. o/p

—My Lady Greensleeves. New York: Ballantine Books, 1955. o/p

—The Book of Eve. Toronto: Macmillan, 1972. cl $6.95 [0-7705-0888-X] ; Boston: Little, Brown

Setting: a Canadian city

As this book opens, a woman, Eva, has just left her husband after forty years of faithful marriage and servitude. Written with a humorous and sensitive perception of personal relationships, the novel describes Eva's thoughts and actions during the weeks that follow: her initial feelings of freedom and exhilaration, her subsequent fear and attempts at survival (both physical and emotional), the recollections of her past life, and her involvement and interactions with people she meets during the course of her life alone.

CW OX

BERLIN, Bernard

—Call heaven to witness. Bonanza Books. Don Mills, Ont.: Musson, 1970. pb $1.00 [0-7737-0010-2]

Setting: Montreal

Jonathan Temple and Arnie, the narrator of this book, are partners in a law firm and have been close friends since childhood. According to Arnie, however, Jonathan is slowly being destroyed by the woman he married—a possessive, ambitious, coldhearted bitch. Also involved with this trio is Blaze Scotland, the beautiful actress that Jonny has always truly loved. This novel traces the progression of Jonathan's eventual defeat and destruction.

BESSETTE, Gérard 1920—

—Not for every eye / Le Libraire. 1960. Tr., Glen Shortcliffe. Toronto: Macmillan, 1962. cl. $4.95 [0-7705-0008-0] ; pb $2.95 [0-7705-1016-7]

Setting: a small Quebec town

Written as a diary (on Sundays, because "there is nothing else to do in St. Joachim"), this short novel adopts a sober style. A scandal erupts when the diarist, Hervé Jodoin, sells a book forbidden by the Catholic church to a young seminarian. Jodoin is forced to leave town. *Not for every eye* satirizes the reactionary force present within rural and village Québec on the eve of the Quiet Revolution. The translation is good; Bessette and Shortcliffe were friends and colleagues at Queen's University.

—**Incubation / L'Incubation.** 1965. Tr., Glen Shortcliffe. Toronto: Macmillan, 1967. cl $4.50 [0-7705-0007-2]
Setting: London, Montreal, "Narcotown"
The heroine has an affair with a Canadian whom she meets in a bomb shelter. Her husband is killed, and the affair ends. The underground scenes are played out in an atmosphere of darkness and alienation; life there is separate and quite different from that on the surface. After the war, the heroine goes to Montreal to find the man who once loved her and to give coherence to her memories. Bessette writes in a poetic style which clearly conveys his pessimistic and satirical view of life. This is an excellent translation of a difficult book.

CW FC OX OX2

BHATIA, Jamunadeui 1919—
—**Alien there is none.** London, Eng.: Hodder, 1959. o/p
—**The Latchkey kid.** Don Mills, Ont.: Longman, 1971. cl $6.95 [0-7747-0055-6]
Setting: Alberta
Olga Stych, a social-climber, is mortified when her son publishes a supposedly obscene novel. Distracted from her disgrace by an accident, she begins work with retarded children. The novel is a vehicle for the author's conservative views on womanhood.

BIRD, Will Richard 1891—
—**Private Timothy Fergus Clancy.** Ottawa: Graphic, 1930. o/p
—**Maid of the marshes.** Amherst, N.S.: Author, 1935. o/p
—**Here stays good Yorkshire.** Toronto: Ryerson Press, 1945. o/p
—**Sunrise for Peter.** Toronto: Ryerson Press, 1946. o/p
—**Judgement Glen.** Toronto: Ryerson Press, 1947. o/p

—**The Passionate pilgrim.** Toronto: Ryerson Press, 1949. o/p
—**So much to record.** Toronto: Ryerson Press, 1951. o/p
—**To love and to cherish.** Toronto: Ryerson Press, 1953. o/p
—**The Shy Yorkshireman: a novel.** Toronto: Ryerson Press, 1955. o/p
—**Tristram's salvation.** Toronto: Ryerson Press, 1957. o/p
—**Despite the distance.** Toronto: Ryerson Press, 1961. o/p
—**An Earl must have a wife.** Toronto: Clarke Irwin, 1969. cl $5.95 [0-7720-0108-1]
Setting: Maritimes; London, England
Although this novel is based on the letters of an historical personage, Colonel Joseph Frederick Wallet Desbarres, governor of Cape Breton and Prince Edward Island, at times it seems too funny and outrageous to be true. Desbarres, denied a title because of his refusal to marry either of his two common-law wives, is clearly one of the more extraordinary men in Canadian history.

—**Angel Cove.** Toronto: Macmillan, 1972. cl $6.95 [0-7705-0757-3]
Setting: a Newfoundland outport
This series of interrelated sketches about a small Newfoundland fishing village at the turn of the century reveals Bird's warm feeling for the people, although occasionally the characters seem a little naïve.

CW OX OX2

BIRNEY, Earle 1904—
—**Turvey: a military picaresque.** 1949. NCL. Toronto: McClelland & Stewart, 1963. pb $2.50 [0-7710-9134-6]. Also published as **The Kootenay Highlander,** London: Lansborough, 1960. o/p
Setting: Canada, England, and Belgium
This novel humorously traces the World War II career of a clumsy, simple-minded, but good-natured private named Turvey. In a clear and fast-paced style, the author satirizes army discipline and efficiency while describing Turvey's constantly thwarted attempts to be transferred to his home regiment where his best friend is an officer.

—**Down the long table.** Toronto: McClelland & Stewart, 1955. o/p

Davey, Frank. *Earle Birney.* 1971. SCL. Toronto: Copp Clark, 1974. pb $2.35 [0-7730-3003-4]

Davey devotes the first chapter of this monograph to an account of Birney's career, and the second chapter to a study of Birney's novels. Both *Turvey* and *Down the long table* are discussed, and then compared to each other. A bibliography includes books and articles by and about Birney, up to 1971.

Nesbitt, Bruce, ed. *Earle Birney.* CVCW. Scarborough, Ont.: McGraw-Hill Ryerson, 1974. cl $8.95 [0-07-077364-5]; pb $3.95 [0-07-077788-8]

This collection of reviews and criticisms of Birney's work includes an interesting selection of reactions to his two novels. The most valuable information about the intent and structure of his work is contained in Birney's often indignant and amusing reactions to his critics, including a long passage about the novels in the epilogue. The chapter of essays on the novels includes five essays about *Turvey* and three about *Down the long table.* A selected bibliography covers books, articles and recordings by and about Birney up to 1973.

Robillard, Richard H. *Earle Birney.* CWS. NCL. Toronto: McClelland & Stewart, 1971. pb $1.25 [0-7710-9609-7]

Unlike Frank Davey, Richard Robillard considers *Down the long table* inferior to *Turvey.* The only mention of either novel is made in the brief introductory account of Birney's career. Robillard's study concentrates on Birney's poetry. A selected bibliography lists books, articles and recordings by and about Birney, up to 1971.

CB CW ON ON2 OX OX2

BLAIS, Marie-Claire 1939—

—Mad shadows / La Belle bête. 1959. NCL. Tr., Lawrence Merloyd. Toronto: McClelland & Stewart, 1971. pb $1.75 [0-7710-9178-8]

Setting: a rural area in Quebec

In this dark tale every character seems deformed—either physically or mentally. Louise, beautiful herself, dotes on her beautiful son Patrice and ignores her ugly daughter Isabelle. Isabelle at first seems to escape their scorn by marrying a blind man but he regains his sight and flings her back to her family. She takes a terrible vengeance on them all, but despite this seems the only character who possesses human emotions and reactions. The translation is satisfactory.

—Tête Blanche / Tête-Blanche. 1960. NCL. Tr., Charles Fullman. Toronto: McClelland & Stewart, 1974. pb $1.95 [0-7719-9204-0]

Setting: Quebec City

Tête-Blanche is a young adolescent capable of the worst actions, but also capable of love. He treats some of his friends coldly, as if they were objects, but expresses his more emotional side—his anxiety and despair—in letters to his mother and to Emilie, his first love. Even though *Tête-Blanche* is not as polished as her later work, Blais makes us feel the torments of a young anguished heart. The translation is satisfactory.

—The Day is dark / Le Jour est noir. 1962. Published with Les Voyageurs sacrés. 1962. Tr., Derek Coltman. New York: Farrar, Straus and Giroux, 1967. o/p

—A Season in the life of Emmanuel / Une Saison dans la vie d'Emmanuel. 1965. Tr., Derek Coltman. New York: Grosset & Dunlap, 1966. pb $1.95

Setting: rural Quebec

The newly-born Emmanuel is one of a long stream of babies doomed to a merciful death or a short and miserable life in a poverty-stricken rural family. Despite the novel's somber events, the fierce humour of the family's consumptive young poet, Jean-le-Maigre, saves it from abject pessimism, as does the apparent immortality of his grandmother, who rescues his poetic works from the outhouse after his death. There is a certain amount of hope derived from this rescue as there is in the coming of spring and in Emmanuel's resemblance to Jean-Le-Maigre. Blais's viewpoint, in this her most admired novel, leaves room for the strength of spirit that can laugh at despair. The translation is good.

—David Sterne / David Sterne. 1967. Tr., David Lobdell. Toronto: McClelland & Stewart, 1973. cl $5.95 [0-7710-1543-7]

Setting: "a narrow city with high walls"

David Sterne is eighteen, asocial, living his agony deliberately. He consciously violates society's norms, and, as he expected, society kills him. Michel Rameau, his existentialist companion, is suicidal in thought and action. He succeeds in earning his death. Blais presents us with a dark adolescent picture of life—cruel, parched and intellectual.

—The Manuscripts of Pauline Archange / Les Manuscrits de Pauline Archange. 1968. Vivre! Vivre! 1969. Tr., Derek Coltman. Toronto: Doubleday, 1970. cl $6.95; New York: Farrar Straus and Giroux.

Setting: A city in Quebec

Written from the point of view of a six-year-old girl growing up in a slum, this novel examines the precocious outlook of Pauline Archange and her friends. She observes the misery and destitution around her with an acute and critical eye. By writing, she tries to escape from the feeling of guilt and unworthiness instilled in her by the nuns and her family. The long fluid sentences seem to reflect the heroine's inner musings. The reader receives an interesting insight into some of Blais's ideas about art and writing.

The final eighteen pages of *Vivre! Vivre!* are not reproduced in this translation, which is otherwise faithful to the original.

—The Wolf / Le Loup. 1972. Tr., Sheila Fischman. Toronto: McClelland & Stewart, 1974. cl $6.95 [0-7710-1544-5]

Setting: indeterminate

Sebastien, a young homosexual, describes his relationships. He recognizes that his altruism and idealism often bring out the worst in others, but he never loses his faith in love. Even his violent and unpredictable lover Eric does not crush this faith.

—St. Lawrence blues / Un Joualonais, sa joualonerie. 1973. Tr., Ralph Manheim. Toronto: Doubleday, 1974. cl $8.95 [0-374-26945-9]

Setting: Montreal

A worker meets a writer who wants to learn *joual* from him. As a result, the worker is introduced to the writer's feminist wife and his unusual collection of friends: a lawyer on the make, a family of opportunistic pseudo-Marxists, two homosexuals and two prostitutes. The lives of these people are seen as ridiculous and destructive, but also as having a certain inner logic. Interaction between characters of differing viewpoints produces confrontations bordering on the absurd. Although Blais here for the first time uses *joual*—the highly Anglicized semi-language of the working class—this does not prevent her from regarding them and the literature written in *joual* with a somewhat cynical eye. *Joual* is untranslatable; in addition, the translator has simplified Blais's style, reducing her long sentences to shorter ones, perhaps for greater clarity.

Stratford, Philip. *Marie-Claire Blais.* CWW. Rexdale, Ont.: Forum House, 1970. pb $1.25 [no ISBN]

This introductory study of Blais includes chapters on *Mad shadows; Tête-Blanche; The Day is dark, Three travellers* and the poetry; *A Season in the life of Emmanuel; L'Insoumise; David Sterne* and the plays; *The Manuscripts of Pauline Archange* and *Vivre! Vivre!*, as well as a biographical section. In such a necessarily limited and general work, Stratford has managed to give a good account even of the more subtle and philosophic aspects of Blais's work. (Bibliography.)

CL CW FC OX OX2

BLAISE, Clark 1940—

—A North American education. Toronto & Garden City, N.Y.: Doubleday, 1973. cl $6.95 [0-385-06433-0] ; Paper Jacks. Don Mills, Ont.: General Publishing, 1974. pb $1.95 [0-7737-7055-0]

Each of the three parts of this book of short stories represents a stage of emotional and mental maturity in the hero's life. Beginning with the present, each highly descriptive story journeys deeper into the past. As the adventure proceeds, the hero's memory appears to dim, until a dream-like quality is achieved in the passages recounting childhood experiences. Form and meaning thus coincide to create an intensely interesting, adventuresome, and, finally, mysterious effect.

—Tribal justice. Toronto & Garden City, N.Y.: Doubleday, 1974. cl $6.95 [0-385-01038-9]

Setting: United States and Quebec

Demonstrating the author's fine talent for dialect and characters, these stories capture the different ways of life which he encountered as a child growing up in the United States, and as an adult living in Quebec.

ON2

BLICKER, Seymour 1940—

—Blues chascd a rabbit. Montreal: Warbrooke, 1969. o/p

—Shmucks. Toronto: McClelland & Stewart, 1972. cl $5.95 [0-7710-1570-4]

Setting: Montreal

A strange seige in a Montreal alley reveals, often humorously, people's alienation from each other. In the lonely hours from midnight to dawn all people—millionaires, young executives, immigrants, teenage girls—are seen as losers.

BODSWORTH, Fred 1918—

—The Last of the curlews. 1955. NCL. Toronto: McClelland & Stewart, 1963. pb $1.95 [0-7710-9137-0] ; New York: Apollo
Setting: The Arctic

This simple story makes a plea for the conservation of wildlife more eloquently than any impassioned speech could. In striking juxtaposition, factual material is set against the fictionalized account of a male curlew searching for a mate to fulfil his procreative instincts. The factual sections trace the sightings of curlews from the first notation of them in 1772 to the last sighting in 1954, when they probably became extinct. In the end the curlew is left still waiting for the mate that will never come.

—The Strange one. Canadian Nature Classics. Toronto: McClelland & Stewart, 1959. cl $7.95 [0-7710-1856-8]. Also published as **The Mating call.**
Setting: Toronto, Northern Ontario, Outer Hebrides

The story of a stray barnacle goose and his faithfulness to his mate, a Canada goose native to a different environment, effectively counter-balances the love story of a white biologist and an educated Cree woman. The problems of racial prejudice, materialist aspirations, and the effects of education are explored against a background of scientific observations about nature.

—The Atonement of Ashley Morden. New York: Dodd Mead, 1964. o/p

—The Sparrow's fall. Scarborough, Ont. & New York: New American Library, 1966. pb 75¢
Setting: Northern Ontario

An Indian hunter, caught between native and Christian beliefs, is forced by winter starvation to a rational examination of the ecological balance between predator and prey. The tension of life-and-death necessity and Bodsworth's clear descriptive style offset the geological and zoological information incorporated with the text.

OX OX2

BOWERING, George 1935—

—Mirror on the floor. Toronto: McClelland & Stewart, 1967. pb $2.50 [0-7710-1592-5]
Setting: Vancouver

Beat philosophy inspires the lives of two students at the University of British Columbia in this novel set in the 1950s. The narrator's education includes encounters with police brutality, government bureaucracy, and a neurotic woman.

—Autobiology. Vancouver: Vancouver Community Press, 1972. o/p

—Flycatcher. Ottawa: Oberon Press, 1974. cl $6.95 [0-88750-124-9] ; pb $3.50 [0-88750-125-7]
Setting: B.C., Mexico, Istanbul

This collection of short stories combines the nostalgic atmosphere of *Mirror on the floor* with the experimental prose style of *Autobiology*. The book presents a series of first-person accounts of adolescent and early adult experience. Characters and situations from Bowering's two earlier books reappear in several stories.

CB ON2 OX2

BOYLE, Harry J.

—Mostly in clover. 1961. Paper Jacks. Don Mills, Ont.: General Publishing, 1972. pb $1.50 [0-7737-7707-0]
Setting: rural Ontario

This is a collection of articles previously published in the Toronto newspaper, *The Telegram.* Nostalgic, informative, and pleasantly quaint, they tell simple tales of boyhood in rural Ontario.

—Homebrew and patches. 1963. Paper Jacks. Don Mills, Ont.: General Publishing, 1972. pb $1.25 [0-7737-7006-2]
Setting: rural southern Ontario

A sequel to *Mostly in clover,* this selection of short stories deals with life in rural Ontario during the Depression. Many episodes in the author's teenage life appear in these stories which nostalgically describe the joys and hardships of the times. Historical information is imparted in a style well suited to this type of descriptive narrative.

—A Summer burning. 1964. Paper Jacks. Don Mills, Ont.: General Publishing, 1973. pb $1.50 [0-7737-7038-0]
Setting: rural Ontario

Like most of Boyle's stories, this is about a homespun country boy growing up, his discovery of the ways of the world, and the yearnings of his heart. When an under-privileged city boy comes to spend the summer in the country, his delinquent nature clashes with the innocence of the farm boy, forcing him to question his moral, ethical and religious upbringing.

—With a pinch of sin. 1966. Paper Jacks. Don Mills, Ont.: General Publishing, 1973.

pb $1.50 [0-7737-7032-1]

Setting: rural southern Ontario

The author delves into his past, evoking a string of experiences from his early childhood. Primarily they concern his strict religious upbringing and the conflicts which arose as he grew older.

—Memories of a Catholic boyhood. 1971. Toronto & Garden City, N.Y.: Doubleday, 1973. cl $6.95 [0-385-08003-4]; Paper Jacks. Don Mills, Ont.: General Publishing, 1974. pb $1.75 [0-7737-7071-2]

Setting: southwestern Ontario

Boyle tells the story of a year spent at a Catholic boys' school after his graduation from elementary school. He relates vividly the humour, frustration and joy of early adolescence, while providing an interesting picture of small-town life during the early part of the Depression.

—The Great Canadian novel. Toronto & Garden City, N.Y.: Doubleday, 1972. cl $6.95 [0-385-08002-6]; Paper Jacks. Don Mills, Ont.: General Publishing, 1973. pb $1.95 [0-7737-7044-5]

Setting: New York and Mexico

An internationally famous advertising agent is incapacitated by an unsatisfied passion to write. Driven to drink by a job he hates and family responsibilities with which he cannot cope, he decides to flee to Mexico to write the Great Canadian Novel. This is a well told story expressing the author's ideas on Canadian identity and the American-Canadian conflict.

BRAITHWAITE, John Victor Maxwell 1911—

—Why shoot the teacher? Toronto: McClelland & Stewart, 1965. cl $6.95 [0-7710-1602-6]; pb $2.95 [0-7710-1599-2]

Setting: Saskatchewan

The author's experiences as a teacher in the Prairies during the Depression provide the material for this novel. Set in an area severely crippled by drought, sand storms and locusts, it realistically portrays the harsh lives of the farmers who survived almost unbearable hardships.

—Never sleep three in a bed. Toronto: McClelland & Stewart, 1969. cl $6.95 [0-7710-1605-0]; pb $2.95 [0-7710-1606-9]; London, Eng.: Allen & Unwin

Setting: Manitoba

This autobiographical novel consists of a series of recollections of the author's boyhood.

—The Night we stole the Mountie's car. Toronto: McClelland & Stewart, 1971. cl $6.95 [0-7710-1601-8]; pb $2.95 [0-7710-1603-4].

Setting: Saskatchewan

Life in a small Prairie town is described in fourteen comic episodes. The book is autobiographical, evoking the details of the author's experiences during the Depression as a young teacher, husband, and writer.

—A Privilege and a pleasure. North Vancouver: J.J. Douglas, 1973. cl $7.95 [0-88894-040-8]

Setting: southern Ontario

A car salesman's inability to cope with the reality of a rapidly changing and materialistic society results in the breakdown of his home and his business, and makes him a social outcast.

BRANDIS, Marianne

—This spring's sowing. Toronto: McClelland & Stewart, 1970. cl $6.95 [0-7710-1611-5]; London, Eng.: Harrap

Setting: the coast of British Columbia

Jane Farrow, a shy schoolteacher who discovers she has an incurable disease, gives up her job and goes to live in a deserted seaside cabin. Her only neighbours are her doctor and his wife, but she also befriends a man who arrives on her doorstep. Written in the form of her journal, this book deals in a simple and direct way with the last months of a lonely woman's life.

—A Sense of dust. Illus., G. Brender à Brandis Carlisle, Ont.: Brandstead, 1972. Limited ed. $9.50. Not seen

BRENNAN, Anthony

—The Carbon copy. Toronto: McClelland & Stewart, 1973. cl $7.95 [0-7710-1615-8]

Setting: indeterminate

Harry Carbon is either a rebel leader or an amnesiac. He finds himself in a country where he bears a striking resemblance to a famous guerilla leader whose face is on hundreds of wanted posters. He undergoes a series of adventures—hair's breadth escapes, various sexual encounters and brushes with death which sometimes seem real, sometimes fantastic. By the end of the novel, the reader is gripped in the same agonizing dilemma as the hero: half-believing in both alternatives and unable to choose which role—madman or rebel—masks Harry Carbon's real identity.

BREWSTER, Elizabeth 1922—

—**The Sisters.** Ottawa: Oberon Press, 1974. cl $6.95 [0-88750-118-4], pb $3.50 [0-88750-119-2]

Setting: New Brunswick

The story of three sisters who grew up during the Depression and World War II is told mostly from the point of view of the youngest. Though the family's history involves several moves and all three narrators tend to be loquacious, coherence is achieved through their recurring fascination with one of their homes.

CW OX2

BRIGGS, Margaret

—**Lost identity.** Toronto: McClelland & Stewart, 1968. cl $5.95 [0-7710-1650-6]

Setting: England and Switzerland

A victim of amnesia sets out to discover his identity. As details of his past life come back to him, it becomes increasingly apparent that he is blocking some painful but important memories.

BROOKE, Frances 1724-1789

—**The History of Lady Julia Mandeville.** London, Eng.: Dodsley, 1763. o/p

—**The History of Emily Montague.** 1769. NCL. Toronto: McClelland & Stewart, 1961. pb $2.75 [0-7710-9127-3]; New York: Garland Publications

Setting: Quebec City and England

This epistolary novel primarily details Colonel River's courtship of and marriage to Emily Montague. The letters offer a clear picture of Quebec high society after Wolfe's victory over the French and before the American Revolution. Of great interest are the characters' impressions of life in Canada, the climate, landscapes and Indians.

—**The Excursion.** London, Eng.: Cadell, 1777. o/p

CB CL CW ON OX

BRUCE, Charles Tory 1906-1971

—**The Channel shore.** 1954. LL. Toronto: Macmillan, 1974. pb $4.95 [0-7705-1179-1]

Setting: rural Nova Scotia

This novel studies the history of two generations of families interrelated by an illegitimate pregnancy. Bruce explores the self-awareness of uneducated people credibly and respectfully. The mutual support developed in the small, stable community is depicted with a sound sense of the underlying currents of time.

—**The Township of time.** Toronto: Macmillan, 1959. o/p

CW OX OX2

BRUCE, John 1922—

—**Breathing space.** Toronto: Anansi, 1974. cl $6.50 [0-88784-432-4]; pb $3.25 [0-88784-330-1]

Setting: rural Ontario

A middle-aged writer invites three friends for a weekend at his isolated country home. While they indulge in sophisticated conversation and eccentric private reveries, a wounded murderer makes a hiding place for himself in the cellar below them. In its violent conclusion, the novel makes a bleak, symbolic comment on the moral aspects of intellectual freedom.

BUCKLER, Ernest 1908—

—**The Mountain and the valley.** 1952. NCL. Toronto: McClelland & Stewart, 1961. pb $1.95 [0-7710-9123-0]

Setting: Annapolis Valley, N.S.

Using Biblical symbolism and a lyrical prose style, Buckler follows the Canaan family's progress to maturity and death. David Canaan's desire to realize himself as an artist involves him in a choice between two worlds—one the rural valley of his childhood, the other the isolated mountain peak of inspiration.

—**The Cruelest month.** 1963. Toronto: McClelland & Stewart, 1974. pb $4.95 [0-7710-1765-0]

Setting: Granfort, N.S.

Seven people, all suffering from traumatic losses, meet at a country inn. Buckler's characters gain self-knowledge by analyzing their problems. The plot is structured to emphasize the tension between chance occurrence and individual psychological make-up.

—**Ox bells and fireflies.** Toronto: McClelland & Stewart, 1968. cl $7.95; NCL 1974 pb $2.75 [0-7710-9199-0]

Setting: Nova Scotia

Buckler's fictionalized memoirs of his upbringing on a Nova Scotia farm are written in the form of impressionistic vignettes. A fusion of descriptive detail and grass-roots philosophy is achieved through the lyrical style.

Cook, Gregory M., ed. *Ernest Buckler.*
CVCW. Scarborough, Ont.: McGraw-Hill
Ryerson, 1972. Trade ed. pb $4.25; Educa-
tion ed. $3.25 [0-07-092958-0]
This book presents Buckler as an important
stylist and a writer's writer. His three prose
works are categorized chronologically as a
"novel", an "anatomy", and a "confession".
The study is especially useful for its inclusion of descriptions by the author of the
genesis of his characters and themes. The
three chapters begin with Buckler's own
commentaries, followed by mainly favour-
able reviews and critical essays.

Young, Alan R. *Ernest Buckler.* CWS. NCL.
Toronto: McClelland & Stewart, 1976. pb
$1.75 [0-7710-9622-4]. Not seen

See also Sinclair Ross, *Sinclair Ross and
Ernest Buckler,* by Robert D. Chambers.

CB CW ON OX OX2

BUELL, John 1927—

—**The Pyx.** 1959. New York: Popular Library, 1970. pb 60¢; London, Eng.: Quartet
Books
Setting: Montreal
This tale of drugs and prostitution is told
in the past from the point of view of a girl
who dies violently, and in the present from
the point of view of the policeman who investigates her death.

—**Four days.** New York: Farrar, Strauss and
Giroux. 1962. o/p

—**The Shrewsdale exit.** Toronto: Doubleday,
1972. cl $7.75 [0-374-26342-6]; New York:
Farrar, Strauss and Giroux; Pocket Books.
New York: Simon & Schuster; London,
Eng.: Angus & Robertson
Setting: eastern United States
When his wife and child are raped and mur-
dered by a motorcycle gang, Joe Grant sets
out to revenge their deaths.

OX2

BULLER, Herman

—**One man alone.** Toronto: Canadian
National Book Club, 1963. o/p

—**Quebec in revolt, the Guibord affair.**
Toronto: Centenniel Press. 1965. o/p

—**Days of rage: Quebec today and the
revolution underground.** Willowdale, Ont.:
October Publications, 1973. cl $6.95

[0-919660-00-2]; pb $3.95 [0-919660-01-0]
Setting: a Quebec mining town; Montreal
Buller has reversed the geographical sequence
and up-dated his characters, but has retained
many of the same socio-political themes and
situations of his first novel. Pierre leaves a
squalid mining town to join the FLQ in Montreal, where he becomes involved in revolutionary activities leading to his attempt to
assassinate Queen Elizabeth. The excitement
of the story is frequently interrupted by ex-
cursions into the hero's separatist-socialist
ideology.

BULLOCK, Michael

—**Sixteen stories as they happened.** Delta,
B.C.: Sono Nis Press, 1969. cl $5.95; Red
Bluff, CA: Kanchenjunga Press
These strangely fascinating stories force the
reader to restructure his conceptions of
reality and of the conventional short story.
The writing and the imagery are surrealistic:
"1: Tell me, what is the age of time?
2: A freight train crossing the desert.
1: With a mustard plaster.
2: And a basket of eggs."
Despite the often disturbing, even supernatural imagery, the author seems to maintain a light and humorous touch. The specific physical setting of the stories is unimpor-
tant, but certain universal symbols reappear
constantly: the river, the sea, the mountain.

—**Green beginning, black ending.** Delta, B.C.:
Sono Nis Press, 1971. cl $6.95; Red Bluff,
CA: Kanchenjunga Press
As in his other collection of short stories,
Bullock's writing contains a strange mixture of fantastic surrealism and matter-of-
fact observation. His usual technique in
these stories is to use a first person narrator
who passively observes (but sometimes par-
ticipates in) dream-like occurrences and
supernatural happenings. Particularly fascinating is the first and longest story titled
"The Green girl" in which a man is visited
by a forest being who lives with him and
leads him into final destruction.

BURNFORD, Sheila

—**The Incredible journey.** 1961. Paper
Jacks. Don Mills, Ont.: General Publishing,
1973. pb $1.25 [0-7737-7040-2]; Boston:
Little, Brown; New York: Bantam; London,
Eng.: Hodder & Stoughton; Pilot Books.
London, Eng.: University of London Press

Setting: northern Ontario

Separated from their owners, two dogs and a cat travel over 250 miles of rough northern wilderness. Their adventures are described simply without any attempt to invest the animals with human characteristics. As the story involves interaction between animals and people it provides insight into both animal and human behaviour.

—**Without reserve.** Illus., Susan Ross. Toronto: McClelland & Stewart, 1969. cl $6.95 [0-7710-1799-5]; Paper Jacks. Don Mills, Ont.: General Publishing, 1974. pb $1.75 [0-7737-7060-7]; Boston: Little, Brown; London, Eng.: Hodder & Stoughton

Setting: northwestern Ontario

This book documents a time the author and artist Susan Ross spent among the Cree and Ojibwa Indians in northwestern Ontario. Such events as the harvesting of wild rice and fishing for pickerel are described. Burnford concludes with an assessment of the injustices done to Canadian Indians.

—**Mr. Noah and the second flood.** Illus., Michael Forman. Toronto: McClelland & Stewart, 1973. cl $2.95 [0-7710-1789-8]; New York: Praeger; Buffalo, N.Y.: Washington Square Press; London, Eng.: Gollancz.

Setting: an imaginary mountain

Although it has the appearance of a children's story, this short tale is a contemporary fable. It tells of the gradual flooding of the earth due to pollution, and laments the dying out of many species of animals. In the end the world is overwhelmed with garbage. A final twist indicates the futility of man's attempts to control his world.

—**One woman's Arctic.** Illus., Susan Ross. Toronto: McClelland & Stewart, 1973. cl $6.95 [0-7710-1825-8]; Boston: Little, Brown; London, Eng.: Hodder & Stoughton

Setting: the Canadian Arctic

Burnford records another trip she made with artist Susan Ross, this time in the Arctic gathering information on the people, wildlife and land. Her study of the Eskimo people reveals the same curiosity and understanding with which she approached the Indians in *Without reserve.*

BUTLER, Juan 1942—

—**Cabbagetown diary: a documentary.** Toronto: Peter Martin, 1970. pb $2.95 [0-88778-040-7]

Setting: Toronto

In a fast-moving, surrealistic, photomontage style, Butler captures every facet of Cabbagetown slum life from street smells to Saturday night brawls. Michael, bartender and "hero" of this book, keeps a daily record of his life, local crimes and criminals, street personalities and class anecdotes, all of which are mingled with flashbacks of his own youth.

—**The Garbageman.** Toronto: Peter Martin, 1972. cl $6.95 [0-88778-063-6]; pb $2.95 [0-88778-071-7]

This first person narrative records the journeys and obsessions of a young writer whose only certainty is that everyone else is unreal. It is difficult to tell whether or not he is acting out the fantasies described in long hallucinatory passages filled with sadistic violence. In a frenzied attempt to control the direction of his life he travels to Europe and back to Canada, ending in a mental hospital. The connections between alienation and violence are examined in this kaleidescopic and potent novel.

—**Canadian healing oil.** Toronto: Peter Martin, 1974. cl $8.95 [0-88778-101-2]

Setting: Quebec City, Toronto, the West Indies

A Quebec bookstore manager, St. John the Eagle, the evangelist Christ loves best, abandons his customers (who include Frankenstein and Charlotte Brontë) to search for the meaning of life. This surrealistic quest contains elements of the Gothic novel, the Keystone Cops and Roman Catholic piety, and is interspersed with graphics, photographs, newspaper clippings and fragments of witty conversation concerning the nature of tree vipers and genitality, an anecdote about a man who was served wine improperly, and lyrical descriptions of love and fruit. Butler seems to have moved from the style of his earlier novels to something resembling, at least in its emphasis on unusual style and unusual sainthood, Cohen's *Beautiful losers* or bp Nichol's *Martyrology* and *Two novels.*

ON2 OX2

CALLAGHAN, Morley 1903—

—**Strange fugitive.** 1928. Edmonton: Hurtig, 1970. rev. ed. cl $5.95 [0-88830-024-7]; LL. Toronto: Macmillan, 1973. pb $1.95 [0-7705-0948-7]

Setting: Toronto

Harry Trotter, the central character of this novel, is the "strange fugitive". Restless in his job as foreman of a lumber yard, he is at last fired; this event is the first in a sequence leading to his final destruction. His pursuit of self-aggrandizement and drama causes him to leave his wife and begin a career of violence as a bootlegger. Although he becomes successful in his new career, he is haunted by the loss of his wife and by a feeling of impending doom. The circumstances of the second half of this novel are melodramatic, but the alienation of the hero and the spare style are sometimes reminiscent of Camus's *L'Etranger*.

—**An Autumn penitent/In his own country.** 1928-1929. LL. Toronto: Macmillan, 1973. pb $2.25 [0-7705-1031-0]

Setting: a small town in northern Ontario

The first of these two stories concerns the moral insensitivity of a man who is responsible for the suicides by drowning of his wife and niece. He escapes uneasiness only after he has been baptized into his wife's religion in the river in which she drowned. The second centres on a man whose studies alienate him from his wife. The shock of finding her with another man precipitates in him a kind of catatonia. Only after Bill has become "one of the most interesting people in town" does she return to care for him. The stories reveal how one can avoid discovering the motives and consequences of one's own acts.

—**A Native argosy.** 1929. Short Story Index Reprint Series. Plainview, N.Y.: Books for Libraries. Facsimile ed. cl $12.00

This book includes "An Autumn penitent", "In his own country", and fourteen short stories, twelve of which also appear in *Morley Callaghan's stories*.

—**It's never over.** 1930. LL. Toronto: Macmillan, 1972. pb $1.95 [0-7705-0945-2]

Setting: Toronto

John Hughes, whose friend has been hanged for murder, is haunted by the past in the form of Isabelle, sister of the hanged man. She pursues John and those who knew her brother well, twisting their memories and lives so drastically that John is forced to think of murdering her. He thus falls heir to his friend's violent history.

—**No man's meat.** Paris, France: E.W. Titus, 1931. o/p

—**A Broken journey.** New York: Scribner, 1932. o/p

—**Such is my beloved.** 1934. NCL. Toronto: McClelland & Stewart, 1957. pb $1.75 [0-7710-9102-8]

Setting: Toronto

When a naïve young priest befriends two prostitutes, he confronts the hypocrisy of his bourgeois parishioners and the expediency of his bishop. He is finally broken by his compassionate efforts to help the women in the face of an indifferent society.

—**They shall inherit the earth.** 1935. NCL. Toronto: McClelland & Stewart, 1969. pb $1.95 [0-7710-9133-8]

Setting: Toronto

In this novel of the prodigal son, Mike Aikenhead allows his stepbrother to drown and his father to accept the responsibility. Mike's growing love for Anna, by whom he has a child, revives not only his conscience (he asks his father's forgiveness), but also his consciousness of the meaning of death and life.

—**Now that April's here and other stories.** New York: Random House, 1936. o/p

—**More joy in Heaven.** 1937. NCL. Toronto: McClelland & Stewart, 1970. pb $1.75 [0-7710-9117-6]

Setting: any North American city

Kip Caley, a former bank robber, is paroled and accepted back into society. The welcome quickly fades when people tire of his stories of the underworld. When he is denied permission to work on the parole board as a liaison between convicts and the law, Kip realizes the city has merely used him.

—**The Varsity story.** Toronto: Macmillan, 1948. o/p

—**The Loved and the lost.** 1951. LL. Toronto: Macmillan, 1970. pb $1.95 [0-7705-0254-7]

Setting: Montreal

Jim McAlpine, on the verge of social success, falls in love with a girl who is neither socially acceptable nor willing to be possessed. Her innocent affection belongs to everyone, despite the confusion and hatred aroused by her association with the city's black community. Jim's desire to change and possess her leads him to doubt her honesty, and in the end he becomes a by-stander to tragedy.

—The Many-coloured coat. 1951. LL. Toronto: Macmillan, 1960. pb $1.95 [0-7705-0787-5]
Setting: Montreal
Scotty Bowman, an aging bank manager, meets Harry Lane, a popular young PR man, and is suddenly exposed to a new and glamorous social scene. His attempts to join this world lead to financial disaster, a jail sentence, and eventually, his suicide. Harry is held morally responsible for Scotty's downfall—in particular, by Scotty's friend Mike. In a long and bitter public feud with Mike, Harry attempts to estab-lish his innocence and regain esteem. The lack of communication between these two is mirrored in the relationships between many of the characters.

—Morley Callaghan's stories. 1959. LL. Toronto: Macmillan, 1967. pb $1.25 [0-7705-0250-4]
Setting: various North American small towns and cities
Each of these stories deals with everyday bourgeois or working class people and the moral repercussions that arise from the "slice of life" events related. The moral dilemmas are credible because Callaghan is adept at quickly developing convincing characters and situations. Twelve of these fifty-seven stories are from *A Native argosy*, and thirty-two from *Now that April's here*.

—A Passion in Rome. Toronto: Macmillan, 1961. cl $7.95 [0-7705-1123-6]
Setting: Rome
Sam, a failed painter, is a newspaper photo-grapher covering the death of the Pope. He meets Anna, a once successful singer who has since become an alcoholic. Sam rehabil-itates her, and she is forced to leave him. The novel hinges on the assumption that Sam's redemption of Anna is a great achieve-ment akin to art.

—That summer in Paris. 1963. Toronto: Macmillan, 1973. pb $3.95 [0-7705-1108-2].
Setting: Toronto and Paris
Callaghan's reminiscences of his relation-ships with F. Scott Fitzgerald and Ernest Hemingway have the psychological depth and suspense of a novel. With a flair for *reportage*, Callaghan re-examines his efforts

to be included in the social and literary milieu of 1929 Paris. His return to Toronto is a result of his belief that the writer's first responsibility is to describe that part of the world he knows best.

Conron, Brandon. *Morley Callaghan*. Twayne World Authors Series. Boston: Twayne, 1966. cl $5.95
Conron uses a biographical and critical approach to examine concisely each of Callaghan's books in chronological order. Since it relates mostly plots, it is useful as an introductory survey rather than an in-depth study. (Bibliography.)

Hoar, Victor. *Morley Callaghan*. SCL. Toronto: Copp Clark, 1969. pb $2.35 [0-7730-3004-2]
This short study is divided into two sections: "Technique" and "Themes". Part two is especially thorough, casting Christian human-ism and Sartre's existentialism as players in Callaghan's development.

Sutherland, Fraser. *The Style of innocence: a study of Hemingway and Callaghan*. Tor-onto: Clarke, Irwin, 1973. cl $4.00 [0-7720-0556-7]; pb $2.75 [0-7720-0580-X]
The literary and personal relationships of Ernest Hemingway and Morley Callaghan are examined in this detailed biographical and evaluative comparative study. The two men shared experiences, a writing style and a friendship in the Paris of the Lost Genera-tion. Sutherland looks at their failures as well as their successes and their differences as well as their similarities.

Weaver, Robert. *Morley Callaghan*. CWW. Toronto: Forum House, 1969. o/p

———

The Short stories of Morley Callaghan. Audio-tape.
Introduced and read by the author. Thirteen stories. CBC Cat. Nos. 610, 622 30 min. ea.
CB CL CW ON OX OX2

CAPE, Judith see P.K. Page

CARR, Emily 1871-1945

—Klee Wyck. 1941. Fwd., Ira Dilworth. Toronto: Clarke, Irwin, 1965. pb $1.75 [0-7720-0194-4]
Setting: the east coast of Vancouver Island, Victoria. B.C.
Emily Carr developed her writing style by trying to put clearly in words exactly what she wished to achieve in paint. The result was

clear, exceptionally powerful and unambig-
uous writing. This first collection of stories
is autobiographical, and tells of the many
trips the young Carr made to capture in paint
and words the dying culture of the totem
pole carving tribes. Travelling by gas boat
and canoe, she risked drowning, mosquitoes
and censure by "polite" Victoria society in
order to portray a culture she understood in
a way that was exceptional for her time. Her
ability to laugh at herself and her little dog
in the many precarious and tense situations
she encounters, her acceptance of another
culture as valid and her bravery in moments
of danger all confirm the words of the old
chief who "named" her; he said she had no
fear, was not stuck up and knew how to
laugh.

—The Book of Small. 1942. Toronto: Clarke,
Irwin, 1966. pb $1.95 [0-7720-0223-1]

Setting: Victoria, B.C.

This autobiographical work records the
author's childhood in a proper, religious and
British household. It is also a description of
Victoria in its early days, just barely past the
stage of a garrison. The city gradually succumbed to progress—the slow creep of land
fill, paved roads and modern conveniences.
The child "Small" never succumbed to her
repressive Victorian upbringing and continued
to love animals, dirt and singing off key. She
devotes much attention to animals and to
people—especially Indians, Chinese and
eccentrics.

—The House of all sorts. 1944. Toronto:
Clarke, Irwin, 1967. pb $2.50 [0-7720-0204-5]

Setting: Victoria, B.C.

All sorts come to live in Emily Carr's rooming house during the First World War. Although she had hoped to make enough
money from the project to allow her time
to paint, rents declined and taxes rose,
forcing her to become her own janitor. The
period proved artistically unproductive but
her menagerie, including a kennel of bob-
tail dogs bred for sale, provided her with
some comfort. In her simple and forthright
manner she recounts her experiences with
tenants' wiles and British snobbery, both
native and imported.

**—Growing pains: the autobiography of
Emily Carr**. 1946. Toronto: Clarke, Irwin,
1966. pb $2.50 [0-7720-0219-3]

Setting: Victoria, B.C., San Francisco,
London, Paris

In this autobiography, Emily Carr describes
her development as an artist. Her creative

aspirations unappreciated by her family and
in contemporary Victoria, she saved enough
money to study in San Francisco, London,
and finally Paris. Throughout her life she
concentrated on capturing the essence of
the huge forests of British Columbia, first by
copying Indian totem poles, then by using
her own eye to penetrate from the surface to
the reality. The selection from her correspondence with Lawren Harris makes clear how
important a role this member of the Group
of Seven played in her artistic growth.

—The Heart of a peacock. Ed., Ira Dilworth.
Toronto: Oxford University Press, 1953. o/p

**—Hundreds and thousands: the journals of
Emily Carr**. Toronto: Clarke, Irwin, 1966.
cl $10.00 [0-7720-0033-6]

Emily Carr named her journal after the tiny
English sweets because it was a record of the
small delights that made up the pattern of
her life. It begins with her trip east in 1927
when she met the Group of Seven and ex-
hibited some of her works in the National
Gallery, and ends in March 1941. The 1927
trip was the beginning of her second period
of painting, and she vividly describes her
methods and the encouragement given her
by Lawren Harris and others. Here the reader
encounters the "unvarnished" Carr.

———

Hembroff-Schleucher, Edythe. *M.E.; a
Portrayal of Emily Carr*. Toronto: Clarke,
Irwin, 1969. o/p

Pearson, Carol. *Emily Carr as I knew her*.
Toronto: Clarke, Irwin, 1954. o/p
CL CW ON OX

CARRIER, Jean-Guy

—My father's house. Ottawa: Oberon Press,
1974. cl $5.95 [0-88750-116-8]; pb $2.95
[0-88750-117-6]

Setting: St. Camille, Quebec

These stories describe the relationships between a boy and his father, and a husband
and wife in rural Quebec. The short sentences and paragraphs create a visually
fragmented style which reflects the episodic
nature of the stories. As well, the strong
clear language nicely mirrors the simple
rectilinear lives being described.

CARRIER, Roch 1937—

—La Guerre, yes sir! / La Guerre, yes sir!
1969. Tr., Sheila Fischman. Anansi Spiderline Editions. Toronto: Anansi, 1970. cl
$5.00 [0-8878-410-3]; pb $2.95
[0-88784-310-7]

Setting: a village in Quebec

A soldier's funeral vigil turned drunken wake is the setting for this serio-comic account of French-Canadian anti-conscription feelings during an "English" war. Drunk, the men express their feelings of anger against the church and the *maudits Anglais*; sober they conform. The translation is a good one.

—**Floralie, where are you? / Floralie, où es-tu?** 1969. Tr., Sheila Fischman. Toronto: Anansi, 1971. cl $6.50 [0-88784-417-0]; pb $2.50 [0-88784-317-4]

Setting: Quebec, near the American border

Floralie wanders in a land that is filled with horrible dream-like visions. Her husband, Anthyme, has reluctantly abandoned her because he is convinced that she was not a virgin when he married her. Carrier sets the stage in a rural area in the 1920s where people are tempted by the easy life in the United States and are afraid of both God and the devil. Floralie becomes a living symbol of the history of the province of Quebec.

—**Is it the sun, Philibert? / Il est par là, le soleil.** 1970. Tr., Sheila Fischman. Toronto: Anansi, 1972. cl $6.50 [0-88784-420-0]; pb $2.95 [0-88784-321-2]

Setting: a Quebec village, Montreal

Philibert runs away from a rural village and a brutal father. In Montreal, he quits a succession of menial jobs, unable to accept the position to which "the big guys" have condemned him. Then he meets the Ninth Wonder of the World, Boris Rataploffsky, the Man with the Face of Steel, and becomes his manager. For a while it seems as if Philibert might escape his fate. The translation is good, although the change in title from statement to question clouds Carrier's intention.

—**They won't demolish me! / Le Deux-millième étage.** 1973. Tr., Sheila Fischman. Toronto: Anansi, 1974. cl $6.50 [0-88784-429-4]; pb $3.25 [0-88784-328-X].

Setting: Montreal.

"They won't demolish me!" is the defiant cry of Duval, a roomer in an overcrowded two-storey house which is to be demolished to make room for a high-rise. Duval tries to create a collective offensive against progress, the capitalists in general and the English in particular. A Frenchman, two wrestlers, an old lady, a black, a whore, the landlord and his wife are all drafted into Duval's army. The translation is a good one.

OX2

CHARNEY, Ann

—**Dobryd.** Toronto: New Press, 1973. cl $8.95 [0-88770-140-X]

Setting: Poland

The Russian army rescues a group of Polish Jews hidden in a barn. Among them is a five-year-old girl who has no memories of another place or other children. Gradually she develops an awareness of what it is to be a child. All around her are adults who live in the past, who can never forget what she has never known. New fears of new repression finally drive them out of Europe to Montreal.

CHARTERS, Michael

—**Victor victim.** Toronto: Anansi, 1970. cl $5.50 [0-88784-411-1]; pb $2.50 [0-88784-311-5]

Setting: Scotland, England and Toronto

In a bizarre attempt to confess to an apparently non-existent murder, a man in a hospital tells the story of his life to a doctor. The character which emerges is totally perverse, paranoid and twisted, but nevertheless compelling.

CHILDERHOSE, Robert James

—**Splash one tiger.** 1961. CBL. Toronto: McClelland & Stewart, 1967. pb 95¢ [0-7710-1985-8]

Setting: Canadian air base in Germany

A Canadian war-trained fighter pilot has difficulty adjusting to the safety-oriented behaviour of a NATO base during peacetime. Despite the opportunity offered by plot and character, there is little discussion of political, social, or moral issues. Much of the dialogue consists of airborne radio communications.

—**Winter racehorse.** Toronto: Peter Martin Associates, 1968. o/p

CLARK, Delwin Mark

—**Inside shadows.** Toronto: McClelland & Stewart, 1973. cl $6.95 [0-7710-2136-4]

Setting: British Columbia

Lost on a mountain during a hunting trip, a man reflects unhappily on his family and his own crumbling will to live. Descriptions of the bleak, wintry terrain are interspersed with memories of growing up on a dairy farm and of how his artistic aspirations were thwarted by the banal compromises of marriage. Though he considers suicide as a way out, he eventually finds a road back to civilization, which he takes with a sense of hopeless resignation.

CLARKE, Austin 1932—

—The Survivors of the crossing. Toronto: McClelland & Stewart, 1964. o/p

—Amongst thistles and thorns. Toronto: McClelland & Stewart, 1965. o/p

—The Meeting point.* 1967. Boston: Little, Brown, 1972. cl. $6.95

—When he was free and young and he used to wear silks. Toronto: Anansi, 1971. cl $7.50 [0-88784-418-9] ; pb $2.95 [0-88784-318-2] ; Boston: Little Brown

Setting: West Indies and Toronto

Displaying a variety of techniques and styles, these short stories provide many insights into lives of West Indians both at home and in Toronto. The author, a West Indian, communicates his deep understanding of West Indian hardships, joys, traditions and prejudices.

—Storm of fortune.* Toronto & Boston: Little, Brown, 1973. cl $8.95 [0-316-14700-1]

Setting: Toronto

*These are the first two volumes of a trilogy about a group of West Indian immigrants in Canada. The novels focus on the tensions, problems and comedy which arise when cultures collide in their struggle for economics and cultural security. With a flair for dialogue and characterization, the author perceptively explores West Indian, Anglo-Saxon, and Jewish traditions.

CLARKSON, Adrienne

—A lover more condoling. Toronto: McClelland & Stewart, 1968. cl $5.95 [0-7710-2123-2]

Setting: a small village in France

Sara Rainier goes to France for the unveiling of a memorial to her dead war-hero husband. She rents a house in a village and soon finds herself inundated by relative and friends, but her most interesting encounter is with a sophisticated and amusing man who teases her about her "Anglo-Saxon shy". The book captures the stillness and dream-like quality of a hot and idly-spent summer.

—Hunger trace. Toronto: McClelland & Stewart, 1970. cl $5.95 [0-7710-2164-X]. Also published as Love affair. New York: Pyramid Publications, 1971. pb 95¢.

Setting: Toronto

The "hunger trace" is the mark on hawks' feathers caused by lack of food. Regina Adler's hunger trace is left by the loss of a man called Tiercel (a hawk's name—hers means eagle). Their love had all the wildness of the falcons Regina and her father loved to fly.

COBURN, Kathleen 1905—

—The Grandmothers. Toronto & New York: Oxford University Press, 1949. pb $1.65 [0-19-540117-4]

Setting: Ontario and Bohemia (Czechoslovakia)

This novel traces the ancestry of the author's grandmothers—one Irish and the other Czechoslovakian. Going back four generations, it describes and compares the economic and cultural progress of each family.

COHEN, Leonard 1934—

—The Favourite game. 1963. NCL. Toronto: McClelland & Stewart, 1970. pb $1.95 [0-7710-9175-9] ; Toronto & New York: Bantam, 1971. pb $1.25; London, Eng.: J. Cape; Panther Books. St. Alban's, Eng.: Granada

Setting: Montreal, the Quebec resort area and New York

This portrait of an artist develops the childhood and adolescence of Lawrence Breavman in cinematic flashes. Edited down from a much longer work, the novel is tight, poetic and witty. Games, disguises and play fascinate the romantic in Breavman; but as he ages he is able to distance himself enough to be ironic about them. His total involvement in childhood games slowly gives way to a new involvement in the adult game of sex, but he never loses his nostalgia for the purity and magic of the old games.

—Beautiful losers. 1966. Toronto & New York: Bantam, 1971; New York: Viking Press; London, Eng.: J. Cape

Setting: Montreal

A parallel is made between saint and con man and between sexual and religious ecstasy in this account of a man's search for release from his own shell of self-consciousness. Cohen's exuberant, varied and involving style is the focal interest for the reader, since the plot is outlined in the first few pages. "F", insane, sensual, saintly, domineering (whose rhetorical excesses increase as his brain is eaten away by syphilis) tries to help the narrator break the barriers

in his mind between past and present, imagination and reality, self and other; that is,
to become a beautiful loser—a saint.

Ondaatje, Michael. *Leonard Cohen.* CWS.
NCL. Toronto: McClelland & Stewart, 1970.
pb $1.25 [0-7710-9630-5]

In this introductory study, Ondaatje concentrates on what he calls the "sainthood"
aspects of Cohen's writing and the ways in
which these aspects tell one about Cohen's
concept of the poet's role. He also traces
changes in Cohen's work from 1956 to
1970, using one chapter for each of the
books. (Bibliography.)

CB CL CW ON ON2 OX OX2

Angel. Film.
Music by Leonard Cohen.

NFB   col   7 min   16mm

Ladies and gentlemen: Mr. Leonard Cohen.
Film.
NFB b&w 44 min. 16mm: dist. CFI.

Poems. Canadian poets I. Record.
CBC

Prose poem from "Beautiful losers". Film.
Read by Cohen.
NFB   b&w   4½ min   16mm

Songs. Record
New York: Amsco

Songs from a Room. Record
New York: Columbia C79767

Songs of Leonard Cohen. Record.
New York: Columbia CL2733

See also Hugh MacLennan, *The Immoral
Moralists,* by Patricia Morley.

COHEN, Matt 1942—

—**Korsoniloff.** Toronto: Anansi, 1969. cl
$5.00 [0-88784-405-5]; Spiderline Edi-
tions, pb $1.95 [0-88784-306-9]
Setting: Toronto

Korsoniloff is a man whose many selves
confront each other and confuse his sense
of reality. He describes in a kind of diary
his relationship with Marie and how it
comes to an end. In his kaleidoscopic
writing he attempts to attain a state of
mind where all conflicts cease to exist.

—**Johnny Crackle sings.** Toronto: Mc-
Clelland & Stewart, 1971. cl $6.95

[0-7710-2217-4]; pb $2.95 [0-7710-2218-2]
Setting: Canada and Europe

A boy from the Ottawa Valley becomes a
rock star and is then returned to obscurity
after suffering a psychotic experience. The
story is told in stream of consciousness
style punctuated with wry humour.
Journalistic reporting, fantasy, drug hallucination and realism produce a complex
effect.

—**Columbus and the fat lady.** Toronto:
Anansi, 1972. cl $8.50 [0-88784-423-5];
pb $3.25 [0-88784-324-7]

Cohen's collection of short stories, written
from an interior perspective, is witty,
surreal, and satirical. He creates a convincing reality in stories which record the
struggle to define personality.

—**Too bad Galahad.** Toronto: Coach House
Press, 1972. pb $2.50 [0-88910-097-7].

A cyclical, whimsical account of Sir Galahad's attempts to find the Holy Grail, this
short novel combines contemporary nonsense with historical and mythical content. The elusive and illusory Holy Grail can
only be perceived by poor Galahad at the
moment of death, and so the story is re-
peated over and over as Galahad continues
his quest in his many reincarnations (figura-
tive and literal). The book is beautifully
produced: the writing is accompanied by
appropriate illustrations.

—**The Disinherited.** Toronto: McClelland
& Stewart, 1974. cl $8.75 [0-7710-2219-0].
Setting: Toronto, Kingston, and a farm
north of Kingston

As Richard Thomas, the last of a line of
farmers, lies dying in hospital, he relives
memories and stories of his, his father's
and his grandfather's lives. The pattern of
disinheritance is established by alienating
experiences ranging from immigration to
city living. Richard's son in turn isolates
himself by rejecting the farm and trying to
make a new beginning in the city. More
than Cohen's other books, this one is
anchored in a realistic landscape.

—**Peach melba.** Toronto: Coach House Press,
1974. cl $3.00
Setting: indeterminate

This short, often playful book charts the
progress of a love affair between the narrator and a married nightclub singer.
Bizarre juxtapositions of highly tangible
images give the prose its poetry-like flow,
as does the inclusion of several lyrics. The

story could be interpreted allegorically as the artist's relationship to the workings of his imagination.

ON2 OX2

COLLINS, David M.
—The Mending man. Toronto: Coach House, 1972. pb $4.50 [0-88910-084-5]
Setting: a city
A childhood accident has left "the mending man" with one leg shorter than the other; his mother and schoolmates reject him. He studies under Dr. Bliss, a pseudo-healer, and opens his own "Health Institute". Pushed into performing an illegal abortion, he is jailed when the girl dies. Despite the stupidity and cruelty of the crime, some understanding of the hero's motives is conveyed through the device of first person narration—he writes with the clarity and emotional logic of a child. Bliss had said, "Man, not some men, is broken." The mending man fails because like all men he is broken himself.

CONAN, Laure (pseud. for Marie-Louise-Félicité Angers) 1845-1924
—Angéline de Montbrun / Angéline de Montbrun. 1884. Tr. and intro., Yves Brunelle. Toronto: University of Toronto Press, 1974. cl $15.00 [0-8020-2126-3]; pb $5.50 [0-8020-6234-2]
Setting: Québec City, a Gaspé village
Laure Conan was the first Canadian writer to attempt a *roman d'analyse* or psychological novel. Much of the novel is composed of letters written by the major characters—the young and beautiful Angéline, her father, her fiancé Maurice Darville and his sister Mina. Early critics held that the novel's major theme was the suffering that leads to God, and saw Angéline as the holiest of heroines. Later critics find her much more ambiguous. Her renunciation of Maurice's love is seen as a result of her excessive love for her father and his memory. The final ambiguity is an unresolvable one—was Conan herself aware of the Oedipal implications of her novel, or were they the unconscious expression of her own troubled mind?

CW

CONNOR, Ralph (pseud. for Charles W. Gordon) 1860-1937
—Beyond the marshes. Toronto: Westminster, 1898. o/p

—Black rock. 1898. New York: Avon, 1973. pb 95¢
Setting: a mining and logging town in British Columbia
One of Connor's favourite themes appears in this novel—reprobate men saved from damnation by the efforts of a beautiful good woman. The story is narrated by an artist who comes to town to draw sketches for the impending railroad. He describes the reformation of several men who drown their past bad deeds in drink, but who are finally cured through the ministrations of the Reverend Mr. Craig and the woman he loves, the widowed Mrs. Mavor. The novel includes interesting descriptions of such events as a sleigh race and a barroom fight.

—Gwen's canyon. Toronto: Westminster, 1898. o/p

—The Sky pilot. Chicago: Revell, 1899. o/p

—Michael McGrath, postmaster. London, Eng.: Sharpe, 1900. o/p

—The Man from Glengarry. 1901. NCL. Toronto: McClelland & Stewart, 1960. pb $2.25 [0-7710-9114-1]
Setting: eastern Ontario, Quebec City and British Columbia
This story of post-confederation Ontario centres on the lives of loggers and farmers of the Glengarry district. The protagonist, young Ranald MacDonald, must choose between a sinful life and the Christian ideals illustrated in the life of the district minister's wife, Mrs. Murray. In choosing the Christian life he is able to convert numerous loggers, even the villainous Le Noir, who contributed to the death of Ranald's father. The novel is at its best when describing community activities.

—Glengarry school days. 1902. Toronto: McClelland & Stewart, 1968. trade (cl) $4.95; text $2.50; NCL pb $2.95 [0-7710-9218-0]
Setting: eastern Ontario
Set in the late nineteenth century, this novel describes school life of a group of boys and girls and their teaching masters. The central character is Hughie Murray, the son of a minister and his angelic wife. There are some interesting details, such as descriptions of a bear hunt and a game of shinny, but the tone is often excessively sentimental and didactic.

—Breaking the record. New York: Revell, 1904. o/p

—**Gwen.** New York: Revell, 1904. o/p

—**The Prospector.** New York: Revell, 1904. o/p

—**The Swan Creek blizzard.** New York: Revell, 1904. o/p

—**The Pilot at Swan Creek.** London, Eng.: Hodder, 1905. o/p

—**The Doctor.** Toronto: Westminster, 1906. o/p

—**The Foreigner.** 1909. Toronto: University of Toronto Press, 1974. o/p

Setting: Winnipeg and the West

This story concerns the adaptation of Russian immigrants to life in Canada, and the problems that a Russian nihilist's son has in moving from a vengeful to a forgiving view of life. Connor suggests that the foreigner can retain a link with his roots while becoming a Canadian.

—**Corporal Cameron of the N.W.M.P.** New York: Hodder, 1912. o/p

—**The Patrol of the Sun Dance Trail.** New York: Doran, 1914. o/p

—**The Major.** Toronto: McClelland & Stewart, 1917. o/p

—**The Sky pilot in no man's land.** Toronto: McClelland & Stewart, 1919. o/p

—**To him that hath.** New York: Doran, 1921. o/p

—**The Gaspards of Pine Croft.** Toronto: McClelland & Stewart, 1923. o/p

—**Treading the winepress.** Toronto: McClelland & Stewart, 1925. o/p

—**The Friendly four and other stories.** New York: Doran, 1926. o/p

—**The Runner.** Garden City, N.Y.: Doubleday. 1929. o/p

—**The Rock and the river.** New York: Dodd Mead, 1931. o/p

—**The Arm of God.** New York: Dodd Mead, 1932. o/p

—**The Girl from Glengarry.** New York: Dodd Mead, 1933. o/p

—**Torches through the bush.** New York: Dodd Mead, 1934. o/p

—**The Rebel Loyalist.** Toronto: McClelland & Stewart, 1935. o/p

—**The Gay crusader.** New York: Dodd Mead, 1936. o/p

—**He dwelt among us.** New York: Revell, 1936. o/p

—**Postscript to adventure: the autobiography of Ralph Connor.**1938. Intro., Clara Thomas. Toronto: McClelland & Stewart, 1975. pb $4.95 [0-7710-2228-X] Not seen

CL CW ON OX

CORMACK, Barbara Villy 1903—

—**Local rag.** Toronto: Ryerson, 1951. o/p

—**The House.** Toronto: Ryerson, 1955. o/p

—**Westward ho: 1903.** Don Mills, Ont.: Burns & MacEachern, 1968. cl $3.50; pb $1.75 [0-88768-010-0]

Setting: Lloydminster, Sask.

A minister responsible for organizing the settlement of hundreds of people on the Canadian Prairies, shortchanges many of them. The novel centres on the family of a Manchester mill-worker that manages to survive, unscathed by hard work, cold weather, wild animals and prairie fires. The book simplifies and glorifies the life of a pioneer family.

CRAIG, John 1921—

—**Wagons west.** Toronto: Dent, 1955. o/p

—**The Long return.** Toronto: McClelland & Stewart, 1959. o/p

—**The Pro.** Toronto: Peter Martin, 1968. Reprinted as: **Power play.** Toronto & New York: Dodd, Mead, 1973. cl $7.95 [0-396-06761-1] ; New York: Warner Paperback Library

Setting: an Ontario city

The action scenes in this story of a hockey player's search for happiness might be of interest to hockey fans.

—**If you want to see your wife again . . .** New York: Putnam, 1971. cl $5.95; New York: Dell, 1974, pb $1.25

Setting: Toronto and southern Ontario

The plot involves a kidnapping and has some unusual twists. However, the characters remain two-dimensional.

—**In council rooms apart.** New York: Putnam, 1971. cl $5.95. Not seen.

—**Zach.** New York: Coward, 1972. cl $5.95; London, Eng.: Gollancz.

Setting: northern Ontario and midwestern United States

When Zach Kenebec's only relatives die in a fire, he discovers that he is not an Ojibway Indian, as he had always believed, but is the last survivor of an Agawa band that had come to Canada from the United States. Zach goes in search of his origins and is joined by a young girl and a young black man who are also looking for meaning in their lives.

—**How far back can you get?** Toronto & Garden City, N.Y.: Doubleday, 1974. cl $6.95 [0-385-00384-6]

Setting: Peterborough, Ontario

John Craig has written a series of stories about growing up in Peterborough during the Depression years. In these brief anecdotes he highlights the details, the many minor events, and the warmth and humour of small-town life during the thirties.

CRAVEN, Margaret

—**I heard the owl call my name.** Toronto: Clarke, Irwin, 1967. cl $4.95 [0-7720-0049-2]

Setting: an island off the coast of British Columbia

An Anglican bishop, learning that one of his young priests has only two years to live, sends him to a remote Indian village for his final parish duties. The simple, moving story describes the development of love and trust between the priest and his Indian parishioners. The title refers to the Indians' belief that each person hears the owl call his name when it is time for his death. In the end the young priest hears the owl, and having found peace with himself and with his fellow men, is ready to accept the call.

CREIGHTON, Luella 1901–

—**High bright buggy wheels.** Toronto: McClelland & Stewart, 1951. o/p

—**Turn east, turn west.** 1954. CBL. Toronto: McClelland & Stewart, 1968. pb 95¢ [0-7710-2358-8]

Setting: a small Ontario town

Fresh from the west, the beautiful Laura Paparin scandalizes the strait-laced people of Kinsail, Ontario. Her disregard for their petty conventions means she has a difficult time, until, of course, the right young man comes along.

CUTLER, Ebbitt

—**The Last noble savage.** Illus., Bruce Johnson. Montreal: Tundra. 1967. cl $4.00. Also published as **I once knew an Indian woman: the last noble savage.** Illus., Bruce Johnson, 1967. Montreal: Tundra, 1974. cl pb $1.95 [0-88776-000-7] ; Boston & New York: Houghton Mifflin; Boston: G.K. Hall.

Setting: a village in Quebec

This brief novel is a poignant account of a middle-aged Indian woman's daily life and her ability to face tragedy with dignity. It is written from the point of view of a young boy—one of the many summer vacationers in the sleepy Laurentian village where the story takes place.

DANTIN, Louis. (pseud. for Eugène Seers) **1865-1945**

—**Fanny / Les Enfances de Fanny.** 1951. FWCS. Tr., Raymond Chamberlain. Montreal: Harvest House, 1974. pb $2.50 [0-88772-143-5]

Setting: Greenway, Va. and Boston, Mass.

Fanny, a black girl, is married at the age of fifteen to the thirty-year-old schoolteacher in her village. Eventually he takes a mistress. Fanny moves to Boston with three of their four sons to live in dignified poverty. Finally, Fanny finds happiness with a white man, but dies shortly after.

CW OX

DARIOS, Louise 1913–

—**Strange tales of Canada / Contes étranges du Canada.** 1962. Tr., Philippa C. Gerry. Scarborough, Ont.: McGraw-Hill Ryerson, 1965. cl $6.95 [0-7700-0199-8]

Folk tales—one from each province, the Yukon and the Northwest Territories—make up this collection. Some stories appear to have been cut to the point of near-incomprehensibility, while others are excellent, conveying a flavour of mystery and exoticism.

DAVIES, Peter

—**Fly away Paul.** New York: Crown Publishers. 1974. cl $6.95 [0-517-51437-0]. Distributed by General Publishing, Don Mills, Ont.

Setting: Montreal

Fourteen-year-old Paul plans to run away from a Montreal children's home. The sexual and psychological sordidness of his situation, unrelieved by either proper physical or emotional care, seems realistic. As social protest, the novel lacks passion, while remaining one-dimensional in its character development, perhaps in part because of its narrative voice, that of an underprivileged, underdeveloped child.

DAVIES, Robertson 1913–

—Tempest-tost. Toronto: Clarke, Irwin, 1951. pb $2.50 [0-7720-0191-X]

Setting: a small Ontario city

The first in a series of three comic novels set in the city of Salterton, this one explores the problems of a group of upper middle-class Ontarians involved in a little theatre production of *The Tempest*. Central to the action are disappointed romances, artistic jealousies and the secret wine-making of the precocious daughter of the city's wealthiest resident. As is usual in his humorous novels, Davies presents characters whose problems, no matter how serious, are part of a fantasy world in which everything turns out for the best.

—Leaven of malice. Toronto: Clarke, Irwin, 1954. pb $2.25 [0-7720-0190-1]; Philadelphia: Curtis Books

Setting: southern Ontario

In the university town of Salterton a Hallowe'en prank initiates a series of misunderstandings and quarrels among several residents. The pettiness and provincialism of a small English-Canadian city is probed in this humorous exposure of its middle class.

—A Voice from the attic. 1960. NCL. Toronto: McClelland & Stewart, 1972. pb $2.95 [0-7710-9183-4].

A book about reading, this volume contains short pieces, mainly humorous, concerning books both past and present.

—Samuel Marchbanks' almanack. Toronto: McClelland & Stewart, 1967. cl $6.95 [0-7710-2275-0]; NCL. Toronto: McClelland & Stewart, 1968. pb $2.75 [0-7710-9161-3]

Setting: Peterborough

This almanac, selected for the most part from a weekly column printed in the *Peterborough Examiner* during the late forties and early fifties, outlines the astronomical and astrological year. It also contains extracts from the correspondence, musings, pensées, *obiter dicta*, apothegms and ruminations of Wizard Marchbanks. The Wizard, his head filled with obscure, arcane and fascinating trivia, carries on an eccentric, crotchety and humorous correspondance with friends, enemies, relatives and the world at large.

—A Mixture of frailties. LL. Toronto: Macmillan, 1968. pb $1.95 [9-7705-0252-0]; Philadelphia: Curtis Books

Setting: southern Ontario and England

When a rich old woman dies and leaves an unusual will, several people in the city of Salterton are affected, including a young woman who receives a scholarship to study singing in England. The story centres on her development into a concert artist.

—Fifth business. Toronto: Macmillan, 1970. cl $7.95 [0-7705-0081-1]; Scarborough, Ont. & New York: New American Library pb $1.25; London, Eng.: Macmillan.

Setting: a small Ontario town

Dunstan Ramsay, a retired schoolteacher, writes his autobiography, which is essentially the story of his quest for wisdom. He sees himself as having played a secondary but crucial "fifth-business" role in the lives of several people, especially Mary Dempster and her son. His attempts to decide how much responsibility he bears for their lives leads him into esoteric fields of study—magic, saints' lives, religious art and the relation of myth to history. The development of the plot is informed by the theories of Jungian psychology, although this presents no difficulties for readers who are unfamiliar with them. Davies has invested a small town and its "ordinary" inhabitants with mystery and romance.

—The Manticore. Toronto: Macmillan, 1972. cl $7.95 [0-7705-0891-X]; New York: Viking Press; Philadelphia: Curtis Books; London, Eng.: Macmillan

Setting: Toronto, Zurich, Switzerland

Fifth business ends with a voice shouting, "Who killed Boy Staunton?" The voice belongs to David Staunton, the hero of this book, a highly successful criminal lawyer and an alcoholic. His insecurity about his father peaks after his father's mysterious death, and he decides to go to Switzerland for Jungian analysis. The rest of the story deals with his search through his memories and his unconscious for clues to his emotions and behaviour.

Buitenhuis, Elspeth. *Robertson Davies*. CWW. Rexdale, Ont.: Forum House, 1972. pb $1.25 [no ISBN]

After a brief biographical chapter, Buitenhuis discusses the Samuel Marchbanks books, the plays, *Tempest-tost, Leaven of malice, A Mixture of frailties* and *Fifth business*. In the conclusion she examines the tension between romance and satire in Davies's work

and traces a development from the predominantly authoritarian voice of the earlier works to the more organically-developed narrative voice of Dunstan Ramsay in *Fifth business*. She gives a good account of the development of Davies's ideas and characters. (Bibliography.)
CB CL CW ON OX OX2

DAY, Frank Parker 1881-1950

—**River of strangers.** New York: Doubleday, Doran, 1926. o/p

—**Rockbound.** 1928. Literature of Canada. Poetry and Prose in Reprint. Toronto: University of Toronto Press, 1973. cl $12.50 [0-8020-1995-1] ; pb $4.50 [0-8020-6200-8]
Setting: an island off the coast of Nova Scotia
Rockbound, the island setting of this novel, is so isolated that it is hard to locate the story in time or space; it becomes, like legend, timeless and universal. David Jung, the hero, challenges his old uncle Uriah, the rich and grasping "king" of the island, and after performing the fisherman's equivalent of the labours of Hercules wins back his inheritance. The contrast between the ignorant, quarrelsome and superstitious nature of the islanders and their strength, diligence and courage emerges in the clear description of their daily life.

—**John Paul's rock.** New York: Minton, Balch, 1932. o/p

DE LA ROCHE, Mazo 1885-1961

—**Explorers of the dawn.** New York: Knopf, 1922. o/p

—**Possession.** 1923. New Portway Reprints. Bath, Eng.: C. Chivers
Setting: rural Ontario
In this romantic tale of love and jealousy set at the turn of the century, Derek Vale, an idealistic young Nova Scotian full of naïve hopes, comes to take possession of an uncle's farm by Lake Ontario. In turn, he is possessed by two women—the young sylph-like Indian, "Fawnie", and his aristocratic neighbour, Grace Jerrolds. Reminiscent of some of Thomas Hardy's early writing, the book provides many picturesque descriptions of rural life.

—**Delight.** 1926. NCL. Toronto: McClelland & Stewart, 1961. pb $1.95 [0-7710-9121-4]
Setting: Ontario
Delight Mainprize's presence in a small Ontario town creates an uproar in the hotel where she works, and finally involves the whole community in an extravagant battle of the sexes. Delight's beauty and naïve impetuosity are depicted with verve.

—**Jalna.*** Toronto & London, Eng.: Macmillan, 1927. cl $7.50 [0-7705-0087-0] ; Don Mills, Ont.: Collins, 1952. pb $1.25; Boston: Little, Brown; London, Eng.: Pan Books.

—**Whiteoaks of Jalna.*** Toronto & London, Eng.: Macmillan, 1929. cl $6.50 [0-7705-0096-X] ; Don Mills, Ont.: Collins, 1929. pb $1.25 [0-330-20198-0] ; Boston: Little, Brown

—**Finch's fortune.*** Toronto & London, Eng.: Macmillan, 1931. cl $6.50 [0-7705-0086-2] ; Don Mills, Ont.: Collins, 1955. pb $1.25 [0-330-20200-6] ; Boston: Little, Brown; London: Pan Books.

—**Lark ascending.** Boston: Little, Brown, 1932. o/p

—**The Thunder of new wings.** Boston: Little Brown, 1932. o/p

—**The Master of Jalna.*** Toronto & London, Eng.: Macmillan, 1933. cl $6.50 [0-7705-0089-7] ; Don Mills, Ont.: Collins. pb $1.25 [0-330-20262-6] ; Boston: Little, Brown; London, Eng.: Pan Books

—**Beside a Norman tower.** London: Macmillan, 1934. o/p

—**Young Renny.*** Toronto & London, Eng.: Macmillan, 1935. cl $6.50 [0-7705-0100-1] ; Don Mills, Ont.: Collins, 1948. pb $1.25: Boston: Little, Brown.

—**The Very house.** London: Macmillan, 1937. o/p

—**Whiteoak harvest.*** Toronto & London, Eng.: Macmillan, 1937; cl $6.50 [0-7705-0098-6]. Don Mills, Ont.: Collins, 1971. pb $1.25 [0-330-10118-8] ; Boston: Little, Brown; New York: Fawcett World; London, Eng.: Pan Books.

—**Growth of a man.** Boston: Little, Brown, 1938. o/p

—**Whiteoak heritage.*** Toronto & London, Eng.: Macmillan, 1940. cl $7.50 [0-7705-0099-4] ; Don Mills, Ont.: Collins, 1970. pb $1.25 [0-330-10157-9] ; Boston: Little, Brown; New York: Fawcett World; London, Eng.: Pan Books

—**Wakefield's course.*** Toronto & London, Eng.: Macmillan, 1941. cl $6.50 [0-7705-0095-1] ; Don Mills, Ont.: Collins, 1971. pb $1.25 [0-330-10050-5] ; Boston: Little, Brown; New York: Fawcett World.

—**The Two saplings.** London, Eng.: Macmillan, 1942; New Portway Reprints. Bath, Eng.: C. Chivers

Setting: Boston and England

Two babies, one British, one American, are born on the same day in a London nursing home. Meeting accidentally thirteen years later, their parents discover that the boys had been exchanged shortly after birth. The resulting attempt to return the boys to their "real" homes reveals differences in British and American temperaments. Though simply written, the story's concern with the effects of heredity and environment gives it wider appeal than the author's other books for young audiences, most of which are now out of print.

The Building of Jalna.* Toronto & London, Eng.: Macmillan, 1944. cl $7.50 [0-7705-0084-6] ; Don Mills, Ont.: Collins, 1971. pb $1.25 [0-330-10158-7] ; Boston: Little, Brown; New York: Fawcett World; London, Eng.: Pan Books

—**Return to Jalna.*** Toronto & London, Eng.: Macmillan, 1946. cl $6.50 [0-7705-0092-7] ; Don Mills, Ont.: Collins, 1960. pb $1.25 [0-330-10060-2] ; Boston. Little, Brown; New York: Fawcett World; London, Eng.: Pan Books

—**Mary Wakefield.*** Toronto & London, Eng.: Macmillan, 1949. cl $6.50 [0-7705-0088-9] ; Don Mills, Ont.: Collins, 1971. pb $1.25 [0-330-10133-1] ; Boston: Little, Brown.

—**Renny's daughter.*** Toronto & London, Eng.: Macmillan, 1951. cl $6.50 [0-7705-0091-9] ; Don Mills, Ont.: Collins, 1951. pb $1.25 [0-330-20201-4] ; Boston: Little, Brown; New York: Fawcett World; London, Eng.: Pan Books

—**The Whiteoak Brothers.*** Toronto & London, Eng.: Macmillan, 1953. cl $6.50 [0-7705-0097-8] ; Don Mills, Ont.: Collins, 1954. pb $1.25 [0-330-20199-9] ; Boston: Little, Brown: London, Eng.: Pan Books.

—**Variable winds at Jalna.*** Toronto & London, Eng.: Macmillan, 1954. cl $6.50 [0-7705-0094-3] ; Don Mills, Ont.: Collins, 1955. pb $1.25 [0-330-02168-0] ; Boston: Little, Brown; London, Eng.: Pan Books.

—**The Song of Lambert.** Toronto: Macmillan, 1955. o/p

—**Ringing the changes.** Toronto: Macmillan, 1957. cl $5.95 [0-7705-0093-5] ; New Portway Reprints. Bath, Eng.: C. Chivers

Mazo De La Roche's autobiography is written in the same expansive, gossipy tone as is much of the Jalna series. She describes her sheltered Victorian upbringing and the connection between her family life and the events in her novels.

—**Centenary at Jalna.*** Toronto & London, Eng.: Macmillan, 1958. cl $7.50 [0-7705-0085-4] ; Don Mills, Ont.: Collins, 1961. pb $1.25; Boston: Little, Brown; little, Brown.

—**Morning at Jalna.*** Toronto & London, Eng.: Macmillan, 1960. cl $7.50 [0-7705-0090-0] ; Don Mills, Ont.: Collins, 1962. pb $1.25 [0-330-10136-6] ; Boston: Little, Brown

*Setting: Ontario, London, Eng., New York, Quebec, Ireland

Mazo De La Roche's sixteen-volume saga has achieved international popularity: besides the editions listed above, there are many translations into other languages. The saga revolves about the love affairs, marriages, births, and deaths of five generations of the Whiteoak family.

The expansion of the original story to its present epic dimensions was somewhat arbitrary. To read the series, one should not follow the order in which the books were written; the order according to the Whiteoak family tree is: *The Building of Jalna, Morning at Jalna, Mary Wakefield, Young Renny, Whiteoak heritage, The Whiteoak brothers, Jalna, Whiteoaks of Jalna, Finch's fortune, The Master of Jalna, Whiteoak harvest, Wakefield's course, Return to Jalna, Renny's daughter, Centenary at Jalna.*

Captain Philip Whiteoak, his Anglo-Irish wife and their first child leave army life in India to come to settle in Canada. After a brief stay in Quebec, they move to Ontario where they buy a thousand acres of land and build the house called Jalna. The growing up of their four children and the lives of neighbours, visitors and servants provide an uninterrupted stream of events.

As an account of pioneer life, the Jalna series, with its focus on the emotional life of the upper class, is far from being a full portrait. Though it spans the better part of a century between the first honeymoon in the mid-1800s and the years following World War II, the saga deals with world wars, the Great Crash and the Depression only insofar as they affect the family's personal relationships. The characters' passionate loves and jealousies take precedence over everything else in their lives.

Geography, more than history, plays an important part in the saga. Separations and reunions are in keeping with the sentimental bias; so are the various regional stereotypes—mysterious Southern plantation owners, Quebec's transplanted French aristocrats, Irish rogues and Indian rajahs.

Although certain dominant personalities act as powerful nucleii for the action, it is Jalna which serves as the central connecting thread. It is over the transmission of the property from generation to generation that the most powerful characters ultimately divide and unite.

Hambleton, Ronald. *Mazo De La Roche of Jalna.* Don Mills, Ont.: General Publishing, 1966. o/p

_____. *The Secret of Jalna.* Paper-Jacks. Don Mills, Ont.: General Publishing, 1972. pb $1.95 [0-7737-7008-9]

Hambleton gives the account of the translation of the Jalna books into a series of TV shows. The many illustrations include samples of the author's handwriting, stills from the TV serial, magazine clippings, and many old photographs. The text explores several unexpected facets of the story's progress from conception to its ongoing reception by the public.

Hendrick, George. *Mazo De La Roche.* World Authors Series. New York: Twayne, 1970. cl $5.95

This biographical-critical study of Mazo De La Roche concentrates on the popular Jalna series. Biographical information has been mostly transferred from Hambleton's *Mazo De La Roche of Jalna;* criticism is mainly in the form of plot summary.

CB CL CW ON OX

DEMERS, James 1942—

—**The God tree.** Don Mills; Ont.: Musson, 1974. cl $7.95 [0-7737-0018-8]

Setting: Ottawa valley, Ontario

An insane and mute killer gives peculiar direction to a boy's childhood in an idyllic farm community. The novel's climax involves the murderer's death in a struggle with the boy, and is followed by a bizarre conclusion in which the boy identifies with the man he has killed. Between highly dramatic scenes, country life is described in a nostalgic tone almost eerie within the context of escalating horror.

DEMILLE, James 1836-1880

—**John Wheeler's two uncles.** New York: Carlton and Porter, 1860. o/p

—**Andy O'Hara.** New York: Carlton and Porter, 1861. o/p

—**The Martyr of the catacombs.** New York: Carlton and Porter, 1865. o/p

—**Helena's household.** New York: Carter, 1867. o/p

—**The Dodge Club abroad.** New York: Harper, 1868. o/p

—**The Dodge Club.** New York: Harper, 1869. o/p

—**Cord and creese.** New York: Harper, 1869. o/p

—**The "B.O.W.C."** (Brethren of the White Cross). Boston: Lee and Shepard, 1869. o/p

—**The Boys of Grand Pré school.** Boston: Lee and Shepard, 1870. o/p

—**The Lady of the ice.** 1870. Toronto: University of Toronto Press, 1974. o/p

Setting: nineteenth-century Quebec City

This is a wildly romantic story tempered with extremely effective touches of humour. It concerns the serious romantic involvement of the narrator, Alexander Macrorie, and the comic multiple love entanglements of his friend and fellow soldier. Among the characters are a mysterious lady with whom Macrorie falls in love after rescuing her from danger, a comic Irishman, and an irrepressible widow. Demille demonstrates his unusual ability to create an immensely interesting tale based on a highly implausible situation.

—**Lost in the fog.** Boston: Lee and Shepard, 1870. o/p

—**Among the brigands.** Boston: Lee and Shepard, 1871. o/p

—**The Cryptogram.** 1871. Toronto: University of Toronto Press, 1974. o/p

Setting: England and Italy

The arrangement by Lord Chetwynde and General Pomeroy of a betrothal between their son and daughter, unlocks a mystery that has been hidden for years. It involves an undecipherable message, confused parentage, and hidden identities. This nineteenth-century mystery story, despite several forced coincidences, is interesting and very readable.

—**Picked up adrift.** Boston: Lee and Shepard, 1872. o/p

—**The American baron.** New York: Harper, 1872. o/p

—**A Comedy of terrors.** Boston: Osgood, 1872. o/p

—**Fire in the woods.** Boston: Lee and Shepard, 1872. o/p

—**The Seven hills.** Boston: Lee and Shepard, 1873. o/p

—**The Treasure of the seas.** Boston: Lee and Shepard, 1873. o/p

—**An Open question.** New York: Appleton, 1873. o/p

—**The Living link.** New York: Harper, 1874. o/p

—**The Lily and the cross.** Boston: Lee and Shepard, 1874. o/p

—**The Babes in the wood.** Boston: Gill, 1875. o/p

—**The Winged lion.** New York: Dillingham, 1877. o/p

—**A Castle in Spain.** New York: Harper, 1883. o/p

—**Old Garth.** New York: Munro, 1883. o/p

—**A Strange manuscript found in a copper cylinder.** 1888. NCL. Toronto: McClelland & Stewart, 1969. pb $2.95 [0-7710-9168-0]
Setting: a fictional Antarctic world
A satirical fantasy in the tradition of *Gulliver's travels and Erewhon,* this novel describes the adventures of a man lost in the Antarctic. He discovers a country at the South Pole where attitudes to life and death opposed those current in nineteenth-century society. Like Swift and Butler, DeMille imaginatively manipulates his fantasy world to act as implied criticism of the real one.

CB CL CW OX

DEWDNEY, Selwyn 1909—
—**Wind without rain.** 1946. NCL. Toronto: McClelland & Stewart, 1974. pb $2.95 [0-7710-9203-2]
Setting: a small town in western Ontario
John Westley begins his career as a high school teacher during the Depression. Despite the warnings of an old friend and of his wife, he attaches his loyalty to a smooth hypocrite who becomes the school's principal. The gradual revelation of the principal's true character provides the narrative line in the novel. Despite some defects in characterization a clear picture emerges of what it was like to be a high school teacher in small-town Ontario before World War II.

DICKSON, Barry 1939—
—**Home safely to me.** Toronto: Anansi, 1973. cl $6.95 [0-88784-428-6]; pb $2.95 [0-88784-326-3]
Setting: Toronto and Ottawa
A young boy is sent back and forth between his separated parents. Finally he rejects both his mother, who lives in poverty in Toronto, and his father, a brutally misanthropic war veteran who lives in an Ottawa rooming house. Written in the first person, the novel gives a particular view of working-class life in the forties.

DOBBS, Kildare 1923—
—**Running to paradise.** 1962. Paper Jacks. Don Mills, Ont.: General Publishing, 1974. pb $1.50 [0-7737-7033-X]
Primarily autobiographical, this is a sequence of reminiscences which begins with the author's childhood. The various settings—India, Ireland, Tanganyika, Ontario—provide a broad scope for his storytelling. With wit and eloquence, he describes many diverse characters and combines adventure, humour and serious sentiment to produce a thoughtful and entertaining account of his life.

OX2

DREW, Wayland
—**The Wabeno feast.** Toronto: Anansi, 1973. cl $7.95 [0-88784-425-1]
Setting: Toronto and northern Ontario
Drew traces the survival of one man in a future world breakdown back to his childhood friendships and learning experiences. Unlike a Victorian ancestor who has left a stoic account of life in the wilderness, and his friends, whose beliefs are crushed by over-technologized society, Paul Henry adapts successfully to nature. The novel is a collage of literary styles and historical and fictional events.

DUNCAN, Sara Jeanette 1861-1922
—**His honour and a lady.** Toronto: Rose, 1889. o/p

—**An American girl in London.** London: Chatto, 1891. o/p

—**The Simple adventures of a memsahib.** New York: Appleton, 1893. o/p

—**The Story of Sonny Sahib.** London: Macmillan, 1894. o/p

—**Vernon's aunt.** London: Chatto, 1894. o/p

—A Daughter of today. New York: Appleton, 1894. o/p

—Hilda. New York: Stokes, 1898. o/p

—A Voyage of consolation. London: Methuen, 1898. o/p

—Those delightful Americans. New York: Appleton, 1902. o/p

—The Pool in the desert. New York: Appleton, 1903. o/p

—The Imperialist. 1904. NCL. Toronto: McClelland & Stewart, 1971. pb $2.35 [0-7710-9120-6]

Setting: a town in southern Ontario

Set in Elgin, a town similar to Duncan's home town of Brantford, the novel concerns a young man, Lorne Murchison, who is an ardent supporter of close ties between England and Canada. As Lorne's personal and political problems are worked out a vividly detailed portrait emerges of small-town society in the late nineteenth century. The novel is most successful when it concentrates on people and culture rather than on prevailing theories about imperialism.

—Set in authority. London: Constable, 1906. o/p

—Cousin Cinderella. 1908. Toronto: University of Toronto Press, 1974

Setting: southern Ontario and London, England

Graham and Mary Trent, a brother and sister from Minnebiac, are sent to London by their father to gain some polish. The resultant contact between new and old world culture is humorously described. Graham and Mary meet various strange and interesting characters, and both experience their first serious romantic entanglements.

—The Burnt offering. London: Methuen, 1909. o/p

—The Consort. London: Stanley Paul, 1912. o/p

—His royal happiness. New York: Appleton, 1914. o/p

—Title clear. London: Hutchinson, 1922. o/p

—The Gold cure. London: Hutchinson, 1924. o/p

CB CW ON OX

DUNHAM, (Bertha) Mabel 1881-1952

—Trail of the Conestoga. 1924. Toronto: McClelland & Stewart, 1970. pb $4.50 [0-7710-2955-1]

Setting: Pennsylvania and Waterloo County, Ont.

Two Mennonite brothers leave their home in Pennsylvania to emigrate to Canada, the land of freedom and promise. After an arduous trip, they finally arrive and settle in Waterloo County. Later many of their friends and family follow them and establish a new Mennonite colony in Ontario.

—Toward Sodom. Toronto: Macmillan, 1927. o/p

—The Trail of the king's man. Toronto: Ryerson Press, 1931. o/p

CW OX

DURKIN, Douglas 1884-1968

—The Heart of Cherry McBain. Toronto: Musson, 1919. o/p

—The Lobstick trail. Toronto: Musson, 1921. o/p

—The Magpie. 1923. SHC. Toronto: University of Toronto Press, 1974. cl $15.00 [0-8020-2150-6]; pb $5.50 [0-8020-6246-6]

Setting: Winnipeg

The "Magpie" is Craig Forrester, a native of Winnipeg—thus nicknamed for his terseness and raucous voice. This is basically a novel about post-World War I disillusionment, set at the time of the Winnipeg General Strike and dealing with the social conflict that ensued from the strike's failure and the dashed hopes of those who believed in a new order after the war. This conflict and its development is worked out through Forrester, who, despite his upper-class wife and surroundings, opts for personal morality and social justice. Eventually, he returns to his childhood farm where he reaffirms his traditional values of honesty and simplicity.

—Mr. Grumble sits up. New York: Liveright, 1930. o/p

DYBA, Kenneth

—Sister Roxy. Vancouver: November House, 1973. cl $7.95 [0-88894-024-6]

Setting: indeterminate

All the macabre events and the grotesque characters of this novel are seen through the eyes of a twenty-eight-year-old man who is apparently psychotic or mentally retarded. His sister's murder and torture of the family's two maids are given limited credibility by the warped narrative perspective. Frequent allusions to old Hollywood movies lead the reader to suspect that the author intends this psychedelic tale as a horror story.

EARL, Lawrence 1915–

—**The Frozen jungle.** Toronto: McClelland & Stewart, 1955. o/p

—**Risk.** Toronto: McClelland & Stewart, 1969. cl $6.95 [0-7710-7500-6]

Setting: an eastern Canadian mining town

Centred on a mine disaster resembling that of Springhill, this novel examines the interaction among several members of the community, and the effects that the mining accident has on their lives. Although the suspense is well-handled, the characters tend to be stereotypes: the town slut, the careless and greedy mine owner, the unsuspected heroes and heroines. Generally, however, the book is successful in its aims.

ELLIOTT, George

—**The Kissing man.** 1962. Toronto: Macmillan, 1971. pb $1.95 [0-7705-0884-7]

Setting: rural Ontario

Family histories and their transmission to the children unify these interlocking stories about a western Ontario farm town. "The Kissing man" and other pieces transcend the realistic mode through mysterious characters who express the human need for infinite compassion. The style is clear and confident, in the best tradition of the Canadian short story.

ON2

ENGEL, Marian 1933–

—**No clouds of glory.** Don Mills, Ont.: Longman, 1968. Also published as **Sarah Bastard's notebook.** Paper Jacks. Don Mills, Ont.: General Publishing, 1974. pb $1.50 [0-7737-7065-8]

Setting: Toronto

Having reached her thirtieth birthday, Sarah Porlock, a "lady Ph.D.", reviews her life and finds that it is time to make a change. Her story unfolds in various humorous flashbacks to the important episodes in her past. After selling her possessions and giving up her job, Sarah heads for Europe and makes a surprising decision about the way to bring some meaning to her life.

—**The Honeyman festival.** Toronto: Anansi, 1970. cl $6.50 [0-88784-413-8]; pb $2.95 [0-88784-313-1]; New York: St. Martin

Setting: a large Canadian city

Minn, almost forty, waits for the birth of her fourth child in a crumbling, cockroach-ridden house. She gives a party after a film festival commemorating the director Honeyman, whose mistress she was at twenty. Her memories are catalysed by the festival, and she muses about her past. In the present she acknowledges her limitations and regrets only the sticky woodwork and the thefts of the hippies in the attic.

—**Monodromos.** Toronto: Anansi, 1973. cl $7.95 [0-88784-427-8]. Also published as **One way street.** Paper Jacks. General Publishing, 1975. pb $1.50 [0-7737-7064-X]

Setting: a Greek island

When Audrey Moore's ex-husband gets into financial trouble on a Greek island, she leaves her lover and her job in London to go and help him. She arrives to find a place which is appealing in many ways, but filled with both Greeks and Europeans who are on a "one-way street" to nowhere. However, out of her sometimes comic experiences with a number of people, such as her homosexual ex-husband, a woman artist, a Greek lover, and a lustful Orthodox bishop, come insights which allow Audrey to retain a desire for life.

ON2 OX2

EPPS, Bernard

—**Pilgarlic the death.** Toronto: Macmillan, 1967. cl $3.25 [0-7705-0108-7]

Setting: Eastern Townships, P.Q.

The imaginary farming community of Stormaway is described through stories and diary accounts of the lives some of its inhabitants. The most prominent of these, a schoolteacher, makes observations about the others, between bouts of philosophizing, drinking, and fighting with his shrewish wife. The novel's often comic episodes are fable-like, with stylized characterization and an underlying concern with social manners and morals.

—**The Outlaw of Megantic.** Toronto: McClelland & Stewart, 1973. cl $6.95 [0-7710-3101-7]; pb $1.50 [0-7710-3102-5]

Setting: Eastern Townships, P.Q.

Major McAulay tricks Murdo Morrison out of the fine farm he wrested from the rocky soil. His son Donald vows to get it back. He learns the hard way not to trust lawyers and the law; his Scottish sense of justice depends on honest men who keep their word; when he encounters the "strictly legal" manoeuvres of Major McAulay he is on the defensive. He ends by defying the entire judicial system of Quebec.

—EVANIER, David

—The Swinging headhunter. Vancouver:
November House, 1972. cl $6.95
[0-88894-010-6] ; pb $2.95 [0-88894-009-2]
This novel describes the literary, sexual,
psychological and political experiences of
Bruce Orav as he grows up. His troubled
mind is more often reflected in the friends
he attracts—the. vague and circumlocutory
Mr. Lieber, the leather-skirted Marian—than
exposed directly. Although Orav plays a
passive role in this world of colourful,
"groovy" characters, he remains at the
centre of the novel.

EVANS, Cicely Louise

—The Newel post. Garden City, N.Y.:
Doubleday, 1967
Setting: a Canadian city
This romantic novel improves on the classic
boy-meets-girl theme. The chief characters
are middle-aged, and the book centres on
the heroine's effort to defeat her approach-
ing nervous breakdown. Some of the complex ways in which humans can neglect their
psychological and physical needs are rather
too simply described.

—Nemesis wife. Toronto: Doubleday, 1970.
cl $6.95
Setting: Europe
In this mystery novel about death, love and
guilt, the heroine marries her brother-in-law,
whom she loved as a teenager, searches for
the cause of her sister's suicide, and brings
happiness to her fortune-hunting husband.

—Shadow of Eva. Milton House Books.
Aylesbury, Eng.: Dolphin Publishing Co.,
1973. Not seen

EVANS, Hubert 1892—

—Forest friends: stories of animals, fish and
birds west of the Rockies. Philadelphia:
Judson, 1926. o/p

—The New front line. Toronto: Macmillan,
1927. o/p

—Derry, Airedale of the frontier. New York:
Dodd Mead, 1928. o/p

—Derry's partner. New York: Dodd Mead,
1929. o/p

—The Silent call. New York: Dodd Mead,
1930. o/p

—Derry of Totem Creek. New York: Dodd
Mead, 1930. o/p

—Mist on the river. 1954. NCL. Toronto:
McClelland & Stewart, 1973. pb $2.95
[0-7710-9186-9]
Setting: Skeena Valley, B.C.
This novel explores the conflict of generations within a small Indian community,
as well as the cultural conflict between
it and white society. The main character is torn between conforming to
the traditional Indian way of life on the
reservation, and conforming to working-
class life away from it.

—Mountain dog. Philadelphia: Westminster
Press, 1956. o/p

OX

FANCOTT, Edmund

—The Shell game. Toronto: Peter Martin,
1967. cl $5.95 [0-88778-014-8] ; Markham,
Ont.: Simon & Schuster, 1971. pb $1.25
[0-671-78089-1]
Setting: Montreal, Alberta, and London,
Eng.
Using stolen and embezzled money, Monty
Banks and his friends come to Canada to
play the biggest confidence game of all: they
open a chartered bank in Montreal. Not content with success in the financial world,
Monty moves into the political scene by
forming a new party and running on a plat-
form of fiscal responsibility. This implausible career ends abruptly however, as Monty
meets the fate of all con-men.

FARMILOE, Dorothy

—And some in fire: a novel based in a
northern Ontario community. Guelph,
Ont.: Alive Press, 1974. pb $3.00
[0-919568-33-5]
Setting: northern Ontario
Trapped in her marriage to an overbearing,
heavy-drinking hotel manager, Vanessa
Norden has an affair with a wealthy tourist/
entrepreneur from Philadelphia. Only after
her daughter is killed in a vicious incident
does Vanessa manage to shake herself free
from her husband and her lover. The novel
deals with the dual issue of sexual/eco-
nomic liberation.

FAUCHER, Claire (née Montreuil) see
Claire Martin

FENNARIO, David (pseud. for David Wiper)

—Without a parachute. Toronto: McClelland
& Stewart, 1974. pb $3.95 [0-7710-3120-3]

Setting: the Montreal slums

Fennario writes in his journal about old drunks crying in 50¢ movies; of kids raised on Kraft dinners, baloney and beatings; of waitresses asleep on their feet. Somehow he emerged out of the pain and craziness of a bad family life to write about the larger pain and craziness of poverty. Despite the despair, there is also spirit. A waitress refuses to serve two lawyers boasting about sending a man to jail for stealing a quart of milk; Fennario, burdened by frequent attacks of the "blues" himself, keeps his pen moving and his friends talking.

FERRON, Jacques 1921–

—**Dr. Cotnoir / Cotnoir.** 1962. FWCS. Tr., Pierre Cloutier. Montreal: Harvest House, 1973. pb $1.95 [0-88772-140-0].

Setting: suburban Montreal

Dr. Cotnoir, a "slum celebrity" and an alcoholic, is not so much described as evoked in this deceptively short and simple account. His young colleague's recollections of his funeral from the distance of ten years form part of the account, Cotnoir's unusual treatment of a mentally retarded man another. Finally there is the "living-dying" testimony of "Dr. Bessette" who goes from doctor's funeral to doctor's funeral, stealing morphine from their offices to feed his addiction. The events of the novel become a symbolic account of Quebec's emerging self-confidence in the 1960s. There are some errors in translation.

—**Tales from the uncertain country** / sel. from **Contes du pays incertain**, 1962, and **Contes anglais et autres** and **Contes inédits**, 1968. Tr., Betty Bednarski. Toronto: Anansi, 1972. cl $6.50 [0-88784-419-7]; pb $2.95 [0-88784-320-4].

Ferron writes about large families, fear of God, a treacherous élite, the English, rural communities, the rhythm of the seasons and love. He writes not only about those things unique to Quebec, but about the things Quebec has in common with other places. Ferron's writing is full of biblical and Freudian symbols and contains many historical and literary allusions. He treats established institutions and deeply-rooted myths ironically. The translation is satisfactory, although Ferron's unique blend of satire and fantasy is difficult to capture.

—**The Saint Elias / Le Saint-Elias.** FWCS. 1972. Tr., Pierre Cloutier. Montreal: Harvest House, 1974. pb $2.50 [0-88772-147-8].

Setting: Batiscan, P.Q., 1869.

The "Saint-Elias", a three-masted merchant ship designed for foreign trade, becomes a symbol of the attempt to open up Quebec to the outside world. In Batiscan, the doctor, the vicar and the merchant-owner of the ship form an alliance which opposes the narrow domination of church and state in Québec.

—**The Juneberry tree / L'Amélanchier.** FWCS. Tr., Raymond Chamberlain. Montreal: Harvest House, 1974. pb $2.50 [0-88772-143-5].

Setting: Montreal

On the surface, this contemporary fable is about the growing-up of Tinamer, a girl whose bent for fantasy is encouraged by her eccentric father. The story of Tinamer's disillusionment demonstrates theories about growth and development, and how the gradual acquisition of identity and memory tends to confuse moral distinctions. Explicit allusions to *Alice In Wonderland* bolster the book's fairytale quality, and give peculiar impact to references to current political and psychological issues.

CW OX OX2

FIELDEN, Charlotte

—**Crying as she ran.** Toronto: Macmillan, 1970. cl $5.95 [0-7705-0110-9]; pb $2.95 [0-7705-0109-5].

Setting: a large Canadian city

The flavour of day-to-day life in a Jewish immigrant household is conveyed in this account of the childhood and adolescence of Sarah Weil and her two sisters.

FORER, Mort

—**The Humback.** Toronto: McClelland & Stewart, 1969. cl $7.95 [0-7710-3164-5].

Setting: Manitoba

The frustrations of daily life in a Métis settlement provide a focus for the story of a resourceful, loving Métis woman who manages to find joy in her numerous children. With a delicate and realistic handling of characterization, Forer explores the lives of 'Toinette and the other members of the community.

FOXELL, Nigel

—**Carnival.** Ottawa: Oberon Press, 1969. pb $3.50 [0-88750-009-9].

Setting: Germany

The main action in this short, comic novel occurs during one evening at a wild, university carnival. Just before the party, Walter Phalts insults the son of the head of the English department where he will be teaching. The son challenges Walter to a duel; he accepts, and spends the rest of the night deciding whether to go through with it.

—**Schoolboy rising.** Ottawa: Oberon Press, 1973. cl $7.95 [0-88750-071-4] ; pb $3.95 [0-88750-072-2] ; London, Eng.: Dobson
Setting: England
Written in a humorous tone, this novel centers on Robin Thrale's upbringing at the boys' school where his father teaches. Through friendship with an artistic boy and through his sexual encounters with an older woman, he progresses from blind submission to rigid family/school authority to assumption of a position of power.

FRANKFURTER, Glen

—**A Stranger in my own country.** Don Mills, Ont.: Longman, 1972. cl $8.95 [0-7747-0093-9]
Setting: a small logging town in northern Ontario
Henry Sparrow founds Sparrow Lake and its logging industry and becomes its petty tyrant. David Bolster, his son-in-law, caught in an affair and unable either to tolerate or challenge Sparrow's domination, deserts his wife and leaves town. Five years later he returns, and all the old problems and gossip erupt again. This time, however, he copes.

FRANKLIN, Stephen 1922—

—**Knowledge Park.** Toronto: McClelland & Stewart, 1972. cl $6.95 [0-7710-3169-6]
Setting: northern Ontario, Quebec and the Prairies
The knowledge explosion has led to speculation about how to best classify, store and use knowledge. In this blend of Utopian novel and science fiction, an area of northern Canadian parkland is set up as a modern equivalent of the famous ancient library at Alexandria. Not only is "Knowledge Park" a repository for all recorded information in any form, it is a domed city organized on ecologically sound concepts.

FRASER, Sylvia

—**Pandora.** Toronto: McClelland & Stewart, 1972. cl $7.95 [0-7710-3177-7] ; Boston:

Little, Brown
Setting: a Canadian city
A child's life in a working-class neighbourhood during the war years is described in warm detail. The socialization of young boys and girls is handled in a specific but light-handed manner.

FREY, Cecelia

—**Breakaway.** Toronto: Macmillan, 1974. cl $7.95 [0-7705-1174-0]
The emotional, sensuous, vulgar world of childhood is recreated in this novel of a little girl living in the harsh land of northern Alberta during the harsh times of the thirties. From the moment of birth her eyes look out on the adult world and her mind struggles to make sense of what she sees.

FRY, Alan

—**How a people die.** Paper Jacks. Don Mills, Ont.: General Publishing, 1974. pb $1.50 [0-7737-7052-6] ; New York: Tower
Setting: British Columbia
The resettlement of a band of Indians is followed by an alarming increase in alcoholism, unemployment and premature deaths. Exasperated by the media attitude that Indians themselves cannot be held responsible for their "problem", an RCMP officer charges a couple with criminal negligence when their baby dies. In a documentary-like tone, the narrator uses this case to expose the attitudes of the police, the government, the newspapers and the Indians toward the deterioration of living conditions in the settlement.

—**Come a long journey.** Toronto: Doubleday, 1971. cl $6.50; New York: Manor Books
Setting: the Yukon Territory
A journey on the Yukon River from Whitehorse to Dawson is made by the narrator and his Indian guide Dave. Interspersed with their adventures are tales told by the guide about both Indians and white man. As the journey progresses the narrator learns the necessity of friendship for both physical and spiritual support.

—**The Revenge of Annie Charlie.** Toronto & Garden City, N.Y.: Doubleday, 1973. cl $5.95 [0-385-06257-5] ; Paper Jacks. Don Mills, Ont.: General Publishing, 1974. pb $1.50 [0-7737-7070-4]
Setting: British Columbia

When Annie Charlie's brother murders another Indian in self-defense, her white lover calls in the RCMP. The ensuing events give Annie a means of revenge for a life-time of submission to repressive white laws and customs. The novel's uneventful beginning leads to desperate conflicts and an energetic comic climax. Fry concentrates on the Indian woman's thoughts and feelings.

—**The Burden of Adrian Knowle.** Toronto & Garden City, N.Y.: Doubleday, 1974. cl $5.95 [0-385-07464-6]

Setting: British Columbia

Living under the shadow of his tyrannical rancher father, Adrian Knowle grows up to be an insecure and frightened adolescent. In spite of his fears, he is determined to win the love and respect of his father. After many painful confrontations and a prolonged absence during which he matures a great deal, he succeeds.

GALLANT, Mavis 1922—

—**The Other Paris: stories.** 1955. Short Story Index Reprint Series. Plainview, N.Y.: Books for Libraries, 1970. cl $10.50

In the title story of this collection Carol, a young woman, is spending a year working in Paris where she has become engaged to another American. She has vague romantic expectations of what it should be like to be in love in Paris, but none of them are fulfilled. The only glimpse she gets of the other side of Paris is through her French friend Odile and her seedy lover. Most of the other stories are also about Americans living in Europe.

—**Green water, green sky: a novel in which time is the principle actor.** Boston: Houghton Mifflin, 1959. o/p

—**My heart is broken.** 1964. Paper Jacks. Don Mills, Ont.: General Publishing, 1974. pb $1.75.

Most of the characters in these stories are women whose lives have essentially been failures. The collection includes a short novel, "Its images in a mirror", in which a middle-aged housewife reviews her life in terms of a consuming jealous fascination with her younger sister's life. Now that they both have families, she consoles herself with pity for her sister's less successful marriage. This story is an excellent example of Gallant's talent for description and characterization.

—**A Fairly good time.** New York: Random House, 1970. cl $5.95; New York: Popular Library, 1973. pb 95¢

Setting: Paris

Shirley Perrigny, a young Canadian, lives in Paris after the death of her first husband. She lives in complete chaos, which her second husband, a Frenchman, finds impossible to understand. When he leaves her, she spends the summer coming to terms with her problems in the company of equally disorganized friends. The book is most interesting for its detailed and sensitive revelations of Shirley's thoughts, actions, and surroundings.

—**The Pegnitz Junction: A novella and five short stories.** New York: Random House, 1973. cl $5.95; London, Eng.: J. Cape.

Setting: Germany and France

The stories included in this volume are about "Germany and Germans either at home or abroad". In the novella, *Pegnitz Junction*, the author describes the modern German parent and the young unmarried woman. Each story examines the cultural effects of World War II on German society and shows how individuals face the responsibility of their past. The writing is infused with a quiet dramatic intensity which effectively underlines the tensions in German society both past and present.

—**The End of the world and other stories.** NCL. Toronto: McClelland & Stewart, 1974. pb $2.95 [0-7710-9191-5]

Setting: Canada and Europe

This collection includes many short stories which have previously been published in *New Yorker* magazine. Each story deals with a character who is in one way or another a foreigner. The situation or environment is described, with particular attention to social detail and its emotional and psychological effects. Clarity and simplicity are achieved through the use of short sentences.

CB OX2

GARBER, Lawrence

—**Garber's tales from the Quarter.** Toronto: Peter Martin, 1969. pb $4.95 [0-88778-030-X]

Setting: Paris and London

Tribal life in the Latin Quarter of Paris is conveyed in a series of anecdotes. The sketches deal with individual women, with the group's bohemian Paris life, and with the author-narrator's experiences in London.

—**Circuit**. Toronto: Anansi, 1970. cl $7.50 [0-88784-414-6] ; pb $2.50 [0-88784-314-X]

In the first of these three stories, Reynolds Hall is a journalist interviewing a former movie idol Bruce Karle. Hall's obsession with Karle grows and is physically manifested in his inability to eat without vomiting; in hospital he can write only about Karle. Hall is gradually devoured by his subject, who seems to grow larger and stronger until he completely dominates the book. The themes of digestion and excretion recur in the second and third stories (the latter aptly titled "Death by toilet").

GARNER, Hugh 1913—

—**Storm below**. 1949. Markham, Ont.: Simon & Schuster, 1971. pb 95¢ [0-671-77464-6].

Setting: the North Atlantic, St. John's, Nfld.

A sailor dies aboard a corvette escorting a convey of supply ships across the North Atlantic during World War II. The captain decides, two days away from St. John's, to have the body buried ashore. Tension mounts as the crew attributes subsequent bad luck to the presence of a dead body on board.

—**Cabbagetown**. 1950. rev. 1968. Markham, Ont.: Simon & Schuster, 1971. pb 95¢ [0-671-7746-4]

Setting: Toronto

Ken Tilling leaves school at sixteen in 1929 with bright hopes for the future. The Depression changes all this; his life becomes a drudgery of back-breaking factory work, riding the rails and marching in the streets. Poverty's impact on him, trapped in North America's largest Anglo-Saxon slum, is described in what is a social document as well as a novel. *Cabbagetown* has become one of Garner's best known works.

—**Present reckoning**. Don Mills, Ont.: Collins, 1951. o/p

—**Waste no tears**. By Jarvis Warwick (pseud.) New Toronto, Ont.: Export, 1951. o/p

—**The Yellow sweater and other stories**. Don Mills, Ont.: Collins, 1952. o/p

—**Silence on the shore**. 1962. Markham, Ont.: Simon & Schuster, 1971. pb 95¢ [0-671-77463-8]

Setting: Toronto

Several people, connected only by the rooming house they share in a rundown area of Toronto, become involved in one another's lives. They interact for a while, but with the sale of the house go on their separate and for the most part, lonely ways.

—**Hugh Garner's best stories**. 1963. Markham, Ont.: Simon & Schuster, 1971. pb $1.25 [0-671-77467-0]

This representative selection of Garner's early work deals with the relationships between parent and child, worker and boss, and man and woman. Perhaps because the stories were written over more than a decade, the collection has more variety than later ones.

—**Men and women: stories**. 1966. Markham, Ont.: Simon & Schuster, 1973. pb $1.25 [0-671-78315-7]

These fourteen stories centre on the relationships between men and women. Garner's plots are based on the lives of "ordinary" people: an old couple soon to be separated by death, love-sick adolescents and those united by love, desperation or the need for revenge.

—**A Nice place to visit**. 1970. Markham, Ont.: Simon & Schuster, 1971. pb 95¢ [0-671-77466-2]

Setting: an Ontario town

Ben Lawlor, an aging free-lance writer who drinks too much, investigates the death of a young girl murdered two years previously. Seeking proof that the supposed sex murderer is innocent, Ben uncovers the real motive for the murder.

—**The Sin sniper: a novel**. Markham, Ont.: Simon & Schuster, 1970. pb 95¢ [0-671-77250-3].

Setting: the Moss Park area of Toronto

A psychopath kills four women, three of them prostitutes, before Inspector McDumont of the Metropolitan Toronto Police discovers the sniper's identity.

—**Violation of the virgins and other stories**. Scarborough, Ont.: McGraw-Hill Ryerson, 1971. cl $3.95 [0-07-092031-9].

Chicanos, hippies, workers, alcoholics, young brides and schizophrenics are among the characters in these stories which encompass a range of place and time from northern Ontario to Mexico, and from the Depression to the present.

———

Fetherling, Doug. *Hugh Garner*. CWW. Rexdale, Ont.: Forum House, 1972. pb $1.25 [no ISBN]

Fetherling briefly describes the literary and social influences on Garner's work and writes a short biographical sketch. He discusses Garner's novels and short stories, as well as some of his non-fiction work. The chapters consist mainly of plot summaries, with very little critical or evaluative comment. (Bibliography.)

The Novel. Audiotape.
Three tapes.
CBC Cat. Nos. 837–839 30 min.

Discussion with Scott Symons and Yves Thériault. Three tapes.

CB CL CW ON2 OX OX2

GIBSON, Graeme 1934–

—**Five legs.** Toronto: Anansi, 1969. cl $6.50 [0-88784-403-0]; pb $2.50 [0-88784-303-4]
Setting: London, Ontario
A winter funeral in a small Ontario town brings together the novel's two narrators— a professor and a graduate student. Both are failures, in work, in love, and in their own eyes. Their confusion is reflected in rapid flashbacks and narrative disjunction. A series of images of deformed animals linked with examples of human failure reinforce the point that to choose the conventional is to become "deformed" or "dead".

—**Communion.** Toronto: Anansi, 1971. cl $6.95 [0-88784-416-2]; pb $2.50 [0-88784-316-6].
Setting: Toronto, northern Ontario and the northern United States
Felix Oswald attempts to free a husky from a pet shop in Toronto and release him in the north, despite the dog's incurable epilepsy. A symbolic parallel is made between the husky's physical abnormality and Oswald's sexual one, as well as between their miserable lives and deaths.

ON2 OX2

GLASS, Joanna M. 1936–

—**Reflections on a mountain summer.** Toronto: McClelland & Stewart, 1974. cl $7.95 [0-7710-3320-6]
Setting: the British Columbia Rockies
A rich and idle middle-aged man recalls his fourteenth summer, when his mother had a love affair with a local man at her mountain lodge. The affair was the narrator's only exposure to love, and his memories and present situation are clearly

revealed in a series of fast-paced, often humorous flashbacks.

GLASSCO, John 1909–

—**Contes en crinoline.** 1930? Paris: Olympia Press, 1959
—**Under the hill.** [with Audrey Beardsley] 1959. New York: Grove Press, 1967. o/p
—**Under the birch: the story of an English governess.** By Miles Underwood (pseud.). 1960 (first published as **The English governess**); Paris, France: Ophelia Press, 1965. o/p
—**Memoirs of Montparnasse.** Don Mills, Ont. & New York: Oxford University Press, 1970. cl $7.95 [0-19-540168-9]; pb $3.50 [0-19-540202-2]; New York: Viking Press
Setting: Montreal and Paris
Written in the 1930s while the author was awaiting a critical operation, these memoirs record a young Montreal poet's impressions of life in Paris and on the Riviera during the late 1920s. His father's withdrawal of financial support, due to disapproval of his hedonistic literary life-style, leads Glassco to take a series of unorthodox and often illegal jobs. Vivid descriptions of characters, settings, and moods bring to life many literary, musical and artistic personalities of a legendary epoch.

—**The Fatal woman: three tales.** Toronto: Anansi, 1974. cl $8.50 [0-88784-433-2]; pb $3.95 [0-88784-331-X]

The first two of these elegant pornographic novellas are delicate explorations of the human sexual behaviour classically represented by Artemis and Electra, while the third tale is about the castration of men in a world populated and run by women. Glassco employs much the same peculiar symbolism and florid language as late nineteenth-century Decadent writing.

CB CW ON2 OX OX2

GLYNN-WARD, Hilda (pseud. for Hilda Glynn Howard) **1887–**

—**The Writing on the wall.** 1922. SHC. Toronto: University of Toronto Press, 1974. cl $12.50 [0-8020-2070-4]; pb $4.95 [0-8020-6202-4]
Setting: British Columbia
This propagandist tract was part of the long campaign in British Columbia against Japanese and Chinese immigration. The ideas expressed by Glynn-Ward, although exaggerated, were seen by many as prophetic; fears were expressed both in legislation and

in newspaper stories. The central character of the novel is an evil capitalist who encourages illegal Oriental immigration to obtain cheap labour.

GODBOUT, Jacques 1933–

—**Knife on the table / Couteau sur le table.** 1965. Tr., Penny Williams. Toronto: McClelland & Stewart, 1968. cl $5.95 [0-7710-3370-2]

Setting: Montreal, Florida

The hero, a French-Canadian deserter, falls in love with Patricia, the daughter of an American millionaire. Slowly, he switches his love, and his political allegiance, closer to home. He lives with a working-class Québécoise pharmacy student and slowly begins to identify with oppressed groups. Essentially a description of the process of politicization, the novel relates love, politics and violence in a poetic and compelling way. There are some weaknesses in the translation.

—**Hail Galarneau! / Salut Galarneau!** 1967. Tr., Alan Brown. Don Mills, Ont.: Longman, 1970. cl $6.95 [0-7747-0038-6]

Setting: Ile Perrot, Lévis, Montreal.

François Galarneau has transformed an old bus into a hot dog stand and runs it almost artistically, calling himself "the king of hot dogs". When his mistress betrays him, he loses faith in life and has a high cement wall built around his house. He records his misery in notebooks. Eventually he emerges and his old bus gets wheels—a symbol of Quebec's emergence from self-isolation. Godbout uses colloquial language in a humorous and down-to-earth manner. The translation is good.

CW OX OX2

GODFREY, Dave 1938–

—**Death goes better with Coca-Cola.** 1967. Erin, Ont.: Press Porcépic, 1973. cl $6.95 [0-88878-012-5].

Most of these stories use the act of hunting or fishing as a metaphor for the larger acts of spiritual and physical aggression committed by the Coca-Cola culture. Godfrey's simple style is deceptive, since there is no simple ending to these stories. Events are related as they occur in life and the meaning of events is conveyed subtly through juxtapositions among and within the stories.

—**The New ancestors.** Don Mills, Ont.: New Press, 1970. cl $10.00 [0-88770-021-7]; pb $1.95 [0-88770-022-5]

Setting: central West Africa

This decentralized novel, with several narrative voices, tells the story of the clash among neo-colonialists, leftists, the army, the Red Chinese and the Americans for the control of a young African state. Time is fragmented and re-fragmented as incidents and characters are picked up, then dropped. Rusk, a CIA agent, is killed several times in different ways—reflecting Godfrey's belief in a variable, rather than an absolute truth. History is seen as events colliding with individuals who have different visions rather than as a linear progression.

CB ON2

GODFREY, Denis 1912–

—**When kings are arming.** Toronto: Clarke, Irwin, 1951. o/p

—**The Bridge of fire.** London, Eng.: J. Cape, 1954. o/p

—**No Englishman need apply.** Toronto: Macmillan, 1965. cl $5.95 [0-7705-0117-6]

Setting: A city in western Canada

Philip Brent, with his wife and son, arrives in Canada to take up a position as professor in a university English department. The problems of the educated Englishman in Canada are explored through Philip's encounters with the jealousies and machinations of academic politics.

GOODSPEED, D.J. see Dougal McLeish

GORDON, Charles W. see Ralph Connor

GOTLIEB, Phyllis 1926–

—**Sunburst.** Greenwich, Conn.: Fawcett, 1964. o/p

—**Why should I have all the grief?** Toronto: Macmillan, 1969. cl $5.95 [0-7705-0119-2]

Setting: a small Ontario town, Toronto

Heinz Dorfman physically survived Auschwitz, but psychological scars remain to threaten his marriage. After years of isolation from his family, he is asked to sit shiva for his dead uncle. A series of emotional shocks causes him to recall the repressed memory of his capture by the Nazis.

CB CW OX2

GRAHAM, Charles Ross see David Montrose

GRAHAM, Gwethalyn 1913-1965

—**Swiss sonata.** London, Eng.: J. Cape, 1938. o/p

—**Earth and high heaven.** 1944. NCL. Toronto: McClelland & Stewart, 1969. pb $2.50. [0-7710-9113-3]; New York: Lancer.

Setting: Montreal

The problems of anti-semitism during the 1940s emerge through the love story of a

Westmount woman and a Jewish man. In fighting for her relationship with Marc Reiser, Erica Drake discovers her preconceptions both about Jews and her father.

CB CW ON2 OX

GRAINGER, M. Allerdale 1874-1941

—Woodsmen of the west. 1908. NCL. Toronto: McClelland & Stewart, 1964. pb $1.75

Setting: Vancouver, and the woods of British Columbia

Mart, the well-educated Englishman who narrates this story, slowly moves from the position of outsider to insider in the masculine world of the logger. Grainger's accuracy concerning the details of logging at the turn of the century has made this a standard source of information on the industry's history. He avoids romanticizing the men who struggle to exploit the primeval forests; the isolation of man within a sometime hostile nature is at times reminiscent of Conrad.

GREEN, Henry Gordon 1912—

—The Praying mantis. Fredericton: Brunswick Press, 1953. pb $1.00

Setting: a farm in southwestern Ontario

Myra, a young woman from a large and poor family, is sent to nurse her dying aunt. Her uncle is a tyrannical, violent, God-fearing farmer and preacher who tries to wield his power over Myra just as he has over everyone else in the community. Myra, who is strong-willed and independent herself, manages to avoid any serious conflict until he interferes in her plans to help his retarded son and to elope with her fiancé.

—A Time to pass over: life with a pioneer grandmother. 1962. CBL. Toronto: McClelland & Stewart, 1968. pb 95¢ [0-7710-3214-5]; Montreal: Harvest House 1966, cl $4.95

Setting: Arthur, Ontario

An old woman dying of pneumonia spends a night in delirium recalling her life: her early marriage, the births of her numerous sons, the constant struggle against poverty. In the end, she wins both her fights: against death and against her evangelical and tyrannical daughter-in-law.

—A Countryman's Christmas. Fredericton: Brunswick Press, 1965. $3.50. Not seen

—Professor go home. Montreal: Harvest House, 1966. cl $4.00 [0-88772-062-5]; pb $2.50 [0-88772-061-7]. Not seen

—Goodbye little town. Toronto: McClelland & Stewart, 1970. o/p

—Diary of a dirty old man. Toronto: McClelland & Stewart, 1974. cl $7.95 [0-7710-3627-2]

Setting: rural Quebec

Written in the form of a diary, this semi-autobiographical book is about a middle-aged farmer who also teaches high school. The first part of the book records his day-to-day experiences at the farm and school, and contains anecdotes about various people and animals. The second deals mostly with an ex-pupil who falls in love with him, and the relationship which develops.

GREEN, Robert

—The Great leap backward. Toronto: McClelland & Stewart, 1968. cl $4.95 [0-7710-3620-5]

Setting: Toronto and rural Ontario

Set in the twenty-first century, this science fiction novel describes a society split into two groups—the city dwellers who are dominated by their machines, and the naturalists who live in small colonies in the countryside. In a futuristic Toronto, a disaffected jazz musician makes an insurrectionary attack on Queen's Park, the automation centre of Canada.

GREY, Francis William 1860-1939

—The Curé of St. Philippe. 1899. NCL. Toronto: McClelland & Stewart, 1970 pb $2.95 [0-7710-9172-9]

Setting: A small town in Quebec

Written in 1899, this novel describes the events surrounding the 1896 federal election in which the Conservative government fell to Wilfrid Laurier and the Liberals. Grey chooses a small French-Canadian parish, St. Philippe, and follows the events through the involvement of the townspeople, the local member of parliament and the new curé. The result is both a detailed historical view of the period and a close look at the lives of people involved in making moral and political decisions.

OX

GREY OWL (pseud. for Archibald Stansfeld Belaney) 1888-1938

—The Men of the last frontier.* 1931. Toronto: Macmillan, 1972. pb $4.95 [0-7705-0763-8]

—Pilgrims of the wild.* 1934. Toronto: Macmillan, 1935. cl $7.95 [0-7705-1168-6];

pb $4.95 [0-7705-1033-7] ; London, Eng.:
P. Davies; Puffin Books. Harmondsworth,
Mddx., Eng.: Penguin

—Sajo and her beaver people.* Toronto:
Macmillan, 1935. cl $7.95 [0-7705-1104-X] ;
pb $4.95 [0-7705-1105-8] ; London, Eng.:
P. Davies. London, Eng.: Heineman Educ.

—Tales of an empty cabin.* 1936. Toronto:
Macmillan, 1972. pb $4.95 [0-7705-0764-6]

—The Tree. By Wa-sha-quon-asin. Toronto:
Macmillan, 1937. o/p

—A Book of Grey Owl: pages from the
writing of Wa-sha-quon-asin.* 1938. 2nd ed.,
E.E. Reynolds. Toronto: Macmillan, 1941.
cl $7.95 [0-7705-0882-0] ; pb $4.95
[0-7705-0762-X] ; London, Eng.: P. Davies

*Setting: Canadian wilderness

All of Grey Owl's books are stories about
the wilderness and the lives and myths of
Indians, trappers and animals. They are
simply told adventures and descriptions of
nature.

Anahero (Gertrude Bernard). *My life with
Grey Owl.* London: Davies, 1940. o/p

Anahero (Gertrude Bernard). *Divil in deer-
skins: my life with Grey Owl.* Toronto:
New Press, 1972, cl $7.50 [0-88770-126-4].
Also published as *Grey Owl and I.* London:
Heineman

Anahero, who lived as Grey Owl's wife
during the most creative part of his career,
writes of their relationship. She was responsible for the final conversion of the
Englishman Belaney into the Indian, Grey
Owl. Her feeling for the wild and its animals
turned him from a trapper and hunter into
a conservationist and protector of the
"beaver people". She describes their found-
ing of a beaver colony, the movies they
made to promote conservation and their
life in Riding Mountain National Park,
Manitoba. (Twenty-six photographs.)

Cory, Harper. *Grey Owl and the beaver
people.* London: Nelson, 1935. o/p

Dickson, Lovat, ed. *The Green leaf.* London:
Lovat Dickson, 1938. o/p

Dickson, Lovat. *Half-breed. The story of
Grey Owl.* London: Davies, 1939. o/p

Dickson, Lovat. *Wilderness man: the strange
story of Grey Owl.* Toronto: Macmillan,
1973, cl $10.00 [0-7705-1043-4]. Also
published as *Wilderness man: the curious
life of Archie Belaney, called Grey Owl.*
New York: Atheneum

Lovat Dickson published several of Grey
Owl's books and organized his tremendously
successful lecture tours in England. When
Grey Owl died, shortly after the second of
these tours which had included a Royal
Command Performance, controversy erupted.
It was revealed that he had no Indian blood
at all, and he was denounced as a fraud, an
imposter and a charlatan. Dickson rushed
to his defence, initiating an investigation
into Grey Owl's life in an attempt to clear
his name. His discovery that Grey Owl was
wholly English, in body if not in spirit, did
not diminish his respect for Grey Owl's
ability as a field naturalist or his mission to
protect Canada's wilderness and its inhabitants. This account of the "Indianization"
of Archie Belaney provides answers to many
of the questions asked about Grey Owl, the
most important being, perhaps, his motiva-
tion in changing not only his identity, but
also his race. This book contains maps,
twenty-eight photographs, an index and a
bibliography.

Polk, James. *Wilderness writers.* Toronto:
Clarke, Irwin, 1972. [0-7720-0565-0]

After a brief discussion of the development
of the animal story, Polk details the lives
of Ernest Thompson Seton, Sir Charles
G.D. Roberts and Grey Owl. His method is
biographical rather than critical, focusing
on the development of these men's interest
in animals and their conflicts with anti-
conservationists. He describes particular
incidents which inspired various stories.
(Bibliographical notes.)

CW OX

GRISDALE, Alex see Nancy Shipley

GROVE, Frederick Philip 1871-1948

—Over prairie trails. 1922. NCL. Toronto:
McClelland & Stewart, 1970. pb $1.95
[0-7710-9191-X]

Setting: Prairies

One winter, while Grove was a teacher in
Manitoba, his job took him thirty-four miles
from his home. He would spend the week at
the school and journey home each weekend
by horse and cutter. The seven sketches in
this book are descriptions of the journeys—
his moods, observations and experiences.
Central to the stories is the theme of Grove's
struggle against nature.

—The Turn of the year. Toronto: McClelland
& Stewart, 1923. o/p

—Settlers of the marsh. 1925. NCL. Toronto:
McClelland & Stewart, 1965. pb $2.25
[0-7710-9150-8]

Setting: Prairies

A young Swedish immigrant settles as a farmer on the Canadian Prairies. His strength and determination make him prosperous, but his innocence and naïveté cause him many problems. Jilted by the woman he loves, he unwittingly finds himself with the town whore, and then feels obliged to marry her. For many years after he lives in the misery of a stringent moral and ethical code. When he denies his wife a divorce she torments him until he finally kills her.

—A Search for America: the odyssey of an immigrant. 1927. NCL. McClelland & Stewart, 1971. pb $2.95 [0-7710-9176-1]

Setting: late nineteenth-century North America

When Phil Branden recovers from the shock of discovering his father's bankruptcy, he leaves Europe's artistic circles to start a life for himself in America. He works as a waiter in Toronto, an encyclopedia salesman in New York, then leaves the cities to tramp through the countryside, finally returning to a Canadian prairie town to teach and counsel immigrants. The book is divided into four main chapters that are sub-divided episodically to emphasize the story's double nature: immigrant saga on the surface, spiritual quest on a symbolic level.

—Our daily bread. New York: Macmillan, 1928. o/p

—The Yoke of life. New York: R.R. Smith, 1930. o/p

—Fruits of the earth. 1933. NCL. Toronto: McClelland & Stewart, 1965. pb $1.95 [0-7710-9149-4]

Setting: Prairies

The material ambitions of a shrewd and idealistic Prairie farmer force him into slavery—first to the soil and then to machinery. Blinded by his ambitions and his struggle with nature, he fails to find happiness in his day-to-day life in spite of his material success.

—Two generations: a story of present-day Ontario. Toronto: Ryerson, 1939. o/p

—Consider her ways. Toronto: Macmillan, 1947. o/p

—In search of myself. 1946. NCL. Toronto: McClelland & Stewart, 1974. pb $2.95 [0-7710-9194-X]

Setting: the United States and Canada

Although D.O. Spettigue has pointed out the fictions in what was thought to be al-most an autobiography, *In search of myself* is still interesting for its revelation of the author. It outlines the story of a young man who comes to America in search of the American dream. In the end he settles in Canada, and it is from this point that the narrative parallels Grove's life most closely. It is a useful view of his life and the picture he had of himself as a writer.

—The Master of the mill. 1944. NCL. Toronto: McClelland & Stewart, 1961. pb $2.95 [0-7710-9119-2]

Setting: Prairies

Senator Samuel Clark is an old man — the last of three generations of mill owners. As he searches the past for a meaning to his life, the history of the mill and each successive generation of its masters unfolds. The central symbol, the mill, represents the power of technology. One discovers how each master has attempted to enforce his will upon the mill, and how the inherent power of the mill has thwarted their endeavours and enslaved them.

—Tales from the margin. Ed., Desmond Pacey. Scarborough, Ont.: McGraw-Hill Ryerson, 1971. cl $8.95 [0-7700-0072-X]

Setting: Prairies

These short stories best show Grove's dexterity in handling the chronicle and narrative style. For example, they describe the hardships of a country woman or tell the story of a farmer who is duped into forfeiting his farm.

The Letters of Frederick Philip Grove. Ed. with intro. and notes by Desmond Pacey. Toronto and Buffalo: University of Toronto Press, 1976. cl $25.00 [0-8020-5311-4]

Pacey, Desmond. *Frederick Philip Grove.* Toronto: Ryerson, 1945. o/p

The new discoveries concerning Grove's life made by Margaret Stobie and Douglas Spettigue make Pacey's biographical sketches and his views on *In search of myself* and *A Search for America* somewhat outdated. However, his chapters on Grove's other novels are still relevant and worth reading. Also included are a chapter on Grove's style and technique, and another which deals with his main themes and ideas. The book ends with a short discussion of Grove's place in Canadian literature.

Pacey, Desmond. *F.P. Grove.* CVCW. Scarborough, Ont.: McGraw-Hill Ryerson, 1970.

pb $3.25 [0-7700-0314-1]

Desmond Pacey has collected nine articles about Frederick Philip Grove written between 1928 and 1963. He also has included excerpts from twelve contemporary reviews of Grove's novels. Three obituary tributes by Northrop Frye, Lorne Pierce and Kay Rowe, followed by a bibliography of Grove's writing conclude the collection. Pacey, in his introduction, surveys Grove's literary reputation and comments briefly on the criticism his works have received.

Spettigue, Douglas O. *Frederick Philip Grove.* SCL. Toronto: Copp Clark, 1969. pb $2.35 [0-7730-3005-0]

The first half of this book discusses the various discrepancies in Grove's alleged autobiographies. The second part consists of a brief critical analysis of Grove's work. It touches upon the style and technique of the chronicle and the narrative, and discusses Grove's concept of the hero.

Spettigue, Douglas O. *FPG: the European years.* Ottawa: Oberon Press, 1973. cl $11.95 [0-88750-099-4]

With the publication of Frederick Philip Grove's supposedly autobiographical novels, the details of his life appeared to be fully outlined. Since then there has been much speculation as to the biographical accuracy of these novels. This well-researched book successfully unveils many interesting facts about Grove, the stylish romanticism in which he indulged, and the literary circles in which he moved. In this description of Grove's life from his birth in 1871 to his flight from Europe in 1909, Spettigue attempts to recreate his true character and to show how the experiences of his early years affected his work.

Stobie, Margaret R. *F.P. Grove.* World Author Series. Boston: Twayne, 1973. cl $5.95

Stobie traces Grove's life from 1913 until his death in 1948. The biographical details offer insights into Grove's contemporaries, his publishing escapades, his family, and his life as a teacher. The critical sections supply clear and comprehensive plot summaries of his novels, sketches of major characters and textual analysis.

Sutherland, Ronald. *Frederick Philip Grove.* CWS. NCL. Toronto: McClelland & Stewart, 1969. pb $1.25 [0-7710-9604-6]

The more recent work of Margaret Stobie and Douglas Spettigue outdates those parts of this book which concern Grove's life. Sutherland devotes a chapter each to Grove's autobiographical writings (*In Search of myself*, *A Search for America* and the essays in *It needs to be said*); his sketches (*Over prairie trails*, *The turn of the year* and the science-fiction-fable-fantasy *Consider her ways*); *The Master of the mill*; three novels of the soil (*Our daily bread*, *Fruits of the earth* and *Two generations*); *Settlers of the Marsh*; and *The Yoke of life*. Sutherland feels that Grove's reputation was limited by the label "prairie writer" and that he had a modernity and a vision of Canada that was unique in the period.

CB CL CW ON OX OX2

GUTTERIDGE, Don 1937—

—**Bus-ride.** Ailsa Craig, Ont.: Nairn, 1974. cl $7.95; pb $3.50

Setting: a Canadian village

Bill Underhill is nineteen years old and on the verge of hockey star fame in 1939. This is also the story of the village he lives in, his struggles to achieve some kind of independence and to grapple with the mysteries of adult life. Although at times the tone of the novel is ironic and detached, even surrealistic, certain scenes in the hockey rink's locker room capture realistically the dialogue and emotions of the moment.

HALIBURTON, Thomas Chandler 1796-1865

—**The Clockmaker.** 1836. NCL. Toronto: McClelland & Stewart, 1958. pb $1.75 [0-7710-9106-0]; Boston: Gregg

Setting: Nova Scotia

This well-known collection of anecdotes satirizes the politics and social habits of the Nova Scotia Bluenoses and Yankees of the early nineteenth century. Most of the effectiveness of Judge Haliburton's satire relies on the contrast between the opinions of an English Tory gentleman and those of the brash American clockmaker, Sam Slick.

—**The Letter bag of the Great Western.** London, Eng.: Bentley/Halifax: Joseph Howe, 1840. Toronto: University of Toronto Press, 1973

Setting: indeterminate.

Prefacing his book with an objection to the contemporary increase in postal rates and ensuing problems, the narrator follows with a series of letters presenting a wide range of subjects and viewpoints. Included are the journal of an actress, a letter from one sailor to another and a letter from an abolitionist to a member of parliament. The final letter is from the author to the reader. As usual, Haliburton succeeds in his role as "a sort of laughing philosopher" of human nature.

—**The Attaché; or, Sam Slick in England.** 1844. St. Clair Shores, MI: Scholarly, 1971. cl $19.75. Not seen

—**The Old judge.** 1849. Ed., Reginald Watters. Toronto: Clarke, Irwin,1968. pb $2.50 [0-7720-0224-X]
Setting: Nova Scotia
When an English gentleman begins his tour of North America with a trip to Halifax he spends some time with a judge whose opinions and beliefs resemble those of the author. In a series of anecdotes Haliburton reveals the humorous aspects of both high and low life in Nova Scotia. Included are ghost stories, tales of popular entertainments and a description of the governor's visit, all told with a satirical touch.

—**Sam Slick's wise saws and modern instances.** London, Eng.: Jurst and Blackett, 1853. o/p

—**Nature and human nature.** London, Eng.: Hurst and Blackett, 1855. o/p

—**The Season ticket.** (Anon.) 1861. Toronto: University of Toronto Press, 1973
Setting: England and Ireland
Through his favourite device of the travelling gentleman who meets interesting fellow travellers. Haliburton comments on the scenery and the social and political life of England, Ireland and the United States. His most successful characters are the Yankees who resemble his most popular creation, Sam Slick. His biased political views are offset by his interesting and humorous view of things.

—**Sam Slick.** 1871. Ed. with intro. and biblio. by Roy Palmer Baker. Toronto: McClelland & Stewart, 1923. o/p

—**Sam Slick the clockmaker.** Intro., E.A. Baker. London, Eng.: Routledge, 1904. o/p

—**Fragments from Sam Slick.** Ed., Lawrence J. Burpee. Toronto: Musson, 1909. o/p

—**Selections from Sam Slick (Judge Haliburton).** Ed., Paul A.W. Wallace. Toronto: Ryerson Press, 1923. o/p

—**The Sam Slick anthology.** Ed., Walter Spencer Avis. Intro., Reginald E. Watters. Toronto: Clarke, Irwin, 1969. pb $2.75 [0-7720-0202-9]
Setting: Nova Scotia and eastern United States
This anthology, selected by R.E. Watters, includes excerpts from each of the original Sam Slick volumes: all three series of *The Clockmaker,* the first and second series of *The Attaché; Sam Slick's wise saws and modern instances* and *Nature and human nature.* Included are an interesting note on Haliburton's interpretation of Sam Slick's speech, and a glossary of the slang and colloquial language used in the stories.

Bengtsson, Elna. *The Language and vocabulary of Sam Slick.* Upsala: Lundequistska Bokhandeln, 1956. o/p

Chittick, V.L.O. *Thomas Chandler Haliburton.* New York: Columbia University Press, 1924. o/p

Crofton, F. Blake. *Haliburton, the man and the thinker.* Winslow, N.S.: Anslow, 1889. o/p

Jeffreys, C.W. *Sam Slick in pictures.* Ed., Lorne Pierce. Toronto: Ryerson, 1956. o/p

Liljegren, S.B. *Canadian history and Thomas Chandler Haliburton: some notes on Sam Slick.* Upsala: Lundequistska Bokhandeln, 1969. o/p

Liljegren, S.B. *Canadian history and Thomas Chandler Haliburton: some notes on Sam Slick II.* Upsala: Lundequistska Bokhandeln, 1969. o/p

Logan, J.D. *Thomas Chandler Haliburton.* Toronto: Ryerson Press, 1923. o/p

CB CL CW ON OX

HARDEN, Peter see Louis Vaczek

HARDY, William George 1896–

—**Father Abraham.** London, Eng.: Lovat Dickson, 1935. Also published as **Abraham, prince of Ur.** New York: Dodd, Mead, 1935. o/p

—**Turn back the river.** New York: Dodd, Mead, 1938. o/p

—**All the trumpets sounded: a novel based on the life of Moses.** New York: Coward McCann, 1942. o/p

—**The Unfulfilled.** Toronto: McClelland &

Stewart, 1951. cl $5.95 [0-7710-3990-5]
Setting: Toronto and New York
The problems and traumas of a Canadian liberal are outlined in this novel set during and after World War II. Gregory Rolph, a newspaper columnist and novelist, is confronted by the ideological problems raised by the atomic bomb and the cold war. He faces blackmail from a Canadian industrialist who is using the war and post-war devaluation of the dollar to build a business empire in opposition to the interests of Canadian consumers. As well, Rolph must choose between Canada, family and integrity, and Hollywood, sex and success. This is a realistic document of a seldom explored period in Canadian intellectual history.

—City of libertines. 1957. New York: Popular Library, 1964. pb 75¢
Setting: ancient Rome
This historical novel, typical in its dialogue and sexual emphasis, depicts a love affair and the political manoeuvering in Rome during the rise to power of Julius Caesar.

CW OX

HARKER, Herbert
—Goldenrod. 1972. Scarborough, Ont. & New York: New American Library, 1973. pb $1.25; New York: Random House; Boston: G.K. Hall
Setting: Alberta
Jesse Gifford, a rodeo champion, is demoralized when a serious injury ruins his career and his marriage. Jesse eventually returns triumphantly to competition, using his prize money from the Calgary Stampede to buy a farm; the family reunites. The story is told in the style of a modern western romance-thriller.

HARLOW, Robert G.
—Royal Murdoch. Toronto: Macmillan, 1962. o/p
—A Gift of echoes. Toronto: Macmillan, 1965. o/p
—Scann. Delta, B.C.: Sono Nis Press, 1972. cl $9.95; Red Bluff, CA: Kanchenjunga Press
Setting: a small town in northwestern Canada and an RCAF base in England
Scann writes a documentary novel about the small town where he lives and the people who discovered and built it. This novel within a novel is enriched with a subtle metaphysical style that concentrates on detailed observation. Relationships both in the stories he tells and in his real life provide strong ironic and dramatic tension. Scann plays the truth-telling role of an Elizabethan fool.

HARRISON, Charles Yale 1898-1954
—Generals die in bed. 1930. Hamilton, Ont.: Potlatch, 1974. pb $1.95 [0-919676-02-2]
Setting: Montreal, France, London
Acclaimed on publication as "the best of the war books", Generals die in bed focuses on that part of the war left out of official histories. In a stark unemotional style, Harrison describes atrocities committed by Canadian troops worked into a killing rage by lies about the "Huns", the looting of a French town and the killing of a tyrannical officer by his own men. He writes that the men eventually realized that their true enemies were "the lice, some of the officers, and Death". A bleak picture arises of the common man fighting a war for another class, a war that meant nothing to him except death and mutilation.

—A Child is born. New York: Cape & Smith, 1931. o/p
—Meet me on the barricades: a novel. New York: Scribner's, 1938. o/p
—There are victories. New York: Covici Friede, 1938. o/p
—Nobody's fool: a novel. New York: Holt, 1948. o/p

HARVOR, Beth
—Women and children. Ottawa: Oberon Press, 1973. cl $6.95 [0-88750-090-0]; pb $3.50 [0-88750-091-9]
The female experience is the unifying factor in these stories, some apparently autobiographical, which give clear and sensitive pictures of unusual people. Harvor does not rely on clichés but shows an awareness of the ambiguity of emotions revolving around female sexuality, marriage and motherhood.

HEATH, Terrence
—The Truth and other stories. Toronto: Anansi, 1972. cl $6.95 [0-88784-422-7]; pb $2.50 [0-88784-323-9]
Setting: Prairies
These short prose pieces describe the child's world of outdoor play, sexual exploration, the classroom, and Sunday school. The events described often expose the cruelty among boys and between boys and animals.

Heath has simulated the child's perceptual processes without supplying the moral or thematic framework of many Prairie novels. fiction.

HEAVYSEGE, Charles 1816-1876

—The Advocate. A Novel. 1865. Toronto: University of Toronto Press, 1973. o/p
Setting: Montreal and environs
The Advocate is a typical romance of its time, with a heroine of mysterious birth, a kidnapping, a dramatic death and a frustrated love which finally, however, overcomes all. Heavysege, better known for his versedrama, *Saul*, destroyed all the copies of the book he could find after it had been published.

CB CW OX

HEBERT, Anne 1916—

—The Torrent / Le Torrent. 1950. FWCS. Tr., Gwendolyn Moore. Montreal: Harvest House, 1973. pb $2.50 [0-8872-139-7]
Anne Hébert's famous "closed universe" is evident in this collection of stories, which often resemble parables or fairy tales. Often she creates characters who live in hermetic spheres of habit, oppression or tradition. These victims, either physically or emotionally destitute, are often released by a sudden moment of self-awareness catalysed by a strong and unfamiliar emotion. Often the new self-knowledge produces no joy. It does produce the need to throw off old bonds. This action is seen as incredibly dangerous—often resulting in suicide or self-mutilation, but the old ignorance can never again prevail. It is a cruel world, where refusal to commit suicide is a victory, as is the refusal to accept new oppression or betrayal. The translation is not entirely satisfactory.

—The Silent rooms / Les Chambres de bois. 1958. Tr., Katherine Mezei. Don Mills, Ont.: Musson, 1974. cl $7.95 [0-7737-0020-X]
Setting: an industrial city, Paris, a small village
Catherine leaves the silent authority of her father to marry a tormented young pianist, Michel. They live in a two-room apartment, without love or life. Catherine becomes the fine, soft, pale image Michel wants her to be. Despite this, he pays more attention to his sister Lia. Catherine revolts and meets Bruno, who helps her to escape. In *The Silent rooms*, Hébert wrote in prose much

that she had put in her collection of poems, *Le Tombeau des rois*. The translation of this *roman-poème* does not capture all the poetry of the original, or its musical cadences which was perhaps to be expected. Read in conjunction with *The Torrent* and *Kamouraska*, it is helpful in understanding Hébert's prose.

—Kamouraska / Kamouraska. 1970. Tr., Norman Shapiro. Don Mills, Ont.: Musson, 1973. cl $6.95 [0-7737-0012-9] ; Paper Jacks. Don Mills, Ont.: General Publishing, 1974. pb $1.75 [0-7737-7068-2] ; New York: Crown
Setting: Quebec
A woman's American doctor becomes her lover, and is incited to murder her brutish husband. Though exonerated by the court, Elizabeth is increasingly obsessed by the violent events in her past and by the duplicity of her "respectable" remarriage. Based on an actual murder in 1840, the novel is told as a series of jumbled flashbacks, with emphasis on the heroine's moral and psychological make-up. The translation is very good.

—————

Kamouraska. Film.

Canada, Claude Jutra, 1973.
col 119 min
16mm English: dist. Warner Bros.

16/35mm French dialogue only: dist. France Film

CW FC OX OX2

HEBERT, Jacques 1923—

—The Temple on the river / Les Écoeurants. 1966. FWCS. Tr., Gérald Taafe. Montreal: Harvest House, 1967. cl $4.00 [0-88772-067-6] ; pb $2.00 [0-88772-068-4]
Setting: indeterminate
This is a short novel based on the reflections of a young boy disgusted with life and in particular with the kind of "justice" in operation around him. François Seguoin is the son of a judge and grandson of a judge. He does not accept the prevailing social order but has not engaged in radical activity. Almost by accident he becomes involved in a separatist plot and must face the judicial apparatus.

HELWIG, David 1938—

—The Streets of summer. Ottawa: Oberon

Press, 1969. cl. $7.95 [0-88750-014-5]
Setting: Toronto
A young man, determined to rid himself of his innocence and inhibitions, finds he must pay a hideous price for his gain in maturity. Eleven predominantly descriptive short stories accompany this novella.

—The Day before tomorrow. Ottawa: Oberon Press, 1971. o/p

CB OX2

HEMON, Louis 1880-1913

—Maria Chapdelaine. 1916. Tr., W.H. Blake. Toronto: Macmillan, 1971. cl $6.75 [0-7705-0012-9] ; SMC. Toronto: Macmillan, 1972. pb $1.30 [0-7705-0879-0] ; LL. Toronto: Macmillan, 1973. pb $2.25 [0-7705-1041-8]
Setting: Honfleur, not far from Peribonka
Maria, a sixteen-year-old *paysanne*, has reached the age when she must choose a husband. After her first love dies of exposure in the forest, she receives proposals of marriage from radically different young men. One offers her the harsh life her mother lived, while the other conjures up a glittering image of life in the "States". She finally reconciles herself to living with murderous nature and perpetuating the French-Canadian "race". This novel has become a classic of French-Canadian literature.

—My fair lady. Tr., W.A. Bradley. New York: Macmillan, 1923. o/p

—Blind man's buff. Tr., Arthur Richmond. London, Eng.: Macmillan, 1924. o/p

—Monsieur Repois and nemesis. Tr., W.A. Bradley. London, Eng.: G. Allen and Unwin, 1925. o/p

—Battling Malone and other stories. Tr., W.A. Bradley. London, Eng.: Thornton Butterworth, 1925. o/p

OX

HEPWORTH, R. Gordon 1926—

—The Making of a chief. Delta, B.C.: Sono Nis, 1974
Setting: an Indian reserve on the Prairies
A young British doctor working for the Indian Health Service narrates this story about his work on a small, impoverished Alberta reserve. Another focus of the story is the development of Albert Running Up Hill, who is in line for the post of head chief,

in his understanding of the destitution of his people and the incredible odds against helping them. The feeling of frustration which led to Wounded Knee, the blockade of Alberta Highway 12 and the confrontation in Kenora as the result of government paternalism and bureaucracy come through clearly.

HIEBERT, Paul G. 1892—

—Sarah Binks. 1947. NCL. Toronto: McClelland & Stewart, 1971. pb $1.75 [0-7710-9144-3]
Setting: Saskatchewan
This parody of a critical biography reviews the life and literary achievement of the fictitious "Sweet Songstress of Saskatchewan". The absurdity of an untalented farm girl's transformation into a provincial literary lion is only heightened by her ludicrous, untimely death. By including generous samples of Sarah's "poetry" and serious commentaries on it, Hiebert lampoons both academic scholarship and sentimental regionalism.

CW

HILL, R. Lance

—Nails. Toronto: Lester & Orpen, 1974. cl $7.95 [0-919630-51-0]
Setting: Vancouver, B.C.; Oklahoma
Casual love affairs, drug dealing, violence and murder are the forté of Adams Joseph Black who is portrayed as an attractive "cool" loner with a drive for independence and success. An attempt is made to present him as a rebel against hypocritical society.

HOLDEN, Hélène P.

—The Chain: a novel. Don Mills, Ont.; Longman, 1969. cl $5.95 [0-7747-0010-6]
Setting: Montreal
A loose web of relationships connects the characters in these vignettes. They are mostly French-Canadian women moving in the stress-filled area between the church and the new feminism. One loses a son, one a lover and one a husband, losses which profoundly affect their futures.

HOLMES, Abraham S. 1809-1908

—Belinda; or, the rivals: a tale of real life. By A.S.H. 1843. Richmond, B.C.: Alcuin, 1972. cl $27.50 [0-9190-26-03-6]; Toronto: Anansi, 1975. pb $2.95 [0-88784-333-6].
Setting: a small town in Ontario
Belinda is a wayward Ontario coquette who

cheerfully breaks hearts and drives young men to suicide under a pious facade of maidenly respectability. This parody of the sentimental novel, with its mandatory illegitimate birth, star-crossed lovers and repentant death-bed scene, gives us a close and sometimes satirical look at a small Ontario community in the 1800s. Not surprisingly, all of the first edition except for one copy has mysteriously disappeared.

OX

HOLMES, John see Raymond Souster

HOLMES, Raymond see Raymond Souster

HOLMES, Russell see Arthur J.A. Stringer

HOOD, Hugh John Blagdon 1928—

—**Flying a red kite.** 1962. Ryerson Paperback Series. Scarborough, Ont.: McGraw-Hill Ryerson, 1967. pb $2.95 [0-7700-6019-6]

Several of the eleven stories in this collection use nostalgia as a focus, many taking place in the Toronto of Hood's youth. In the title story an ordinary, somewhat incompetent man buys his daughter a kite, ruefully aware that he is unlikely to be able to fly it for her. When the kite flies, the symbolic value it had for him becomes clear.

—**White figure, white ground.** Toronto: Ryerson Press, 1964. o/p

—**Around the mountain: scenes from Montreal life.** Toronto: Peter Martin, 1967. cl $5.00 [0-88778-012-1]

Setting: Montreal

This is a collection of light, simple sketches about Montreal life, written in a journalistic style reminiscent of Harry Boyle, Don Bell, and Max Braithwaite.

—**The Camera always lies.** Don Mills, Ont.: Longman, 1967. cl. $5.75

Setting: Los Angeles and New York

This description of the making of a major motion picture shows how the movie industry builds up an illusory world around its actors in order to dupe the public.

—**A Game of touch.** Don Mills, Ont.: Longman, 1970. cl $5.95

Setting: Montreal

The idea of becoming a cartoonist appeals to Jake Price's youthful innocence until reality destroys his illusions. The portrayal of the various artists and businessmen Jake encounters is enhanced by alternating the point of view from one character to another.

—**The Fruit man, the meat man and the manager.** Ottawa: Oberon Press, 1971. cl $7.95 [0-88750-037-4]

With the exception of two conversational sketches, this collection of stories is primarily written in the narrative style. Most of the stories describe some aspect of life in and around Montreal.

—**You can't get there from here.** Ottawa: Oberon Press, 1972. cl $7.95 [0-88750-055-2]; pb $3.95 [0-88750-056-0]

Setting: a small island republic in the Caribbean island

American and Russian espionage agents attempt to subvert the political and economic policies of a newly formed republic. Written in a journalistic style, the story illustrates the insanity of modern politics.

CB CW ON2 OX2

The Red Kite. Film
NFB col 17min 16mm: dist. CFI

HORWOOD, Harold

—**Tomorrow will be Sunday.** Garden City, N.Y.: Doubleday, 1966. o/p

—**White Eskimo.** Toronto: Doubleday, 1972. cl $5.95 [0-385-04346-5]; Paper Jacks, Don Mills, Ont.: General, 1973. pb $1.50 [0-7737-7043-7]

Setting: Labrador

This is the story of Esau Gillingham, the man the Eskimos call "White Spirit" who restores to the Eskimo people, by sheer force of personality, some of their original life and dignity. He appears in a world of oral tradition as a figure out of a saga or an epic, championing buoyant paganism as opposed to the life-denying paternalism of the missionaries. Somehow he cures some of the Inuit's soul sickness which has caused them to accept welfare and to stay in crowded settlements where disease flourishes. Horwood seems somewhat unfairly biased against missions and for government.

HOUSTON, James 1922—

—**The White dawn: an Eskimo saga.** Toronto: Longman, 1971. cl. $7.95 [0-15-196115-8]

Setting: Baffin Island, 1876

Three men, their boat separated from their whaling ship, are rescued by a group of Eskimos. The quick erosion of Eskimo customs under the pressure of these three uncomprehending strangers is the focus of the novel. Houston's detailed knowledge of the people and the area is conveyed naturally.

The White dawn. Film.
USA: Philip Kaufman, 1974.
col 109 min
16/35mm English: dist. Paramount

HOWARD, Blanche

—The Manipulator. Toronto: McClelland & Stewart, 1972. cl $7.95 [0-7710-4239-6]
Setting: a small Ontario town
Some mystery surrounds the apparent ability of an architect to manipulate people psychologically to achieve his ambitions.

HOWARD, Hilda Glynn see Hilda Glynn-Ward

HUGHES, (Aubrey) Dean 1908—

—And so they bought a farm. Willowdale, Ont.: Nelson,Foster & Scott, 1972. o/p

—Along the sideroad. Willowdale, Ont.: Nelson, Foster & Scott, 1973. cl $7.95 [0-919324-14-2]
Setting: the country near Toronto
This story of Charles and Millie Brewster is based on Hughes's own life on his farm near Toronto. Charles writes a weekly column on country life for a big-city newspaper and his trips to collect material result in encounters with local eccentrics and the retelling of their tall tales and anecdotes.

HUNTER, Robert

—Erebus. Toronto: McClelland & Stewart, 1968. cl $5.95 [0-7710-4290-6]
Setting: Winnipeg
In this book about a young man's quest for self-knowledge, the author explores the theme of man's ability to acquire real happiness in a transient existence. An island and a slaughterhouse are used as symbols of heaven and hell.

IANORA, Claudio

—Sint Stephen Canada, Polyphemus' cave and the Boobieland Express. Don Mills, Ont.: New Press, 1970. cl $8.50 [0-88770-052-7] ; pb $3.50 [0-88770-053-5]
Setting: Toronto

The mercurial hero, Stephen Canada, titles himself Sint Stephen to indicate his dedication to sin, as opposed to saintliness. The story of Stephen's violent friendships, sexual encounters and marriage, is meant to be a surrealistic saga of his paradoxical spiritual quest. Psychedelic jargon and tone obscure the basically simple plot-theme connection.

IRWIN, Grace 1907—

—Least of all saints.* 1952. CBL. Toronto: McClelland & Stewart, 1967. pb 95¢ [0-7710-4348-1] ; Grand Rapids, MI: Eerdmans

—Andrew Connington.* 1957. Grand Rapids, MI: Eerdmans, 1967. pb $2.25

—In little place. Toronto: Ryerson Press. 1959. o/p

—Servant of slaves. Grand Rapids, MI: Eerdmans, 1961. pb $3.95
Setting: England
The spiritual development of John Newton, an eighteenth century sea captain turned Methodist preacher, is recounted in this biographical novel. The frequent use of interior monologues drawn from Newton's log books, letters and diaries reflects the awakening of his religious consciousness.

—Contend with horses.* Toronto: McClelland & Stewart, 1969. cl $6.95 [0-7710-4330-9] ; Grand Rapids, MI: Eerdmans
*Setting: Toronto
The Andrew Connington trilogy attempts to examine many major theological problems of Christian doctrine, to discuss how they relate to capitalist society, and to expose the hypocrisy of Protestant congregations. The first book, *Least of all saints*, describes the intellectual and spiritual conversion of Andrew Connington, his entrance into the ministry, his marriage and his appointment to an established church. In *Andrew Connington*, the hero's religious convictions estrange him from his wife, and alienate him from prominent members of his congregation. This causes his dismissal. *Contend with horses* describes the problems he is forced to face when his wife dies and his children mature. It culminates in a final and drastic test of his devotion to Christ.

OX

JACK, Donald

—**Three cheers for me: the Bandy papers vol. I.** 1962. Toronto & Garden City, N.Y.: Doubleday, 1973. cl $7.95 [0-385-04882-3]; Paper Jacks. Don Mills, Ont.: General Publishing, 1974. pb $1.50 [0-7737-7075-5]

Setting: Beamington, Ont., England, and Europe

Bartholomew Bandy, cursed with a horse-like face and a strict upbringing, surprises everyone, including himself, when he turns out to be a flying ace in World War I. The amusing events surrounding the moral degeneration of the boy from Beamington tend to ignore the harsher realities of war, despite descriptive passages about trench warfare.

—**That's me in the middle: the Bandy papers vol. II.** Toronto & Garden City, N.Y.: Doubleday, 1973. cl $7.95 [0-385-04901-3]; Paper Jacks. Don Mills, Ont.: General Publishing, 1974. pb $1.50 [0-7737-7076-3]

Setting: London, Eng.

In this sequel to *Three cheers for me*, Capt. Bartholomew Bandy, a flying instructor with the Royal Air Force during World War I, is promoted to lieutenant-colonel on a whim of the Secretary of State for Air. His new job turns out to be a farcical administrative one, with his office located in a converted men's washroom. The rest of the novel involves Bandy in a series of mishaps and slapstick situations reminiscent of the humour of P.G. Wodehouse.

JACOT, Michael

—**The Last butterfly.** Toronto: McClelland & Stewart, 1973. cl $7.95 [0-7710-4390-2]

Setting: Czechoslovakia

A clown is forced to entertain children in a Nazi concentration camp. Is it not better to go to one's death with a smile rather than a frown?—this is a question the clown cannot answer. All he understands is the world of the theatre, and thus he feels a duty to entertain while he can. The complexities of the clown's dilemma are clearly and simply outlined.

JAMESON, Anna Brownell 1794-1860

—**Winter studies and summer rambles in Canada.** 1838. Abr. NCL. Toronto: McClelland & Stewart, 1965. pb $1.95 [0-7710-9146-X]; 1838. Coles Canadiana Collection. Rexdale, Ont.: Coles, 1972. 3 vol. pb $12.95

Setting: Ontario

This travel diary contains several factual descriptions of Toronto and Upper Canada in the late 1830s. After leaving Toronto, Jameson encounters Indian, settler and voyageur life first-hand, and her unfavourable first impressions of Canadian society are dramatically reversed. The author's highly personal observations and her sudden adaptation to the new environment give a fictional dimension to her account.

—**Sketches in Canada, and rambles among the red men.** London, Eng.: Longmans, 1852. o/p

———

Erskine, Mrs. Stewart. *Anna Jameson.* London, Eng., 1915. o/p

Thomas, Clara E. *Love and work enough, the life of Anna Jameson.* University of Toronto Department of English Studies and Texts. Toronto: University of Toronto Press, 1967. cl $8.50 [0-8020-5180-4]

Clara Thomas's full-length critical biography of Anna Jameson describes in detail the life of this prolific artist and author, as well as presenting a sound analysis of her work. Extensive quotations from Mrs. Jameson's letters provide a revealing background to the study of her writings, including her best-known Canadian book, *Winter studies and summer rambles in Canada.* Thomas's biography offers an intimate look at the life of a talented woman in regency and Victorian England and in pre-Confederation Canada.

CB CW ON OX

JANES, Percy

—**So young and beautiful.** Ilfracombe, Devon: Stockwell, 1958. o/p

—**House of hate.** Toronto: McClelland & Stewart, 1970. cl $7.95 [0-7710-4400-3]

Setting: Newfoundland

Covering a period of about seventy years, this novel tells the story of two generations of the Stone family of Milltown, Newfoundland. Central to the narration is the idea that poverty breeds hate which can only be destructive to the relationships within a family. The father, Saul Stone, rears his children in such an atmosphere, and the narrator, one of the sons, traces the results on each member of the family. Although the story is one of almost unrelieved unhappiness, it is fascinating for the author's ability to create interesting and generally believable characters.

CL

JASMIN, Claude 1930–

—**Ethel and the terrorist / Ethel et le terroriste.** 1964. FWCS. Tr., David Walker. Montreal: Harvest House, 1974. cl $3.95 [0-88772-024-2] ; pb $2.50 [0-88772-050-1]
Setting: Montreal, New York City
Paul, the terrorist, is in a dilemma: if he plants a bomb in New York as ordered by his organization he will lose the love of Ethel, a beautiful Jewish girl. If he doesn't, he may be betrayed to the RCMP. Paul has already exploded a bomb in Montreal and he and Ethel are running away from the police, but she will accept no more violence on his part. Jasmin makes the idea of conflict between loyalty to a cause and individual freedom as important as the events in the novel, which parallel the actual fatal injury of a French-speaking night watchman by an FLQ bomb. The translation is good.

CW FC OX OX2

JOLLIFFE, Edward B.

—**The First hundred.** Toronto: McClelland & Stewart, 1972. cl $7.95 [0-7710-4458-5]
Setting: Ontario
The son of Métis and Québécois parents imposes his humanitarian beliefs on a community of chronically feuding Catholics and Methodists. His attempts to keep peace in the community end in a grotesque misunderstanding, and in violent death. As well as a dynamic plot the book offers an energetic reconstruction of pre-Confederation Ontario society.

JOUDRY, Patricia 1921–

—**The Dweller on the threshold.** Toronto: McClelland & Stewart, 1973. cl $6.95 [0-7710-4466-6]
Setting: southern coast of British Columbia
Cecelia and Hedleigh meet as thirteen-year-old cousins. She brings discord (some would call it life) into his refined, isolated, intellectual family life. His mother and the old servant compete with Cecelia for his love; she is successful because she is wholly herself, unafraid of looking into her own darknesses, her own mystery. Their relationship begins to take on a deeper meaning—the relationship between masculine and feminine principles.

KIRBY, William 1817-1906

—**The Golden dog.** 1877. Abr. SMC. Toronto: Macmillan, 1931. cl. $1.40 [0-7705-0670-4]. Reprinted as (abridged ed.) **The Golden dog:** a romance of Old Quebec. 1877. NCL. Toronto: McClelland & Stewart, 1969. pb $2.95 [0-7710-9165-6]
Setting: New France
Written in what seems to modern taste an almost amusingly exaggerated romantic style, with its full quota of duels, languishing beauties, debauches, poisoners and passionate love, this novel nevertheless shrewdly depicts the economic realities of Quebec as a French colony.

———

Pierce, Lorne. *William Kirby: the portrait of a Tory Loyalist.* Toronto: Macmillan, 1929. o/p
Riddell, William R. *William Kirby.* Toronto: Ryerson Press, 1923. o/p

CB CW OX

KIRIAK, Illia 1888-1955

—**Sons of the soil.** 1959. 2nd ed. Tr. from the Ukrainian. Winnipeg: Trident, 1973. 3 vols. Set $12.35; vol. 1 $4.25; vol. 2 $3.85; vol. 3 $4.25
Setting: the Prairies
An old man on the verge of death muses on his past. One of a small group of Ukrainian immigrants who settled on the virgin soil of the Prairies, he remembers the early struggles and hardship. Leaving the old country to find a better future for their children and to avoid heavy taxes, conscription, and rapacious landlords, these people faced the bare prairie with determination. Some were self-reliant and tough; others who allowed themselves to become depressed by the difficulty of life were supported by the rest of the community. Many of the old customs, festivals and religious practices were imported into the new country.

KLEIN, Abraham Moses 1909-1972

—**The Second scroll.** 1951. NCL. Toronto: McClelland & Stewart, 1969. pb $1.75 [0-7710-9122-2]
Setting: Canada, Europe, Casablanca, Israel
The story of Melech Davidson's journey from loss of faith to its renewal takes place during the years of greatest tribulation for the Jewish people in the twentieth century: 1917 to 1949. Both Melech's journey and that of his nephew, who goes in search of him, represent the movement of the Hebrews from exile in Egypt to the Promised Land. Klein creates in *The Second scroll* a kind of modern equivalent to the Pentateuch, using Biblical language and symbolism. The book provides insight into the dilemma of the

modern Jew who wishes to return both spiritually and physically to the Promised Land.

Fischer, Gretl K. *In search of Jerusalem: religion and ethics in the writings of A.M. Klein.* Montreal & London: McGill-Queen's 1975. cl $8.50 [0-7735-02271-0] Not seen

Marshall, T.A., ed. *A.M. Klein.* CVCW. Scarborough, Ont.: McGraw-Hill Ryerson, 1970. pb $3.25 [0-7700-0310-9]
This collection of essays and reviews concentrates on Klein's poetry. It provides a broad perspective of criticism of Klein's work from W.E. Collin's essay in 1936 to essays written in the late sixties. The most useful section of the book for readers of Klein's sole novel, *The Second scroll,* is Marshall's introduction. Other critical views are provided by John Sutherland, Louis Dudek, Irving Layton, Margaret Avison and Dorothy Livesay. (Bibliography.)

Waddington, Miriam. *A.M. Klein.* 1970. Rev. ed. SCL. Toronto: Copp Clark, 1974. pb $2.35 [0-7730-3034-4]. Rev. ed. not seen
Klein's language and diction is the focus of this chronologically arranged study. Despite her reservations about the novel's politics, Waddington provides an excellent analysis of *The Second scroll.* She includes a critique of M.W. Steinberg's well-known introduction to the New Canadian Library edition and gives an interesting account of the function of Hebrew and Yiddish syntax in the novel. (Bibliography.)

KNIGHT, David

—**Farquharson's physique and what it did to his mind.** New York: Stein & Day, 1971. cl $7.95; New York: Fawcett Books, 1973. pb $1.25
Setting: Ibadan, Nigeria
This long novel covers the chaotic last year in the life of an English professor. Juggling his disintegrating marriage, Nigerian politics, his mistress, and a teaching job, Henry Farquharson ultimately causes his own gory and tragic death. Farquharson's physique is the book's central focus: its death-directed career as a demanding lover, an affectionate father, and a murderer parallels the desperate, anarchic struggles of the world around him.

KNISTER, Raymond 1899-1932

—**White narcissus.** 1929. NCL. Toronto: Mc-Clelland & Stewart, 1962. pb $1.50 [0-7710-9132-X]
Setting: rural southern Ontario
Richard, a successful writer, returns to his town to persuade his first love, Ada, to marry him. She is torn between her love for him and the duty she feels toward her estranged parents who depend upon her for companionship. In this short poetic work Knister presents the conflict between the romanticism of man and the realism of nature.

—**My star predominant.** Toronto: Ryerson Press, 1934. o/p

—**Selected stories of Raymond Knister.** ed., Michael Gnarowski. Canadian Short Story Series. Ottawa: University of Ottawa Press, 1972. pb $3.75 [0-7766-4332-0]
Setting: rural southern Ontario
The first of these six selections, "The One thing", is the story of a farmer who is alienated from his neighbours by his small stature and ugly features. The following two stories describe the initiation rites of a farm boy to manhood and to evil. Although these three are the most imaginative, all of the stories are interesting psychological studies.

CB CW OX

KOCH, Eric

—**The French kiss.** Toronto: McClelland & Stewart, 1969. o/p

—**The Leisure riots.** Montreal & Plattsburgh, N.Y.: Tundra, 1973. cl $7.50 [0-88776-020-1]
Setting: Montreal and Washington, D.C.
This futuristic satire is presented as the first-hand account of a presidential advisor's disgrace. The advisor, a notorious ex-Nazi, heads a think tank which is put to work on the problem of "leisure riots". These 1980 riots are deliberate interruptions of leisure activities, and are instigated by bored but wealthy businessmen. The main target of Koch's brisk attack is the Protestant work ethic; he also lampoons social and sexual attitudes.

KREISEL, Henry 1922—

—**The Rich man.** 1948. NCL. Toronto: McClelland & Stewart, 1971. pb $2.50 [0-7710-9124-9]
Setting: Austria
Using his life's savings to visit his family in

Vienna, Jacob Grossman, a tailor, plays the role of rich relative until events force him to face this and other deceptions in his life. In the end his naïveté is shattered by his new awareness of the problems of the Jews in Austria in 1935.

—The Betrayal. 1964. NCL. Toronto: Mc-Clelland & Stewart, 1971. pb $2.95 [0-7710-9177-4]

Setting: Edmonton

Narrated by a young history professor, Theodore Stappler, this is a story of guilt and redemption. While tracking down the man who betrayed his family to the Nazis Stappler, an Austrian Jew, discovers that he himself took part in betrayal. Kreisel handles a rare but very important theme in Canadian literature with compassion and insight.

CW ON2 OX

KROETSCH, Robert 1927—

—But we are exiles. Toronto: Macmillan, 1965. pb $2.95 [0-7705-1005-1]

Setting: northern Alberta

While working on a boat on the Mackenzie River, Peter Guy meets a man who had been a profound influence on his life several years earlier. The man dies mysteriously, and his body is lost in the river. The central action of the story takes place while the men on the boat try to recover the body before winter freeze-up. Through the events that occur during the search, Guy learns many things about himself and his relationships with others.

—The Words of my roaring. Toronto: Macmillan, 1966. cl $5.95 [0-7705-0177-X]

Setting: central Alberta

In a desperate move to win an election, a small-town undertaker promises rain to the drought-stricken farmers of his area. The novel traces past and present events from the perspective of Johnnie Backstrom, the undertaker. With ironic humour Kroetsch outlines the trials and frustrations of life during the Depression.

The Studhorse man. 1969. Pocket Books. New York: Simon & Schuster, 1971. pb 95¢

Setting: central Alberta

A quest for perfection animates this rowdy, funny and finally pathetic story of a man who lives only for his search for the ideal mare to mate with his prize stud. Told by the man's nephew who is writing

in a mental hospital, the entertaining story of Hazard Lepage reveals as much about the narrator as it does about the subject of his tale.

—Gone Indian. Toronto: New Press. 1973. cl $7.95 [0-88770-193-0]

Setting: central Alberta

An American graduate student goes to Edmonton to apply for a teaching job and finally attempts to escape the pressures of his world. His unusual story is told through the tapes he sends to his professor and through the comments of the professor himself. Kroetsch's usual ironic humour is given full play in this story of self-discovery.

CB CW ON2 OX2

LADOO, Harold Sonny 1945-1973

—No pain like this body. Toronto: Anansi, 1972. cl $8.50 [0-88784-421-9]; pb $2.95 [0-88784-322-0]

Setting: West Indies

The hostility of nature, of their father and even, it seems, of God, conditions three children to the death of their brother. Written mainly in the pidgin English of the poverty-stricken Hindu family it describes, this is an involving account of life lived against heavy odds.

—Yesterdays. Toronto: Anansi, 1974. cl $6.50 [0-88784-431-6]; pb $3.25 [0-88784-329-8]

Setting: West Indies

In pungent dialect, Ladoo describes the life of a poor East Indian community in the West Indies. A comic approach is taken to the difficulties of Choonilal, unwilling to mortgage his house to a corrupt Hindu priest. His son wants the money to go to Canada to get revenge for years of beatings in a Canadian mission school. He plans to set up Hindu schools in Canada equipped with torture chambers. Despite the surface humour, the grim truth of poverty and colonial oppression is revealed through the son's attempts to escape a life of frustration.

LANGEVIN, André 1927—

—Dust over the city / Poussière sur la ville. 1953. NCL. Tr., John Latrebe and Robert Gottleib. Toronto: McClelland & Stewart, 1974. pb $2.50 [0-7710-9213-X]

Setting: a small town

A young doctor, Alain Dubois, settles down in a small mining town. His beautiful, inconsistent wife Madelaine betrays him with another man. Langevin creates a strong analogy between the asbestos dust almost burying the town and the dark cloud of jealousy and indifference which is settling over the marriage. Social tension is generated by the class differences between the Dubois and the miners. The translation is good.

CW OX OX2

LAURENCE, (Jean) Margaret 1926—

—**This side Jordan.** Toronto: McClelland & Stewart, 1960. o/p (NCL pb forthcoming.)
Setting: Gold Coast, Ghana

An African schoolteacher tries to reconcile the tribal culture of his people with modern society. His efforts to improve the educational standards of his school and help his needy students find jobs bring him into conflict with both white and black societies. This novel about a society in transition clearly portrays the hardships which evolve from fear and misunderstanding.

—**The Stone angel.**Toronto: McClelland & Stewart, 1964. cl $7.50; NCL. Toronto: McClelland & Stewart, 1968. pb $1.95 [0-7710-9159-1]; New York: Knopf; London, Eng.: Macmillan
Setting: a Prairie town

At ninety, Hagar Shipley looks back on her life and painfully begins to come to terms with her pride, her inability to express love and her sharp tongue. Threatened with incarceration in a "home" she runs away, and in this last act of independence the final breakthrough of long-repressed emotions begins. Throughout she is tough, believable and, despite her failings, a sympathetic human being—a woman who rages against the dying of the light as long as she can.

—**The Tomorrow-tamer.** 1963. NCL. Toronto: McClelland & Stewart, 1970. pb $2.50 [0-7710-9170-2]; New York: Knopf
Setting: Ghana, West Africa

Filled with the colour and life of West Africa, these stories focus on the misunderstandings inevitable when two races, two cultures or even two people meet. Sometimes the misunderstanding is trivial or humorous, sometimes tragic or fatal. Although Africa provides an obviously suitable backdrop for such encounters, the stories are concerned with human problems, not simply African ones.

—**A Jest of God.** Toronto: McClelland & Stewart, 1966. pb $2.25 [0-7710-4701-0]; NCL. Toronto: McClelland & Stewart, 1974. pb $2.25 [0-7710-9211-3]; New York: Knopf; London, Eng.: Macmillan. Also published as **Now I lay me down.** London, Eng.: Granada, 1968. o/p
Setting: a small town in southern Manitoba

Rachel Cameron, a thirty-four-year-old schoolteacher in Manawaka, tries in various ways to escape the stifling atmosphere of a small Prairie town. An attempt to become involved in religion proves an embarrassment, and an affair only ends in increased loneliness. In the end, Rachel finds that she must leave the town in order to allow herself the opportunity for a new life.

—**The Fire-dwellers.** Toronto: McClelland & Stewart, 1969. cl $5.95 [0-7710-4699-5]; NCL. Toronto: McClelland & Stewart, 1973. pb $2.50 [0-7710-9187-7]; New York: Knopf; New York: Popular Library; London, Eng.: Macmillan; London, Eng.: Granada
Setting: Vancouver

The fire-dwellers are those who, in a parody of St. Paul's words, marry *and* burn. One of these is Stacey McAindra, a middle-class mother who can't communicate with her children or husband. Brief affairs and several brushes with death allow various characters to break through their verbal blocks and show their feelings. Alive with references to fire, hell and death, the novel deals with the strong feelings often held under the flabby, ordinary surface of life.

—**A Bird in the house.** Toronto: McClelland & Stewart, 1970. cl $5.95 [0-7710-4732-0]; NCL. Toronto: McClelland & Stewart, 1974. pb $1.95 [0-7710-9196-6]; New York: Knopf; New York: Popular Library; London, Eng.: Macmillan
Setting: a Prairie town

The growing consciousness of Vanessa McLeod unites these sketches of a childhood spent in a small Prairie town. The stiff unyielding authoritarian figure of Vanessa's Grandfather McLeod focuses her hate and her fascination. Gradually she comes to the realization that there are different kinds of strength, and that those most apparently strong are perhaps the most vulnerable.

—**The Diviners.** Toronto: McClelland & Stewart, 1974. cl $8.95 [0-7710-4748-7]; New York: Knopf

Setting: Manitoba, Toronto, Vancouver and rural southern Ontario

Morag Gunn, a writer in her forties, worries about her own future and that of her teenage daughter. As she tries to deal with the crisis in their relationship, she makes a mental journey through her past, recalling the major experiences of her life. Through the journey she is able to come to terms with her past and present, and to free herself and her daughter from their mutual misunderstandings.

Thomas, Clara. *Margaret Laurence.* CWS. NCL. Toronto: McClelland & Stewart, 1969. pb $1.25 [0-7710-9603-8]

This short survey of Laurence's work provides a useful introduction to the African material, *The Stone angel, A Jest of God* and the stories that make up *A Bird in the house.* Clara Thomas provides both critical and biographical insight into the author's works. (Bibliography.)

Thomas, Clara. *The Manawaka world of Margaret Laurence.* Toronto: McClelland & Stewart, 1975. cl $10.00 [0-7710-8460-9]

The first full book-length examination of the works and background of Margaret Laurence, this critical volume meticulously explores the development of her work from *The Prophet's camel bell* to *The Diviners.* One of Thomas's central concerns is the ways in which Laurence creates the small town of Manawaka, a place that is at once Canadian and universal. One full chapter is devoted to this aspect of her fiction. Other chapters discuss each of her works, including her critical book on Nigerian writers, *Long drums and cannons.* A bibliographic checklist of works by and about Margaret Laurence is included.

CB CL CW ON OX OX2

Rachel, Rachel. Film.
USA, Paul Newman, 1968
col 104 min
16mm English: Warner Bros.

LEACOCK, Stephen 1869-1944

—**Literary lapses: a book of sketches.*** 1910. NCL. Toronto: McClelland & Stewart, 1957. pb $1.95 [0-7710-9103-6] ; Short Story Index Reprint Series. Plainview, N.Y.: Books for Libraries

Nonsense novels.* 1911. NCL. Toronto: McClelland & Stewart, 1963. pb $1.75

[0-7710-9135-4] ; New York: Dover; Gloucester, MA: Peter Smith

—**Sunshine sketches of a little town.*** 1912. Toronto: McClelland & Stewart, 1958. cl $12.95; NCL. Toronto: McClelland & Stewart, 1960. pb $1.50 [0-7710-9115-X] ; Short Story Index Reprint Series. Plainview, N.Y.: Books for Libraries

—**Behind the beyond and other contributions to human knowledge.*** 1913. NCL. Toronto: McClelland & Stewart, 1969. pb $1.75 [0-7710-9167-2]

—**Arcadian adventures with the idle rich.*** 1914. NCL. Toronto: McClelland & Stewart, 1959. pb $1.95 [0-7710-9110-9]

—**The Methods of Mr. Sellyer: a book store study.** New York: Lane, 1914. o/p

—**Moonbeams from the larger lunacy.*** 1915. NCL. Toronto: McClelland & Stewart, 1964. pb $1.95 [0-7710-9143-5]

—**Further foolishness: sketches and satires on the follies of the day.*** 1916. NCL. Toronto: McClelland & Stewart, 1968. pb $1.95 [0-7710-9160-5]

—**Frenzied fiction.*** 1918. NCL. Toronto: McClelland & Stewart, 1965. pb $1.95 [0-7710-9148-6] ; Short Story Index Reprint Series. Plainview, N.Y.: Books for Libraries

—**The Hohenzollerns in America with the Bolsheviks in Berlin and other impossibilities.** London, Eng.: Lane, 1919. o/p

—**Winsome Winnie and other new nonsense novels.*** 1920. Short Story Index Reprint Series. Plainview, N.Y.: Books for Libraries. Facsim. ed. $8.00

—**My discovery of England.*** 1922. NCL. Toronto: McClelland & Stewart, 1961. pb $1.95 [0-7710-9128-1]

—**College days.** New York: Dodd, Mead, 1923. o/p

—**Over the footlights and other fancies.** London, Eng.: Lane, 1923. o/p

—**The Garden of folly.** Toronto: Gundy, 1924. o/p

—**Winnowed wisdom: a new book of humour.** 1926. NCL. Toronto: McClelland & Stewart, 1971. pb $1.95 [0-7710-9174-5]

—**Short circuits.*** 1928. NCL. Toronto: McClelland & Stewart, 1967. pb $1.95 [0-7710-9157-5]

—**The Iron man and the tin woman with other such futurities. A book of little** sketches of today and tomorrow.   New York: Dodd, Mead, 1929. o/p

—Laugh with Leacock: an anthology of the best works of Stephen Leacock.* 1930. Toronto: McClelland & Stewart, 1968. pb $1.50 [0-7710-5014-3] ; New York: Apollo

—The Leacock book. Being selections from the works of Stephen Leacock.   London, Eng.: Lane, 1930. o/p

—Wet wit and dry humour. Distilled from the pages of — — — —. New York: Dodd, Mead, 1931. o/p

—Afternoons in Utopia: tales of the new time.   Toronto: Macmillan, 1932. o/p

—The Dry Pickwick and other incongruities.   London, Eng.: Lane, 1932. o/p

—The Perfect salesman. Ed., E.V. Knox. New York: McBride, 1934. Also published as Stephen Leacock. London, Eng.: Methuen, 1934. o/p

—Funny pieces: a book of random sketches. New York: Dodd, Mead, 1936. o/p

—Here are my lectures and stories.* New York: Dodd, Mead, 1937. o/p

—Model memoirs and other sketches from simple to serious.* 1938. Essay Index Reprint Series. Plainview, N.Y.: Books for Libraries. cl $12.50

—Too much college.   New York: Dodd, Mead, 1939. o/p

—Laugh parade: a new collection of the wit and humour of Stephen Leacock.* 1940. New York: Apollo. $2.25. (Originally published as Stephen Leacock's laugh parade in 1940.)

—My remarkable uncle and other sketches.* 1942. NCL. Toronto: McClelland & Stewart, 1965. pb $1.95 [0-7710-9153-2]

—Happy stories just to laugh at.   New York: Dodd, Mead, 1943. o/p

—The Boy I left behind me. Garden City, N.Y.: Doubleday, 1946. o/p
This is four chapters of posthumous, unfinished autobiography.

—Last leaves.* 1945. NCL. Toronto: McClelland & Stewart, 1970. pb $1.95

—The Leacock roundabout. A treasury of the best works of Stephen Leacock.* New York: Dodd, Mead, 1946. cl $7.95

—The Bodley Head Leacock.* Ed. and intro., J.B. Priestly. London, Eng.: Bodley Head, 1957. Also published as The Best of Lea-

cock. Toronto: McClelland & Stewart, 1957. cl $6.95 [0-7710-7182-5]

—The Unicorn Leacock. Ed., James Reeves. London, Eng.: Hutchinson, 1960. o/p

—The Feast of Stephen: a Leacock anthology.* 1970. Ed., Robertson Davies. Toronto: McClelland & Stewart, 1974. pb $1.95 [0-7710-9195-8]

*Although there are many books of humour by Stephen Leacock in print in many languages, it is accepted that Sunshine sketches of a little town, Arcadian adventures with the idle rich and several much-anthologized stories such as "My financial career" are the cream of his humorous work. In Sunshine sketches, Leacock looks at life in the small town of Mariposa in a nostalgic, albeit ironic, light. The sinking of the steamer the Mariposa Belle in six feet of water is compared with the sinking of the Lusitania, and the narrator is hard pressed to say which event is the more dramatic. In its account of Plutoria and its idle rich, Arcadian adventures shows the influence of Thorstein Veblen, the economist who wrote The Theory of the leisure class. Most of Leacock's other books are collections of humorous sketches on diverse topics.

———

Cameron, D.A. Faces of Leacock, an appreciation. Scarborough, Ont.: McGraw-Hill Ryerson, 1967. cl $8.95 [0-7700-0061-4]
Cameron covers the major aspects of Leacock's life and looks at his "faces" as critic, theorist, essayist, traveller, ironist and satirist. He gives thoughtful answers to the major critical questions about Leacock.

Curry, Ralph L. Stephen Leacock: humorist and humanist. New York: Doubleday, 1959. o/p

Davies, Robertson. Stephen Leacock. CWS. NCL. Toronto: McClelland & Stewart, 1970. pb $1.25 [0-7710-9607-0]
Davies divides this work into three sections: one biographical, one critical and the third a summary of Leacock's achievement. He discusses selected works, producing a useful introduction to Leacock's humour, as well as dealing with important critical questions. (Bibliography.)

Kimball, Elizabeth. The Man in the Panama hat. Toronto: McClelland & Stewart, 1970. cl $6.50 [0-7710-4489-5]
Elizabeth Kimball reminisces about her

famous uncle in this informal biography. Her early memories, family stories and factual details are interesting and reveal some of the past about which Leacock was at times reticent.

Legate, David M. *Stephen Leacock*. Toronto: Doubleday, 1970. cl $9.25 [0-385-06634-1]

Legate has written a scholarly biography of Leacock, with index, bibliography, extensive notes and fifty-six photographs. A basically sympathetic picture of Leacock is presented in this biography which is the most detailed available.

McArthur, Peter. *Stephen Leacock*. 1923. Folcroft,PA: Folcroft Library Editions. Library binding $10.00

McArthur's book is divided into three sections: biography, anthology and appreciation. The biography is partially composed of passages from Leacock's writings and the anthology wholly so. Observations of those who knew Leacock or saw him lecture are quoted extensively. The appreciation, although not analytical, provides a good indication of the contemporary reception given Leacock's humour.

CB CL CW ON OX

Bernard Braden reads Stephen Leacock.
Record
Malton, Ont.: Capitol Records

John Drainie reads Stephen Leacock.
Record
Toronto: Melbourne SMLP4015

My financial career.
Film
NFB col and b&w 7 min. 16mm: dist. CFI

Stephen Leacock: a collection of contemporary documents. Jackdaw Kit.
Ed., Stephen Franklin. Toronto: Clarke Irwin, 1970 $4.50 [Jackdaw C24]
16 pieces; illustrations, facsimiles, portraits, etc.

LECLERC, Félix 1914—

—**Allegro / Allegro.** 1944. NCL. Toronto: McClelland & Stewart, 1974. pb $2.25 [0-7710-9190-7].

The fable is a literary genre well suited to Leclerc's purpose. He wants to tell people about the peaceful and simple order of rural life, about the acceptance of death as a part of the grand cycle of life, about the search for freedom and also, of course, about

love. In these fables man's constant search for God, beauty, and light is expressed in a simple, poetic, parabolic style. The moral of the fables is that the French-Canadian race should be preserved through the protection of its idiosyncratic language, and its faith and traditions.

OX OX2

LEE, Ronald

—**Goddam gypsy: an autobiographical novel.** Montreal: Tundra, 1971. cl $7.95 [0-88776-014-7] ; Don Mills, Ont.: Collins, 1973. pb $1.50; New York: Bobbs-Merrill
Setting: Montreal

Lee's pride in his carefree Gypsy heritage leads him into several brawls which he describes along with lengthy commentaries on the evils of Canadian government and society. Praising "non-conformity" and criticizing Canadian liberalism, Lee gives accounts of his marriage to an Indian woman, and of his ethnic, artistic, and radical friends. The arbitrary nature of the ideological outbursts tends to multiply confusion in an already disjointed narrative sequence.

LEMELIN, Roger 1919—

—**The Town below / Au pied de la pente douce.**1944. NCL. Tr., Samuel Putnam. Toronto: McClelland & Stewart, 1961. pb $2.95 [0-7710-9126-5]
Setting: Lower Town in Quebec City

In *The Town below* the poor live cruelly close to the rich upper town. This socioeconomic situation gives birth to much frustration and ambition. The teenagers are the only ones who have not accepted their almost inevitable future of poverty. Lemelin presents a panoramic view of the people of the city and their concerns—those which appear again and again in Quebec literature. The speech of the workers is inadequately rendered in translation, so much of the flavour is lost, but the book is still worth reading.

—**The Plouffe family/ Les Plouffe.**Toronto: McClelland & Stewart, 1948

—**The Quest of splendour / Pierre le magnifique.** 1952. Tr., Harry Lorin Binsse. Toronto: McClelland & Stewart, 1955. o/p

LEPAN, Douglas 1914—

—The Deserter. 1964. NCL. Toronto: Mc-Clelland & Stewart, 1973. pb $2.95 [0-7710-9188-5]

Setting: a large anonymous city

A young war hero's desertion of modern society is founded upon his belief that its final destiny is war. He searches the underworld for the cause of society's moral imperfection. However, his discovery that the underworld is a society distinct in itself leads him back to the conventional world to construct his own private life. The novel suggests that the perfection of society is dependent upon the moral perfection of the individual.

CB CW OX OX2

LEPROHON, Rosanna Eleanor   1829-1879

—Antoinette de Mirecourt: or, secret marrying and secret sorrowing. 1864. NCL. Toronto: McClelland & Stewart, 1973. pb $2.50 [0-7710-9198-3]

Setting: Montreal in the 1760s

When a young heiress, Antoinette de Mirecourt, comes to Montreal to stay with her frivolous cousin, Mme. d'Aulnay, she becomes involved with and secretly marries a British officer. The story proceeds to show the folly of loose morality as conceived by the Victorians.

—Armand Durand: or, a promise fulfilled. Montreal: Lovell, 1868. o/p

—Clive Weston's wedding anniversary. Montreal: Lovell, 1872. o/p

CW OX

LEVINE, Norman   1924—

—The Angled road. Toronto: McClelland & Stewart, 1952. o/p

—Canada made me. London: Putnam, 1958. o/p (autobiography)

—One way ticket. Toronto: McClelland & Stewart, 1961. o/p

From a seaside town. Toronto & London, Eng.: Macmillan, 1970. cl $6.95 [0-333-11317-9]

Setting: England, Ottawa, Montreal

Joseph Grand, a writer who has moved to a small English town, finds he is tired of doing freelance travel articles and of living in poverty. Visits with eccentric friends in the London art scene, and a business trip to Canada only drive Joseph deeper into his private life of memories and domestic ups-and-downs. Levine records the complexities of married life and artistic despair in an uncluttered linear narrative style.

—I don't want to know anyone too well and other stories. Toronto & London, Eng.: Macmillan, 1971. cl $6.95 [0-333-1259-8]

Setting: Quebec, Ottawa, and England

These hauntingly bleak stories about the lives of solitary men—airforce trainees, undirected university graduates, English tutors, journalists—are mostly narrated in the first person. Encounters between protagonists and other characters are related with extreme detachment.

CB CW OX OX2

LEWIS, David E.

—A Lover needs a guitar: and other stories. Toronto: McClelland & Stewart, 1973. cl $6.95 [0-7710-5295-2]

Setting: Bridgetown, N.S.

In the guise of reminiscences of his childhood, the author has portrayed universal small-town character-types of forty years ago. The stories are light and amusing with brief passages of intellectual speculation about the nature of perception.

LIVESAY, Dorothy   1909—

—A Winnipeg childhood. Winnipeg: Peguis Press, 1973. cl $6.00 [0-919566-21-9]

Setting: Winnipeg

Dorothy Livesay, better known for her poetry, has written a fictionalized account of her childhood in Winnipeg during the years of World War I and the General Strike. The impact of the adult world on a sensitive little girl is described with warmth.

CB CW ON2 OX OX2

LOWELL, Robert Traill Spence   1816-1891

—The New priest in Conception Bay. 1858. NCL. Toronto: McClelland & Stewart, 1974. pb $2.95 [0-7710-9201-6]

Setting: Newfoundland

The arrival of a new Roman Catholic priest in a Maritime community sparks the beginning of several mysteries involving romantic and religious situations. The book is both a novel of intrigue and a tract attempting to illustrate the superiority of Protestantism over Roman Catholicism.

LOWRY, Malcolm 1909-1957

—**Ultramarine.** 1933. Philadelphia: Lippincott, 1962. $4.95; London, Eng.: J. Cape, 1963

Setting: at sea

Dana Hilliott signs on as a hand on a tramp steamer, full of romantic notions about life at sea. The mundane reality and the hostility of his fellow seamen, who can't understand why an educated "toff" like Hilliott is trying to fit in with them, force Hilliott to a better knowledge of himself. His efforts to gain the respect of the men are described clearly and realistically. Lowry was, in this first novel, already beginning to use symbolism in a powerful way.

—**Under the volcano.** 1947. Toronto: McClelland & Stewart, 1965. cl $7.50; Philadelphia: Lippincott; New York: New American Library; London, Eng.: J. Cape; Harmondsworth, Mddx. Eng.: Penguin

Setting: Mexico

The alcoholic British ex-consul Geoffrey Firmin vainly tries to defeat the dark forces within him. His wife, separated from him for a year, returns, but he cannot express his love for her. The consul's struggle comes to represent not only the struggle of the individual soul against evil, but also the struggle of mankind. The novel, Lowry's most powerful, resounds with symbolic and allusive meaning reinforced by the brooding landscape of Mexico on the Day of the Dead.

—**Hear us O Lord from Heaven Thy dwelling place.** Toronto: McClelland & Stewart, 1961. cl $5.75; New York: Putnam; Philadelphia: Lippincott; London, Eng.: J. Cape

These seven novellas were considered by Lowry as a unit. More like discursive prose poems than stories, they contain much slightly changed material from Lowry's journals and are interesting for the light they cast on the psychology and literary philosophy of the author. "Forest path to the spring" is widely accepted as the best written story in the collection.

—**Lunar caustic.** 1963. Ed., Margerie Lowry and Earle Birney. London, Eng.: J. Cape, 1968

Setting: New York City

An alcoholic jazz pianist ends up in Bellevue Hospital in New York, suffering from the delusion that he is a ship. His friendship with an old man and a boy is cut short when he is discharged because he is an alien. This short book was intended by Lowry to be the "Purgatorio" section of a series in which Under the volcano was the "Inferno" and a lost novel, In ballast to the white sea the "Paradiso".

—**Dark as the grave wherein my friend is laid.** Ed., Douglas Day and Margerie Lowry. Don Mills, Ont.: General Publishing, 1968. pb $1.49 [0-7736-0006-X] ; London, Eng.: J. Cape; Harmondsworth, Mddx., Eng.: Penguin

Setting: Mexico

In another semi-autobiographical novel, Lowry describes the journey of Sigbørn Wilderness and his wife Primrose from Vancouver to Mexico. Sigbørn is revisiting Mexico, the setting of his new novel about an alcoholic. He is continually beset by unhappy memories and continually tempted to drink. Near the end of the novel he discovers that the friend he came to visit is dead. This novel, incomplete at his death, is mainly of biographical interest or in the study of Under the volcano.

—**October ferry to Gabriola.** New York: New American Library, 1968. $3.50; London, Eng.: J. Cape

Setting: Oakville, Ont. and the coast and islands of British Columbia

A husband and wife lose one home through fire and another through threat of eviction. Driven by a need for security and permanence, they travel in search of a new home to Gabriola, an island off the B.C. coast, alternating between hope and despair. There is very little action, but much reflection and internal monologue in this incomplete and posthumous novel.

———

Bradbrook, Muriel C. *Malcolm Lowry: his art and early life.* London: Cambridge University Press, 1974

Bradbrook writes from the point of view of one born in the same town in the same year and as a graduate of the same university (Cambridge) as Lowry. In the introduction, she reviews other works of criticism about Lowry, especially Douglas Day's biography, which she feels her work supplements. Unlike most critics, she defends the novels Lowry wrote after Under the volcano. She discusses the influence of Nordahl Grieg, Conrad Aiken and others on the young Lowry and gives an account of contemporary Cambridge. In her "psychological" approach, she points out discrepancies between Lowry's accounts of his early life and what other family members saw as the truth. The appendixes consist of a summary of Lowry's famous letter to his publisher, Jonathan Cape, defending *Under the volcano* and two early stories from the *Leys School magazine*. Included is a detailed chronology of Lowry's early life, an index and a bibliography of Lowry's works and manuscripts, and of other biographical, critical and bibliographical books.

Day, Douglas. *Malcolm Lowry: a biography.* New York: Oxford University Press, 1973. cl $10.00.

Any biography of Lowry must deal with his novels and stories which contain much barely transformed autobiographical material. Day, in this official biography, untangles many inaccuracies in former biographical accounts and has worked hard to separate fantasy from fact. He deals with the important question of how Lowry converted his life into his work. There are many photographs, an index and a selected bibliography. Day discusses much unpublished and draft material not mentioned by other critics.

Dodson, Daniel B. *Malcolm Lowry.* Essays on Modern Writers. New York: Columbia University Press, 1970. pb $1.00

A short account of Lowry's work which surveys the most important points, this book is useful only to those who want a very general introduction to Lowry.

Epstein, Perle. *The Private labyrinth of Malcolm Lowry: Under the volcano and the Cabbala.* New York: Holt, Rinehart & Winston, 1969. cl $6.95

As the title indicates, Epstein's major concern is the Cabbala. A lengthy introduction contains a brief biography of Lowry, an explanation of his involvement with Cabbalistic studies and a detailed history of the Jewish and Christian Cabbalas. A short section about the symbolism of *Under the volcano* precedes the main body of the work which discusses, chapter by chapter, the relationship between the novel and the Cabbala. Epstein's work, although thorough, because of its focus sometimes gives the impression that the Cabbala is the only defining structure of *Under the volcano*. There are several useful appendixes, a bibliography of Lowry and one of the Cabbala, and an index.

Kilgallin, Tony. *Lowry.* Erin, Ont.: Press Porcépic, 1973. cl $8.95 [0-88878-014-1]

Lowry is divided into three sections: the first is about Lowry's life, the second deals with his novel *Ultramarine* and the third his

monumental *Under the volcano*. Kilgallin concentrates on tracing influences and allusions, both of prime importance in Lowry's work.

Lowry, Margerie and Breit, Harvey, eds. *Selected letters.* Toronto: McClelland & Stewart, 1965. cl $11.50; Philadelphia: Lippincott; London, Eng.: J. Cape

New, William H. *Malcolm Lowry.* CWS. NCL. Toronto: McClelland & Stewart, 1971. pb $1.25 [0-7710-9611-9]

Following a brief biography of Lowry, New discusses all of Lowry's work, published and unpublished. Although his chapters are brief, he presents a good survey of what is important in Lowry, concentrating especially on the links among the works and those between Lowry's life and work. Lowry's use of the Tarot is discussed, as is his imagery. (Bibliography.)

Woodcock, George, ed. *Malcolm Lowry: the man and his work.* CLS. Vancouver: University of British Columbia Press, 1971. pb $4.50 [0-7748-0006-2]

Apart from Lowry's valuable letter to Jonathan Cape in defence of *Under the volcano*, most of the articles in this collection concern his other works. There is also a section on "The Man and the sources" made necessary because of Lowry's extensive use in his novels and stories of his own life and other men's work.

Costa, Richard Hauer. *Malcolm Lowry.* Twayne World Authors Series. New York: Twayne, 1972. cl $6.95

The first half of this book deals with *Under the volcano* and how the several versions originated and finally meshed. In the second half, Costa examines Lowry's life in Canada and the works of that period. He then discusses the relationship of life and work in Lowry and tries to account for his failure to equal or surpass *Under the volcano*. The final chapter is a study of the novels from the point of view of the work of Carl Jung.

CL CW OX OX2

LUDWIG, Jack Barry 1922—

—**Confusions.** CBL. Toronto: McClelland & Stewart, 1963. pb 95¢ [0-7710-5377-0]

Setting: Cambridge, Mass., and California

When Joe Galsky leaves his orthodox Jewish family to go to Harvard, he changes his name, his wardrobe and his vocabulary in order to fit into the WASP Ivy League social scene. As the title suggests, he does not quite manage to shake off his past, and his "confusion" is increased by a troubled marriage and a teaching position at an outrageously pretentious West Coast college.

—**Above ground.** 1968. NCL. Toronto: McClelland & Stewart, 1974. pb $2.95 [0-7710-9200-8]

Setting: a northern city, Los Angeles, and New York

Joshua spends most of his childhood in and out of hospitals. Because he survives, he clutches at life and all its trivialities in a hedonistic sexual manner. The story is told in a persistently staccato and allusive style.

—**A Woman of her age.** Toronto: McClelland & Stewart, 1973. cl $7.95 [0-7710-5379-7]

Setting: Montreal

The main character of this novel is a Jewish Montreal dowager named Doba. Though old and wealthy, Doba remembers the anarchist leanings of her earlier days with nostalgia, and spends much of her time being chauffeured around in a limousine looking for rich runaway teenage leftists. Structured symmetrically, the book has twelve chapters titled with Doba's name and those of five other characters whose lives are somehow influenced by her.

CW ON2

McCLUNG, Nellie L. 1873-1951

—**Sowing seeds in Danny.** 1908. Don Mills, Ont.: Allen, 1965. cl $2.95 [no ISBN]

Setting: Manitoba

A story that revolves around the lives of a few people in a small Prairie town, this novel is filled with sudden reformations and happy endings. It succeeds in holding interest mainly through the sense of humour which Nellie McClung allows most of her characters.

—**The Second chance.** New York: Doubleday, 1910. o/p

—**The Black Creek stopping-house and other stories.** Toronto: Briggs, 1912. o/p

—**Purple springs.** Toronto: Allen, 1921. o/p

—**When Christmas crossed "the Peace".** Toronto: Allen, 1923. o/p

—**The Beauty of Martha.** London: Hutchinson, 1923. o/p

—**Painted fires.** New York: Dodd Mead, 1925. o/p

—**All we like sheep and other stories.** Toronto: Allen, 1926. o/p

—**Be good to yourself. A book of short stories.** Toronto: Allen, 1930. o/p

—**Flowers for the living. A book of short stories.** Toronto: Allen, 1931

—**Leaves from Lantern Lane.** Toronto: Allen, 1937. o/p

—**More leaves from Lantern Lane.** Toronto: Allen, 1937. o/p

—**Clearing in the west. My own story.** Toronto: Allen, 1935. o/p

—**The Stream runs fast. My own story.** 1945. Toronto: Allen, 1965. $2.98 [no ISBN]

Setting: Manitoba and Alberta

The second book of McClung's autobiography, this one begins with the move, with her new husband, to the town of Manitou in Manitoba. She describes her experiences as a wife, mother and politician, with emphasis on the last role and on the fight for female suffrage in Canada during the first few years of the twentieth century.

CW OX

McCOURT, Edward Alexander 1907-1972

—**Music at the close.** 1947. NCL. Toronto: McClelland & Stewart, 1966. pb $1.95 [0-7710-9152-4]

Setting: Alberta

As a child, Neil Fraser is inarticulate, independent, and wildly idealistic. A series of reversals forces him to become involved in the world outside his tiny rural one; in turn, these involvements lead him to a reunion with the woman he loves. But since he has become more realistic, their marriage provides only a tenuous bond against anxiety and social upheaval.

—**The Flaming hour.** Toronto: Ryerson, 1947. o/p

—**Home is the stranger.** Toronto: Macmillan, 1950. o/p

—**The Wooden sword.** McClelland & Stewart, 1956. o/p

—**Walk through the valley.** Toronto: McClelland & Stewart, 1958. o/p

—**The Ettinger affair.** London, Eng.: Macdonald & Co., 1963. Published in Canada as **The Fasting friar.** Toronto: McClelland & Stewart, 1963. o/p

CB CW OX OX2

McCULLOCH, Thomas 1776-1843

—Colonial gleanings : William and Melville. Edinburgh: Oliphant, 1826. o/p

—The Stepsure letters. 1860. NCL. Toronto: McClelland & Stewart, 1960. pb $1.95 [0-7710-6587-6] . (Orig. published as **Letters of Mephibosheth Stepsure.**)

Setting: The Maritimes

This series of satirical letters was first published in the *Acadian Recorder,* Halifax, 1821. Written by "Mephibosheth Stepsure", a lame orphan who, by hard work and careful farming, is now prosperous, the short sketches of various town characters extoll thrift, sobriety, work and religion as the path to rural prosperity. Delicate characterization, a leisurely tone, and a subtle satire which never becomes bitter make these letters a first-class and enjoyable example of nineteenth-century Maritime writing. As Northrop Frye says, the cultural attitudes exposed by McCulloch are still traceable in present-day Canada.

McCulloch, William. *The Life of Thomas McCulloch, D.D.* Truro, N.S.: The Albion, 1920. o/p

CB CW OX

McDOUGALL, Colin Malcolm 1917—

—Execution. LL. Toronto: Macmillan, 1958. pb $1.95 [0-7705-0247-4]

Setting: Sicily

A group of Canadian soldiers in the invasion of Sicily executes, somewhat arbitrarily, two Italian deserters. Later one of the Canadians, a simple-minded ordinary soldier, is executed for blackmarketeering, as an "example". These executions, even more irrational than the slaughter of the enemy, have a profound affect on the other soldiers.

MacEWEN, Gwendolyn 1941—

—Julian the magician. Toronto: Macmillan, 1963. o/p

Setting: a small town and surrounding countryside

Julian's reputation as a great magician is extended to divinity when he cures a village idiot. With his three disciples, he travels to a town; after their arrival here parallels between Julian's life and Christ's are intensified. Eventually, he is completely possessed by his divine self and is crucified accordingly. This book deals with the roles that art, magic, and religion must play in our divided

natures. An annotated diary provides the epilogue.

—King of Egypt, king of dreams. Toronto: Macmillan, 1971. pb 95¢ [0-7705-1051-5]

Setting: ancient Egypt

Akhenaton watched his empire crumble around him while he attempted to create a new religion from within. He did not believe in war and refused to acknowledge evil, but in order to purify his land, had to destroy the old gods. This inevitably turned his people against him. MacEwen portrays Akhenaton as a man possessed by a vision of his god—an innocent who struggled to establish a dream. This novel of many tensions creates with a poet's care for words a very personal reality from a historical figure.

—Noman. Ottawa: Oberon Press, 1972. pb $2.95 [0-88750-060-9]

Setting: Toronto, and various imaginary settings

The mysterious Noman has the power to invest ordinary people and places with transcendental qualities which seem innate once he points them out. Noman's power to leap from the ordinary to the magic is MacEwen's as well. In the other stories in this collection, simple things—pinking shears, a fireplace, snow, a piece of red cloth—possess people with mythic force.

CB CW ON2 OX2

McLEISH, Dougal (pseud. for D.J. Goodspeed)

—The Traitor game. Toronto: Macmillan, 1969. pb $2.95 [0-7705-0193-1]; Boston & New York: Houghton Mifflin; New York: Popular Library. Not seen

—The Valentine victim. Boston & New York: Houghton Mifflin, 1969. cl $4.95; New York: Popular Library, 1970. pb 60¢

Setting: a small Ontario town

Inspector John Rodericks of the Ontario Provincial Police (a kindly man, who enjoys reading romantic novels and Tolkein) is called out from London to investigate the murder of a young woman in the little town of Farnham.

MacLENNAN, Hugh 1907—

—Barometer rising. 1941. NCL. Toronto: McClelland & Stewart, 1960. pb $1.75 [0-7710-9108-7] ; Impact Books. Toronto: Macmillan, 1969. educ. ed., cl $1.75 [0-7705-0533-3]

Setting: Halifax

Catalysed by the Halifax explosion of 1917, *Barometer rising* is on one level the story of a man's return from the dead and reunion with his love. On another level it is the story of Canada's coming of age. Neil Mc-Crae faces court-martial for disobeying orders, when he is reported killed. He is only wounded, and secretly returns home to clear his name. MacLennan uses generational conflict to represent the conflict between an older militaristic viewpoint which saw Canada as a colony and a newer one which saw her as important in a future new and independent role.

—**Two solitudes.** 1945. SMC. Toronto: Macmillan, 1951. cl $1.95 [0-7705-0702-6]; LL. Toronto: Macmillan, 1968. pb $1.25 [0-7705-0246-6]

Setting: a Quebec parish, Montreal

Perhaps the best-known of MacLennan's novels, *Two solitudes* deals with the difficult question of French-English relations. Two families, the Tallards and the Yardleys, their friendship, conflicts and problems, represent the two cultures. Athanase Tallard is virtual seigneur of the small closely-knit community of St. Marc-des-Erables and a federal M.P. He tries to bridge the cultural gap by his friendship with Captain Yardley, by attempting to compromise on the divisive World War I conscription question and by introducing industry into his rural riding. The crowded second half of the novel deals with the lives of his two sons—the separatist Marius and his younger brother Paul, who eventually marries Heather Yardley.

—**The Precipice.** Toronto: Collins, 1948. o/p

—**Each man's son.** 1951. LL. Toronto: Macmillan, 1971. pb $1.95 [0-7705-0256-3]

Setting: Cape Breton

Archie MacNeil leaves his wife, son and the coal mines to become an unsuccessful prize fighter in the United States. The Calvinist, childless doctor of the village wants to adopt Archie's son, but Mollie MacNeil thinks of marrying a Frenchman and going to France. Her only concern is to rescue her intelligent and frail child from a future of inhuman work in the mines. Archie's sudden return dramatically changes the course of events.

—**The Watch that ends the night.** 1959. Toronto: Macmillan, 1973. cl $8.95 [0-7705-1050-7]; New York: New American Library

Setting: Montreal, northern Canada, Europe

The tension between the public and the private hero is the tension between Catherine's first and second husbands. Jerome Martell, her first husband, a dynamic and vital doctor, leaves her to fight fascism, first in Spain and then in France. When he is reported dead, the quiet and unassuming George Stewart marries her, accepting the fact that she is a chronic invalid and is slowly dying. The return of Martell juxtaposes the different kinds of love and spirit represented by the two men. The Depression, the rise of fascism and communism in both Canada and Europe and the two world wars provide the novel's historical framework.

—**Return of the Sphinx.** LL. Toronto: Macmillan, 1967. cl $7.95 [0-7705-0199-0]; pb $1.95 [0-7705-0255-5]

Setting: Ottawa, Montreal

The clash between French and English Canada takes place on a family and generational level between Alan Ainslie and his separatist son Daniel. Alan Ainslie, a federal cabinet minister, is pressing for an extensive policy of bilingualism, but his efforts are invalidated by his son's attempt to bomb a public building.

———

Buitenhuis, Peter. *Hugh MacLennan.* CWW. Rexdale, Ont.: Forum House, 1969. pb $1.25 [no ISBN]

Buitenhuis discusses all of MacLennan's published work, devoting one chapter to each novel, one chapter to biography and one to non-fiction works. He provides both plot outlines and critical evaluation with particular emphasis on MacLennan's pioneer role in Canada's literary history. (Bibliography.)

Cockburn, Robert H. *The Novels of Hugh MacLennan.* Montreal: Harvest House, 1969. cl $5.95 [0-88772-109-5]; pb. $2.95 [0-88772-108-7]

Cockburn is distinctly critical of MacLennan's artistic capabilities, especially of his tendency to didacticism and his poverty of imagination. Nevertheless, Cockburn does not neglect what he considers MacLennan's best points—his humour, his well-drawn characters and his ability to describe such dramatic events as the Halifax explosion. Cockburn feels that MacLennan, as the first important novelist to write seriously about Canada, has had a great influence on later Canadian fiction.

Goetsch, Paul. *Hugh MacLennan.* CVCW. Scarborough, Ont.: McGraw-Hill Ryerson, 1973. pb $4.95 [0-07-077653-9]

Goetsch's stated purpose in this work is to document the major trends in MacLennan criticism. He includes twenty articles by such well-known critics as William H. New, Douglas Spettigue and George Woodcock. In his introduction he reviews the history of MacLennan criticism and discusses MacLennan's popularity abroad. There is a detailed bibliography of works by and about MacLennan, including articles and reviews.

Lucas, Alec. *Hugh MacLennan.* CWS. NCL. Toronto: McClelland & Stewart, 1970. pb $1.25 [0-7710-9608-9]

Lucas discusses MacLennan's ideas about Canadian identity. In subsequent chapters he discusses MacLennan's use of romance, the young man as hero, types and myths, and social themes. He attempts to evaluate MacLennan's influence on, and place in, the history of Canadian literature.

Morley, Patricia. *The Immoral moralists: Hugh MacLennan and Leonard Cohen.* Toronto: Clarke, Irwin, 1972. cl $4.50 [0-7720-0555-9] ; pb $2.75 [0-7720-0581-8]

Patricia Morley attempts to highlight cultural change in Canada in the last twenty-five years by examining the works of Hugh MacLennan and Leonard Cohen. Her focus is the word "puritan" which she defines in its original and modern senses. She discusses the works of both authors in terms of their attitudes expressed concerning those prime puritan foci—work, sex and the pursuit of pleasure. Although the word has taken on a negative connotation recently, she feels it is a dynamic concept—encompassing the conflict between such opposites as pain and pleasure, materialism and idealism.

Woodcock, George. *Hugh MacLennan.* SCL. Copp Clark, 1969. pb $2.35.

Woodcock writes perceptively about the influence of MacLennan's life and thought on his work. Attention is given to MacLennan's essays, which served as proving ground for many of the ideas found in the novels. Woodcock discusses the novels in terms of their structure and in terms of the Odysseus myth, which he feels to be central to an understanding of MacLennan's work.

Each man's son. Film.
An excerpt from the novel.
NFB b&w 15 min
16mm: dist. CPI

My country, 'tis of Thee. Audiotape. Discussions with Al Purdy, Miriam Waddington and a group of French-Canadian writers. CBC Cat. No. 658L 1 hr.

CB CL CW ON OX OX2

McNAMEE, James

—**Florencia Bay.** Toronto: McClelland & Stewart, 1960. o/p
—**My Uncle Joe.** Toroto: Macmillan, 1962. o/p
—**Them damn Canadians hanged Louis Riel!** Toronto: Macmillan, 1971. cl $6.95 [0-7705-0773-5]
Setting: Prairies
When family business is threatened by the building of the Canadian Pacific and the Northern Pacific Railways, a boy and his uncle come from Montana to the Prairies. Because they are part Indian and because they know Riel personally, they are passionately opposed to the decision to execute the Métis hero. Written in the colloquial, episodic style of a western thriller, the novel animates social and political aspects of 1880s Canada.

MacPHAIL, Margaret 1887–

—**Loch Bras d'Or.** Windsor, N.S.: Lancelot Press, 1970. pb $2.95
Setting: Cape Breton Island, N.S.
This novel describes the hard-working, God-fearing lives of Scottish immigrants forced from their crofts by sheep enclosures. Hamish MacKiel, left motherless, is raised by Protestant neighbours and becomes a Presbyterian minister.

—**The Girl from Loch Bras d'Or.** Windsor, N.S.: Lancelot Press, 1973. pb $3.95
Setting: Cape Breton Island, N.S.
Hard work is the indisputable fact of life in a fatherless Scottish family. Maryann, who tells the story, misses school while she helps her mother cope with the twelve railway workers she boards to make ends meet. The same pride and diligence that enabled her mother to survive allows Maryann to complete her education, become a school principal and leave the past of drudgery behind.

—**The Bride of Loch Bras d'Or.** Windsor, N.S.: Lancelot Press, 1974. pb $2.95. Not seen

MacSKIMMING, Roy

—**Formentera.** Don Mills, Ont.: New Press, 1972. cl $7.95 [0-88770-150-7] ; pb $2.95 [0-88770-151-5]

Setting: a Spanish island

A small community of young adults live on an isolated island in the Mediterranean. Each chapter is devoted to one character's interior monologue, giving an indication of his motives, and emotional and physical needs. The novel is a description of each individual's loneliness as he strives to satisfy these needs and communicate his motives.

McWHIRTER, George

—Bodyworks. Ottawa: Oberon Press, 1974. cl $6.95 [0-88750-100-1]; pb $3.50 [0-88750-102-8]

Setting: indeterminate

These three phantasmagoric "stories" are actually three chapters of highly disjointed prose. In them, McWhirter attempts to transcend the worlds of "water . . . woman . . . earth" by distorting them fantastically. By depicting internal psychological realities rather than external physical ones, the author gives a rendition of perceptions so original and idiosyncratic as to be often inscrutable.

MARAWILLE, Simon

—Fool's gold: the first $1,000,000. Toronto: Pagurian Press, 1974. cl $6.95 [0-919364-31-4]; New York: Scribner's

Setting: Toronto, Montreal

Michael de Shane succeeds in realizing the dream of many immigrants: he makes a million dollars. Arriving in Canada with no assets except charm, an old school tie, ambition and a background of prosperous Dutch colonialist ancestors, he finds a job on Bay Street. He learns to sell himself and spends his time in single-minded pursuit of money. A spectacular crackup teaches him how much he has lost in order to make his million.

MARCOTTE, Gilles 1925—

—The Burden of God / Le Poids de Dieu. 1962. Tr., Elizabeth Abbot. New York: Vanguard Press, 1964. cl $4.50

Setting: a working-class parish in Quebec

A young scholarly curate of Sainte-Eulalie must deal with love and death, two realities he hardly understands. He retires to a monastery with a sense of guilt and failure. He is uncertain and anxious, but finally realizes that difficult as it may be he is committed to God and to the priesthood.

CW OX OX2

MARKOOSIE

—Harpoon of the hunter. Montreal: McGill-Queen's, 1970. $4.95 [0-7735-0102-9]; deluxe ed. $40.00; 1974. pb $1.50.

Setting: the Arctic

This Eskimo tale describes the struggle of a community to maintain its tenuous existence in a harsh and unpredictable environment. The starkness of detail and events makes it, like many other folk tales, a human and powerful story.

MARLYN, John 1912—

—Under the ribs of death. 1957. NCL. Toronto: McClelland & Stewart, 1964. pb $1.95 [0-7710-9141-9]

Setting: Winnipeg, 1913-1929

The first part of this novel deals with the childhood of the son of a poor, idealistic Hungarian immigrant. The second describes his attempt as a young man to achieve material success by concealing his background. Both his marriage to a woman representing his father's ideals, and the disastrous effects of the 1929 market crash suggest an impending reversal of values. The conflict between human and capitalist values is convincingly portrayed, offering penetrating insight into the life of an immigrant.

ON2

MAROIS, Russell

—The Telephone pole. Toronto: Anansi, 1969. cl $5.00 [0-88784-407-3]; Spiderline Editions. pb $1.95 [0-88784-307-7]

Setting: Montreal and Vancouver

The omniscient, third-person narrator of this novel switches identities and neuroses; finally he admits to having murdered his girl friend and to having suffered absolute psychic disintegration. Sexual fantasies and periods of depression are outlined in a disjointed, surrealistic style.

MARQUIS, Helen

—The Longest day of the year. Don Mills, Ont.: General Publishing, 1969. cl $4.95 [0-7736-2000-1]; Paper Jacks. Don Mills, Ont.: General Publishing, 1974. pb $1.25 [0-7737-7056-9]

Setting: northern Saskatchewan

Intended for teenage readers, this morality tale describes the understanding of adult responsibility gained by thirteen-year-old Cissie when she looks after two younger children on an old-fashioned farm during a winter storm. Although leavened by the humorous antics of the children and by a relaxed use of slang, the book has little relevance to the experiences of modern city bred children.

MARTIN, Claire (pseud. for Claire Faucher, *née* Montreuil) **1914—**

—**In an iron glove / Dans un gant de fer.** 1965. Published with **La Joue droite.** 1966. Tr., Philip Stratford. Scarborough, Ont.: McGraw-Hill Ryerson, 1968. cl $9.95 [0-7700-0250-1]

Setting: Quebec City, Côte de Beaupré

This autobiography, written with a novelist's creative intensity, is a true account of an unhappy and oppressed childhood. Her father is freed by the willing or unwilling acquiescence of family, church and society to be a bigot and a petty tyrant. Martin comments that at the time Quebec was "the intersection of every reactionary trend going". It is appropriate that the book's publication coincided with the loosening of traditional controls in Quebec during the Quiet Revolution of the sixties. The translation is a good one.

MEADE, Edward F. **1912—**

—**Remember me.** 1946. NCL. Toronto: McClelland & Stewart, 1965. pb $1.95 [0-7710-9147-8]

Setting: England and Europe

A generally interesting novel of the Second World War, *Remember me* tells the story of a young man, Bob O'Rourke, who leaves the Prairies to train in England, and to fight and die in France. Meade emphasizes the role of the ordinary soldier in wartime and indicates the everyday heroism of these men.

MERKUR, Dan

—**Around and about Sally's shack.** Toronto: Peter Martin, 1973. cl $6.95 [0-88778-076-8]

Setting: Toronto

The narrator of this novel is a self-styled spokesman for the counter-culture. Through conversations with friends, he gives his impressions of communal living.

METCALF, John **1938—**

—**The Lady who sold furniture.** Toronto: Clarke, Irwin, 1970. o/p

—**Going down slow.** Toronto: McClelland & Stewart, 1972. cl $6.95 [0-7710-5830-6]

Setting: Montreal

A young high school teacher who has recently arrived from England comes into personal and ideological conflict with his colleagues and an educational system he regards as antiquated. He is forced to decide whether to resolve his differences by working within the system or to leave it. After a great deal of self-examination, he decides to remain.

OX2

MILLER, Orlo

—**The Donnellys must die.** 1962. LL. Toronto: Macmillan, 1967. pb $1.95 [0-7705-0249-0]

Setting: southwestern Ontario

Using old records and interviews with residents of the village of Lucan, Orlo Miller has reconstructed the events surrounding the murder of five members of the infamous Donnelly family in 1880. The murders were the culmination of a feud between Roman Catholic and Protestant Irish carried over the sea from Ireland. Miller's sympathies are clearly with the Donnellys, but he attempts to present the story objectively. He succeeds in creating an exciting tale of Ontario's past.

MILLS, John

—**From Georgia straight.** Vancouver: Pendejo Press, 1970. pb $1.00. Not seen

—**The Land of Is.** Ottawa: Oberon Press, 1972. cl $7.95 [0-88750-061-7]; pb $3.95 [0-88750-062-5]; Paper Jacks. Don Mills, Ont.: General Publishing, 1974. pb $1.75 [0-7737-7079-8]

Setting: Vancouver

Victorian novelists often claimed that their readers were perusing a long-lost diary rather than an imaginary account. Thus they avoided the accusation that their writing was frivolous—after all, the truth is history and must be taken seriously. Mills makes the same claim for *The Land of Is.* The improbable events and characters of this crime novel are examined through the eyes of a scholar. The reader is presented not only with a satirical and amusing thriller, but also with philosophical questions concerning literary and historical truth.

—The October men. Ottawa: Oberon Press, 1973. cl $6.95 [0-88750-094-3]; pb $3.50 [0-88750-095-1]; Paper Jacks. Don Mills, Ont.: General Publishing, 1974. pb $1.75 [0-7737-7078-X]
Setting: Montreal and environs
As in *The Land of Is*, Mills distances himself from his work by writing it as an edited diary, this time that of a cynical but witty figure who equates crime, business and politics. He is loyal to his friends, however, and attempts to defraud a gangster out of enough money to spring one of them out of jail. Things go wrong, and the hero goes into hiding in a Laurentian *auberge* and writes his diary. Despite his conviction that he will be interrupted by the gangster at any moment, he finds time to discuss his literary problems with the hotel-keeper. Mills uses the reader's (misplaced) faith in the conventions of the novel to keep him in suspense to the end.

MIRVISH, Robert Franklin 1921—

—The Long watch. New York: Sloan, 1954. o/p

—Texana, a novel. New York: Sloan, 1954. o/p

—Woman in a room. London, Eng.: Redman, 1959. o/p

—Dust on the sea. London, Eng.: Redman, 1960. o/p

—Two women, two worlds. New York: Sloan, 1960. o/p

—Holy Loch. 1964. Newcastle-under-Lyme, Eng.: Remploy
Setting: Glasgow
A woman, separated from her husband and teenage son for more than ten years following a marital breakup, comes to live in a hotel. As the story of her unhappy life unfolds, she slowly and at first unwillingly begins to join in the active socializing of the other guests. After an emotionally unsatisfying affair, she finds someone with whom she is prepared to try marriage again— but first she must deal with the problem of her difficult son.

—There you are, but where are you? Toronto: Clarke, Irwin, 1964. o/p

—The Last capitalist. New York: Fawcett, 1966. o/p

—The Eternal voyagers. Markham, Ont.: Simon & Schuster, 1972. pb $1.25 [0-671-78271-1]
Setting: a ship at sea
An American merchant ship sets out on a full year's voyage. The men have had their final fling on shore, and now, as they sober up, must face the monotonous reality of a year spent away from American shores. As the voyage progresses, the individual problems of the crew are exposed as well as the tensions and violence that arise in their isolation from the rest of the world.

—A House of her own. Markham, Ont.: Simon & Schuster, 1974. pb $1.50 [0-671-78689-X]. Not seen

MITCHELL, John see Patrick Slater

MITCHELL, Ken

—Wandering Rafferty. Toronto: Macmillan, 1972. cl $6.95 [0-7705-0895-2]
Setting: towns and cities from Vancouver to Toronto
The story of a heavy-drinking, poetry-quoting wanderer is told by a young self-styled revolutionary. Finally, the friendship that develops between them becomes more important than their political and emotional differences. Despite its numerous political and literary dialogues, the book focuses on both characters' quests for sexual and emotional fulfillment.

MITCHELL, William Ormand 1914—

—Who has seen the wind. 1947. LL. Toronto: Macmillan, 1960. pb $1.95 [0-7705-0946-0]; SMC. Toronto: Macmillan, 1961. pb $1.90 [0-7705-0705-0]
Setting: a small town in Saskatchewan
At the age of four, Brian O'Connal is a precocious, independent and introspective boy who is already struggling to understand the world around him. Over the next eight years, many of his questions about the meaning of life and death are answered— through his relationships with the people in the town, through his contacts with death, and through his love of the Prairies.

—Jake and the kid. 1961. LL. Toronto: Macmillan, 1974. pb $2.95 [0-7705-0962-2]
Setting: rural Saskatchewan
This collection of short stories is written from the point of view of a young boy on a Saskatchewan farm during the Second

World War. Written in a farm boy's rural dialect, the stories deal with the friendship between the boy and Jake the hired hand, and the daily incidents and hardships of life on a farm.

—The Kite. 1962. LL. Toronto: Macmillan, 1974. pb $3.50 [0-7705-1176-7]

Setting: Alberta

A charming but self-willed old man is the focal point of this novel. A magazine writer's interest in him and those who know him allows the novel to move from one episode to another, as different townspeople reveal facets of the old man's character and historical memories. Although this technique is somewhat contrived, it is made less obvious by the humour and humanity of the characters.

—The Vanishing point. Toronto: Macmillan, 1973. cl $9.95 [0-7705-1044-2]; LL. pb$4.50.

Setting: Stony Indian Reserve, Alberta

A white teacher slowly confronts his fear as he reluctantly acknowledges his love for a former Indian student. The frustrations of native people in dealing with alcoholism, vulnerability and demoralization clearly emerge as the teacher begins to accept, but not share, their cultural identity.

Fires of Envy. Film
NFB b&w 3 min.
16mm: dist. CFI

CB CW ON OX

MONTGOMERY, Lucy Maud 1874-1942

—Anne of Green Gables.* 1908. Scarborough, Ont.: McGraw-Hill Ryerson, 1942. cl $4.95 [0-7700-0006-1]; 1968 pb $1.50 [0-7700-0008-8]; New York: Grosset & Dunlap; Bridgeport, CT: Airmont; London, Eng.: Harrap; Peacock Books. Harmondsworth, Mddx., Eng.: Penguin

—Anne of Avonlea.* 1909. Scarborough, Ont.: McGraw-Hill Ryerson, 1942. cl $4.95 [0-7700-0004-5]; 1968 pb $1.50 [0-7700-0005-3]; New York: Grosset & Dunlop; Bridgeport, CT: Airmont; London, Eng.: Harrap

—Kilmeny of the orchard. 1910. Scarborough, Ont.: McGraw-Hill Ryerson, 1944. cl $5.95 [0-7700-0103-3]

Setting: rural Prince Edward Island

As a substitute teacher in a small P.E.I. town, Eric Marshall finds unexpected adventure through involvement with a mysterious mute girl and a vengeful Italian youth.

After a contrived miraculous cure and an attempted murder, everyone, except the Italian boy, lives happily ever after.

—The Story girl.** 1911. Scarborough, Ont.: McGraw-Hill Ryerson, 1944. cl $5.95 [0-7700-0196-3]

—Chronicles of Avonlea.*** 1912. Scarborough, Ont.: McGraw-Hill Ryerson, 1943. cl $4.95 [0-7700-0043-6]; New York: Grosset & Dunlap; London, Eng.: Harrap

—The Golden road.** 1913. Scarborough, Ont.: McGraw-Hill Ryerson, 1944. cl $5.95 [0-7700-0077-0]

**Setting: rural Prince Edward Island

These volumes tell the story of two boys who join their cousins on a farm for a summer and who end up staying for two or three years. Their adventures are usually treated humorously.

—Anne of the Island.* 1915. Scarborough, Ont.: McGraw-Hill Ryerson, 1942. cl $4.95 [0-7700-0009-6]; 1968 pb $1.50 [0-7700-0011-8]; New York: Grosset & Dunlap; London, Eng.: Harrap

—Anne's house of dreams.* 1917. CFS. Toronto: McClelland & Stewart, 1922. pb $2.49 [0-7710-6196-X]; New York: Grosset & Dunlap; London, Eng.: Harrap

—Rainbow Valley.† 1919. CFS. Toronto: McClelland & Stewart, 1923. pb $2.49 [0-7710-6385-7]

—Further chronicles of Avonlea.*** 1920. Scarborough, Ont.: McGraw-Hill Ryerson, 1953. cl $4.95 [0-7700-0071-1]

***Setting: rural and small-town Prince Edward Island

Told from several points of view, these stories relate important events in the lives of some Avonlea people, before and during the time of Anne Shirley.

Rilla of Ingleside.† CFS. Toronto: McClelland & Stewart, 1921. pb $2.49 [0-7710-6406-3]

†Setting: Prince Edward Island

The story of Anne Shirley's life continues in these two novels, with the emphasis shifted to the childhood and youth of her children. The first book recalls some of the interesting aspects of *Anne of Green Gables;* the second degenerates into a chauvinistic tract for Canadian support of Great Britain in World War I.

—Emily of New Moon. 1923. CFS. Toronto: McClelland & Stewart, 1925. pb $2.49 [0-7710-6238-9]

Setting: rural Prince Edward Island

In the tradition of *Anne of Green Gables,* this story tells the life of an orphan from early childhood to her late teens. In the process of growing up she wins over the relatives who have adopted her and begins a career as a writer. Emily has echoes of Anne Shirley, but the novel as a whole is much less successful than the *Anne* books.

—**Emily climbs.** 1925. Toronto: McClelland & Stewart, 1974. pb $2.79 [0-7710-6259-1]. Not seen

—**The Blue castle.** CFS. Toronto: McClelland & Stewart, 1974. pb $2.49 [0-7710-6217-6]

Setting: Muskoka, Ont.

Valency Stirling is twenty-nine and unmarried. The Blue Castle is her imaginary refuge from her dictatorial mother. When a fatal heart condition is diagnosed she discovers she is afraid neither of death nor of her dreary relatives. She breaks free and marries a charming ne'er-do-well. Later, a few convenient twists of the plot ensure that she does not die and that her husband is the heir to an immense fortune.

—**Emily's quest.** 1927. CFS. Toronto: McClelland & Stewart, 1972. pb $2.49 [0-7710-6280-X]. Not seen

—**Magic for Marigold.** Toronto: McClelland & Stewart, 1929. o/p

—**A Tangled web.** CFS. Toronto: McClelland & Stewart, 1931. pb $2.49 [0-7710-6427-6]. Also published as **Aunt Becky began it.** London, Eng.: Hadder, 1931. o/p. Not seen

—**Pat of Silver Bush.**†† 1933. Toronto: McClelland & Stewart, 1974 pb $2.79. [0-7710-6364-4]

—**Mistress Pat.**†† Toronto: McClelland & Stewart, 1935

††Setting: Prince Edward Island

Although Pat has a family, this is another Montgomery story of the life of a young girl from early childhood until the time she realizes that she loves the boy with whom she has grown up. The story is the usual combination of humour and sentimentality.

—**Anne of Windy Poplars.*** CFS. Toronto: McClelland & Stewart, 1936. pb $2.49; New York: Grosset & Dunlap; London, Eng.: Harrap

—**Jane of Lantern Hill.** Toronto: McClelland & Stewart, 1937

Setting: Toronto and Prince Edward Island

A girl whose parents are separated lives with her weak mother and spiteful grandmother in a Toronto mansion. Jane's life changes when her father invites her to spend a summer on Prince Edward Island.

—**Anne of Ingleside.*** CFS. Toronto: McClelland & Stewart, 1939. pb $2.49 [0-7710-6154-4]; New York: Grosset & Dunlap; London, Eng.: Harrap

*Setting: Prince Edward Island

These five books tell the story of the redheaded orphan Anne Shirley, from her adoption to the birth of her first child. The first two volumes are pleasant and humorous; the later ones subside into unending mawkish praise of Anne.

———

Bolger, Frances W.P. *The Years before Anne: the early career of Lucy Maude Montgomery.* Charlottetown: PEI Heritage Foundation, 1975. cl $8.95; pb $4.95

Bolger discusses the life of Lucy Maud Montgomery before 1908 when *Anne of Green Gables* was published. Bolger bases her work on letters written by Montgomery to her intimate friend Penzie Macneil during the years she spent in Saskatchewan, and on two early scrapbooks which contain all her published short stories, serials and poems written in the 1890s. These are supplemented by Montgomery's autobiographical sketch "The Alpine path" and her letters to Ephraim Walker. A brief epilogue discusses the years after 1908. Bolger reprints early poems and sketches and provides many photographs. There is a detailed bibliography of primary and secondary sources relevant to Montgomery's life as well as a list of her published works.

Eggleston, Wilfrid, ed. *The Green Gable letters, from L.M. Montgomery to Ephraim Weber, 1905-1909.* Toronto: Ryerson Press 1960

Ridley, Hilda M. *The Story of L.M. Montgomery.* 1956. Scarborough, Ont.: McGraw Hill Ryerson, 1973. $5.95 [-07-092969-6]

This uncritical biography of Lucy Maud Montgomery is mainly useful in showing resemblances between the novelist's childhood and the childhood of the characters she wrote about.

CB CL CW ON OX

MONTROSE, David (pseud. for Charles Ross Graham)

—**The Crime on Côte Des Neiges.** Don Mills, Ont.: Collins, 1951. o/p

—**The Body on Mount Royal.** Toronto: Harlequin Books, 1953. o/p

—**Gambling with fire.** (by Charles Ross Graham) Don Mills, Ont.: Longman, 1969. cl $5.50 [no ISBN]
Setting: Montreal
Franz Loebek, an ex-squadron leader and member of an aristocratic Austrian family, arrives in Montreal to begin a new life after the war. Eventually he is left a gambling house as a legacy from an acquaintance and becomes involved in the machinations of the Montreal underworld. He also becomes enmeshed in the lives of two women. Written as a conventional thriller-romance, the novel is true to its conventions and has a happy ending.

MOODIE, Susanna 1803-1885

—**Spartacus.** London, Eng.: Newman, 1822. o/p

—**The Little prisoner.** (with Elizabeth Strickland) London, Eng.: 1828. o/p

—**Profession and principle.** London, Eng.: Dean, 1833. o/p

—**Roland Massingham.** London, Eng.: Dean, 1837. o/p

—**The Victoria Magazine, Belleville, 1847.** Vancouver: University of British Columbia Press, 1968. o/p

—**The Little black pony and other stories.** Philadelphia: Collins, 1850. o/p

—**Roughing it in the bush; or, life in Canada.** 1852. abr. NCL. Toronto: McClelland & Stewart, 1962. pb $1.95 [0-7710-9131-1]; Coles Canadiana Collection. Rexdale, Ont.: Coles, 1974. cl $12.95; pb $6.95 [no ISBNs]; Boston: Gregg
Setting: Ontario, near Port Hope and Peterborough
These sketches are based on the actual experiences of the Moodies as settlers in Upper Canada between 1832 and 1839. Originally written for English magazines to discourage

gently bred emigrants from coming to Canada, the book describes very clearly the difficulties encountered by many settlers. Moodie's lively use of dialogue, her eye for detail and her honest portrayal of her own difficulties have made this a widely read book for both its historical and literary interest.

—**Life in the clearings versus the bush.** 1853. Ed., Robert L. McDougall. Pioneer Books. Toronto: Macmillan, 1959. cl $8.95 [0-7705-0242-3]
Setting: Belleville, Upper Canada
Susanna Moodie continues the story of her life in Canada with a description of the experiences she and her husband underwent in Belleville, a more pleasant atmosphere than the isolation of the bush. Some of the bitterness of the earlier experience was eased by the new social environment and the opportunity it gave her to pursue her literary work.

—**Mark Hurdlestone.** London, Eng.: Bentley, 1853. o/p

—**The Soldier's orphan.** London, Eng.: Dean, 1853. o/p

—**Flora Lindsay.** London, Eng.: Bentley, 1854. o/p

—**Matrimonial speculations.** London, Eng.: Bentley, 1854. o/p

—**Geoffrey Moncton.** New York: DeWitt, 1855. Also published as **The Monctons**. London, Eng.: Bentley, 1856. o/p

—**Dorothy Chance.** 1867. o/p

—**The World before them.** London, Eng.: Bentley, 1868. o/p

—**George Leatrim.** Edinburgh: Hamilton, 1875. o/p

—**Life in the backwoods.** New York: Lovell, 1887. o/p

_____

Atwood, Margaret. *The Journals of Susanna Moodie.* Don Mills, Ont.: Oxford University Press, 1970. pb $1.95 [0-19-540169-7]
These are poems based on Moodie's *Roughing it in the bush* and *Life in the clearings.*

Davies, Robertson. *At my heart's core.* 1950. Toronto: Clarke, Irwin, 1966. pb $1.50 [0-7720-0443-9]
A play by Robertson Davies depicting some aspects of pioneer life, with characters portraying Catherine Parr Traill and Susanna Moodie.

Hume, Blanche. *The Strickland sisters.* Toronto: Ryerson Press, 1928. o/p

Morris, Audrey. *Gentle pioneers*. Don Mills, Ont.: Musson, 1968. cl $6.50; Paper Jacks. Don Mills, Ont.: General Publishing, 1973. pb $1.50 [0-7737-7034-8]

Samuel Strickland, his sisters Susanna and Catherine, and their husbands John W. Dunbar Moodie and Thomas Traill, emigrated from England to the Peterborough area in the 1830s. Four major works—Catherine Parr Traill's *The Backwoods of Canada* (1836), Susanna Moodie's *Roughing it in the bush* (1852), Samuel's *Twenty seven years in Canada West* (1853*)*, and John's *Scenes and adventures as a soldier and settler* (1866) tell the story of their early struggles and shed light on early Canadian society. Morris has used these works, supplementing them when necessary for an account of their lives and background. Included is an index and extensive notes.

Needler, G.H. *Otonabee pioneers*. Toronto: Burns & MacEachern, 1953. o/p

---

The Journals of Susanna Moodie. Film.

A dramatic film interpretation of Margaret Atwood's poems.
UEVA Film No. C-29 b&w 15 min 16mm

Mrs. Moodie's Journal. Record.
Poems by Margaret Atwood read by Mia Anderson.

See also Catherine Parr Traill
CB CL CW ON OX

MOORE, Brian 1921—

—**The Lonely passion of Judith Hearne**. 1956. Toronto: McClelland & Stewart, 1964. cl $8.95 [0-7710-6440-3]; NCL (as **Judith Hearne**) pb $1.75 [0-7710-9139-7]; Boston: Little, Brown; London, Eng.: Panther

Setting: Belfast, Northern Ireland
Poverty-stricken and lonely in her forties, Judith Hearne attempts to stem the loneliness of life in a Belfast boarding house with an imaginary romance, heavy drinking and her dying religious faith. Without falling into bathos, Moore reveals, mainly through Judith's mind, the desperation of a woman in a society which offers only marriage or the convent as a means of fulfillment.

—**The Feast of Lupercal**. Boston: Little, Brown, 1957. o/p

—**The Luck of Ginger Coffey**. 1960. NCL. Toronto: McClelland & Stewart, 1972. pb $1.95 [0-7710-9180-X]; London, Eng.: Senior Unicorn; London: Quartet Books

Setting: Montreal
Having failed in business in Ireland, Ginger Coffey tries to fulfill his dreams of being important in his adopted home, Montreal. In the process he almost destroys himself and his marriage, but he finally comes to some understanding of himself and his situation. Through Ginger's thoughts Moore portrays with insight and humour the problems of the disillusioned immigrant.

—**An Answer from limbo**. 1962. PaperJacks. Don Mills: General, 1973. pb $1.50 [0-7737-7035-6]

Setting: New York City
Dominated by Moore's often-used theme of the assimilation of the past by the present, this novel tells of a man's struggle to become an artist and the destructive effects of the struggle on his wife and mother. Moore's handling of this theme here is less interesting than in most of his other novels.

—**The Emperor of ice cream**. 1965. Mayflower Books. St. Albans, Herts.: Granada, 1970

Setting: Belfast, Northern Ireland
Gavin Burke is almost paralyzed by fear that his recent failure to pass his examinations is the foretaste of a desolate future. He becomes a member of the First Aid Party, organized against the threat of German raids in World War II. His first romance his early experiences with drink, and his encounters with the various seedy characters in the party are a prelude to an important maturing experience—a day spent coffining the bodies of the victims of the first air raid. He finds he is strong enough to face life—the "Emperor of Ice Cream" in his favourite Wallace Stevens poem.

—**I am Mary Dunne**. Toronto: McClelland & Stewart, 1968. cl $6.95 [0-7710-6460-8] New York: Viking Press; London Eng.: J. Cape; Harmondsworth, Middx.: Penguin Books.

Setting: New York City
Written in the first person, this novel explores a day in the life of a woman who is suffering from an identity crisis. Although happy with her third husband, she has not been able to reconcile her past experiences with her present. Moore explores, sometime with insight, the mind of a woman who is verging on the realization of herself as a complete individual.

—**Fergus**. Toronto: McClelland & Stewart, 1970. cl $5.95 [0-7710-6430-6] ; London: J. Cape

Setting: southern California

Seeing himself as a failure at thirty-nine, Fergus Fadden, an Irish writer living in California, is suddenly faced with his past in the form of phantoms of his younger self and his family, friends and acquaintances. By wrestling with his past Fergus learns to deal with the present. In depicting this struggle Moore provides an unusual twist to the presentation of man's confusion between past and present.

—**The Revolution script**. Toronto: McClelland & Stewart, 1971. cl $3.95 [0-7710-6431-4] ; Pocket Books. New York: Simon & Schuster; London, Eng.: J. Cape; Harmondsworth, Middx.: Penguin Books

Setting: Montreal

In his account of the kidnapping of James Cross by the FLQ in October, 1970, Moore combines a factual day-by-day account of the crisis with a fictional representation of the thoughts and conversation of the kidnappers. Moore's facile narrative exploits the situation rather than achieving the probing, sensitive examination that he exhibits in his other works.

—**Catholics**. Toronto: McClelland & Stewart, 1972. cl $4.95 [0-7710-6435-7] ; New York: Holt, Rinehart; London, Eng.: J. Cape; Pocket Books. New York: Simon & Schuster

Setting: an island off the west coast of Ireland

Set several years in the future, this novel depicts briefly and movingly the struggle between a new ecumenical, socially-oriented church and a small group of Irish monks who persist in such traditions as the Latin mass. In the centre of the controversy are the abbot, who has lost his faith, and a young priest who must learn more about human nature.

Dahlie, Hallvard. *Brian Moore*. SCL. Toronto: Copp Clark, 1969. pb $2.35 [0-7730-3006-9]

This small volume covers Moore's first six novels chronologically from 1955 to 1968, beginning with a short critical and biographical sketch. Dahlie sees a movement in Moore's work from "despair to affirmation". The discussion is clear and concise and serves as a useful introduction to Moore's work.

Flood, Jeanne. *Brian Moore*. Irish Writers Series. Lewisburg: Bucknell University Press, 1974. cl $4.50 [0-8387-7823-7] ; pb $1.95 [0-8387-7972-7]

Flood describes the key situation in Moore's work as "the guilty dream life of a central figure who has treacherously withdrawn from the morally valid world of the father". The father is represented in Moore's Belfast world by God, religion, family and school. Moore's first four novels were an attack on this Belfast world; later novels often focus on revolution, again the struggle between child and father. (Bibliography.)

The Luck of Ginger Coffey. Film. b&w 100 min 16/35mm English: dist. New Cinema

CL CW

MOSHER, Jack

—**Some would call it adultery**. Montreal: Content, 1972. pb $1.95

Setting: Port Credit, Ont. at the turn of the century

A randy old man amuses his grandsons with local and family history. He also arranges to have his daughter-in-law impregnated, and casts doubt on the image of Upper Canadian society as prim and proper.

MOWAT, Farley 1921—

—**People of the deer**.* Toronto: Little Brown, 1951. cl $8.95 [0-316-58642-0] ; Boston: Little, Brown; New York: Pyramid; rev. ed. Toronto: McClelland & Stewart, 1974. cl $8.50 [0-7710-6589-2] ; pb $5.95 [0-7710-6590-6]

—**Lost in the Barrens**. Toronto: Little Brown, 1956. cl $5.75 [0-316-58638-2] ; Boston: Little, Brown; rev. ed. Toronto: McClelland & Stewart, 1973. pb $2.95 [0-7710-6640-6]

Setting: the northern Barrens

Two boys who set out on a caribou hunting expedition with a group of Chipewyan Indians become separated from them and have to spend several months alone in the Barrens. Jamie and Awasin survive the Arctic winter through skill, determination and some good luck. Although the book is listed as suitable for younger readers, it will be fascinating to readers of almost any age.

—**The Dog who wouldn't be.** Toronto: Little, Brown, 1957. cl $7.95 [0-316-58636-6] ; Boston: Little, Brown; New York: Pyramid

Setting: Saskatchewan

Mowat relates the remarkable and comic adventures of Mutt, the mongrel dog who entered the author's life when he was a child in Saskatoon. Among other feats chronicled in the story are Mutt's development from a chaser of cows into an extraordinary hunting dog, his mastery of fence walking and ladder climbing, and his idiosyncratic methods of dealing with other dogs and humans. The author also includes the exploits of people such as his father who attempts to sail a boat on the virtually dry South Saskatchewan River. This story can be enjoyed by children and adults alike.

—**The Desperate people.*** Toronto: Little Brown, 1959. cl $8.60 [0-316-58635-8] ; Boston: Little, Brown; rev. ed. Toronto: McClelland & Stewart, 1974. cl $8.50 [0-7710-6591-4] ; pb $5.95 [0-7710-6592-2]

*Setting: the northern Barrens

These two books trace the fate of the Ihalmiut Eskimos from the nineteenth century to 1959, concentrating on the period after 1947 when Farley Mowat first met the remaining members of the largely decimated group. The first book describes passionately the terrible results of the white man's invasion of the north. The second book reports more objectively but with even greater effectiveness the circumstances surrounding the disappearance of the Ihalmiut and the indifference of other Canadians to their fate.

—**Owls in the family.** Toronto: Little, Brown, 1961. cl $4.95 [0-316-58641-2] ; Toronto: McClelland & Stewart, 1961. School ed. cl $4.95; [0-7710-6647-3] ; text pb $1.25; Boston: Little Brown; London, Eng.: Piccolo Books

Owls in the family includes the same eccentric cast of animals and people as *The Dog who wouldn't be,* but this time the focus is on Wol and Weeps, the owls. They are not particularly well domesticated, as Wol proves when he arrives at a dinner party with a dead skunk.

—**The Black Joke.** Toronto: Little, Brown, 1962. cl $4.50 [0-316-58631-5] ; Toronto: McClelland & Stewart, 1962. School ed. cl $4.95 [0-7710-6648-1] ; pb $2.95 [0-7710-6649-X] ; Boston: Little, Brown.

Setting: Newfoundland, St. Pierre and Miquelon

In his usual entertaining manner, Farley Mowat tells the story of an adventure involving a boat, "The Black Joke", its owner and his young son and nephew. Set in the 1930s the tale centres on the machinations of rum-running from the French islands to the United States. As in Mowat's other stories, the two children overcome various difficulties to emerge happy and wiser.

—**Never cry wolf.** 1963. Toronto: McClelland & Stewart, 1973. Rev. ed. cl $7.95 [0-7710-6584-1] ; text pb $1.75 [0-7710-6582-5] ; Boston: Little, Brown; New York: Dell; New York: Watts, large type ed.

Setting: northern Canada

Sent on a mission into the "subarctic Barrens" to study the life habits of the wolf, Mowat discovers that the animal's reputation for viciousness is a myth. Living among the wolves for several months convinces him that they are in fact timid in the presence of man. He also learns that rifle-toting men rather than wolves are responsible for the decimation of the northern herds of caribou. Mowat's ability to recognize and communicate the humour in things, especially when the joke is on himself, is well displayed in his comic use of such incidents as his naked romp among the wolves.

—**The Curse of the Viking grave.** Toronto: Little, Brown, 1966. cl $5.95 [0-316-58633- Toronto: McClelland & Stewart, 1966. cl $5.95 [0-7710-6641-4] ; pb $2.95 [0-7710-6642-2] ; Boston: Little, Brown

Setting: northern Manitoba

Many of the characters from an earlier book *Lost in the Barrens*, reappear in this adventure of four teenagers who make their way to the Barren Lands of Manitoba. Carrying some Viking relics discovered on an earlier trip they continue their precarious and adventure-filled journey to Churchill.

—**The Boat who wouldn't float.** Toronto: McClelland & Stewart, 1969. cl $6.95 [0-7710-6586-8] ; pb $2.95 [0-7710-6587-6 Boston: Little, Brown; London, Eng.: Heinemann

Setting: Newfoundland

This is an hilarious account of the author's adventures in buying, attempting to repair and sail a leaky boat with a personality of its own. Mowat also provides humorous insight into the people and culture of Newfoundlan as well as vivid descriptions of the fogs and unpredictable seas of the Atlantic and the Gulf of St. Lawrence.

—**A Whale for the killing.** Toronto: McClelland & Stewart, 1972. cl $6.95 [0-7710-6570-1]; Boston: Little Brown; New York: Penguin Books; London, Eng.: Heinemann

Setting: Burgeo, Nfld.

This, like much of Mowat's writing, falls into the somewhat vague category of fictionalized history, "non-fiction-fiction" or documentary. Based on an actual case of a Fin Whale that became stranded in a pond near a Newfoundland outport, the story also has fictional aspects. The whale, a member of a dying race, dies from numerous wounds inflicted by motor boat and guns. Mowat connects the whale's wanton murder to man's general misuse of nature. He makes a plea not only for the conservation of wildlife, but also for the preservation of the kind of life lived in the outports, gradually being abolished by a centralizing government.

_____

Lucas, Alec. *Farley Mowat.* CWS. NCL. Toronto: McClelland & Stewart, 1976. pb $1.95 [0-7710-9616-X].

CW OX OX2

MUNRO, Alice 1931—

—**Dance of the happy shades.** 1968. Scarborough, Ont. & New York: McGraw-Hill Ryerson, 1973. pb $3.95 [0-07-092967-X]

Setting: Ontario

With one exception, these stories are narrated by girls and young women. Psychological reactions to social pressure and death are expressed in such a way that inner complexity, though not made explicit, is the focal point. The stories are all about fifteen pages long, and written in a direct linear narrative style.

—**Lives of girls and women.** Scarborough, Ont.: McGraw-Hill Ryerson, 1971. cl $7.95 [0-07-092932-7]; Scarborough, Ont. & New York: New American Library. pb $1.25; Large Print Adult Series. Boston: G.K. Hall; London, Eng.: A. Lane

Setting: Ontario

Del Jordan's childhood is spent largely in the company of her friend Naomi and her mother, an eccentric, agnostic encyclopedia saleswoman. After Naomi quits school in quest of a husband, Del turns to high school studies, to the town's various churches, to novel-writing, and to a love affair, in an attempt to understand her place in a stagnant society. Sexual encounters are graphically described, as are the other comic and grotesque events of the book.

—**Something I've been meaning to tell you.**

Scarborough, Ont. & New York: McGraw-Hill Ryerson, 1974. cl $7.95 [0-07-077760-8]

Setting: British Columbia and Ontario

These stories deal mainly with the discrepancies between characters' intentions and their actions. The predominantly female characters tend to be dissatisfied with, or powerless in, their present situations. The most masterful of these stories are about the separation of artistic aspiration and ordinary experience.

CB CW ON2 OX2

MURDOCH, Benedict 1886—

—**The Red vineyard.** Cedar Rapids, IA: Torch, 1923. o/p

—**Souvenir.** Lancaster, Eng.: Wichersham, 1926. o/p

—**Sprigs.** Cedar Rapids, IA: Torch, 1927. o/p

—**Part way through.** Toronto: Mission Press, 1946. o/p

—**Far away place.** Francetown, NH: M. Jones Co., 1952. o/p

—**The Menders.** Francetown, NH: M. Jones Co., 1953. o/p

—**The Murphys come in.** Fredericton: Brunswick Press, 1964. cl $4.00

Setting: New Brunswick

These twenty-three short sketches, written in a simple and humorous style, describe life in the woods as experienced by such characters as lumberjacks, priests, camp cooks and bears. The book is printed in large type and illustrated.

MURRAY, Sinclair see Alan Sullivan

NEWMAN, C.J.

—**We always take care of our own.** Toronto: McClelland & Stewart, 1965.

Setting: Montreal

In revolt against the clannishness of the Montreal Jewish community, Meyer Rabinovitch decides to become a beggar. His search for universal ideals becomes subverted by his pursuit of the Dress King's rich and beautiful daughter, while his own father battles bankruptcy.

—**A Russian novel.** Don Mills, Ont.: New Press, 1973. cl $6.95 [0-88770-175-2] ; London, Eng.: Gollancz

Setting: Moscow

Told in a coherent, even-paced style, this novel relates the experiences of a Canadian author who visits Russia to do research on a pro-Soviet novelist. Intellectual speculation is interspersed with a plot detailing authoritarian censorship and possibilities of revolt and survival in the face of Soviet and Western ways of life.

NEWTON, Norman 1929—

—**The House of gods.** London: P. Owen, 1961. o/p

—**The One true man.** Toronto: McClelland & Stewart, 1963. o/p

—**The Big stuffed hand of friendship.** Toronto: McClelland & Stewart, 1969. cl $5.95 [0-7710-6765-8]

Setting: British Columbia

The author chronicles a short period in a port town during which several lives are intertwined sexually, economically and politically. The tensions in the relationships culminate in ruined reputations, attempted suicide and a riot which involves Indians, fishermen, poets and a minister, among others.

NICHOL, b p 1944—

—**Two novels: Andy / For Jesus Lunatick.** Toronto: Coach House Press, 1969. pb $3.00 [0-88910-036-5]

Setting: Toronto and elsewhere

Andy is a collage of personal letters and excerpts from three pulp novels; its dominant concern is communication, beyond the usual narrative boundaries. *For Jesus Lunatick* develops the techniques hinted at in *Andy,* exploring the perceptions of two men and a woman without resorting to consistency of plot, setting or characterization.

CB ON2 OX2

NOWLAN, Alden 1933—

—**Miracle at Indian River.** Toronto: Clarke, Irwin, 1968. cl $3.95 [0-7720-0073-5]

Setting: a small town in New Brunswick

These short stories about the various hardships of Maritimers contrast the bleakness of the land and the life with the eagerness of the people to find pleasure in new or vicarious experiences. Some stories concentrate on serious character portrayal, others are humorous and others zero in on the emotional significance of particular incidents.

—**Various persons named Kevin O'Brien; a fictional memoir.** Toronto: Clarke, Irwin, 1973. cl $6.75 [0-7720-0588-5]

Setting: Nova Scotia

After an absence of many years, a newspaper editor returns to the village of his childhood. With frequent shifts of viewpoint, the novel concentrates on various scenes from his youth, and on the importance of place. By considering the changes in the hero's perception and understanding of his past, Nowlan creates a past that is a "constant presence"—an idea which is imaginatively developed throughout the novel.

CB CW ON2 OX OX2

O'BRIEN, Bill T. 1943—

—**Summer of the black sun.** 1969. Markham, Ont.: Simon & Schuster, 1971. pb $1.25 [0-671-78093-X]

Setting: indeterminate

Bill Louper is a manic-depressive confined to a hospital. His sun is black; time is confused; memory plays him false. Appropriately, he uses images from Milton's *Paradise lost* to describe the war in his mind. He feels insecure, like a helpless infant. Once a medical student, he can understand what is happening to others around him and sneaks into the office to look at their files. For the outsider he recreates the upside-down chaotic world of the mental hospital.

O'CONNELL, Angela M.

—**The Loveliest and the best.** Markham, Ont.: Simon & Schuster, 1973. pb $1.50 [0-671-78621-0]

Setting: England, Europe, and New York

An upper-class couple are separated by the Nazi invasion of Czechoslovakia. Their adventures while he is in the R.C.A.F. and she is on the fringes of underground resistance are described.

O'HAGAN, Howard 1902–

—**Tay John.** 1939. NCL. Toronto: McClelland & Stewart, 1974. pb $1.95 [0-7710-9205-9]

Setting: Rocky Mountains

Giving up his messianic leadership of the Shuswap people's westward exodus, Tay John stays in the mountains hunting until a woman, cast out from white society, comes along. Only when she dies toward the end of pregnancy does Tay John resume the quest for a western refuge. Circularly structured, the novel juxtaposes the exploits of the mythic Shuswap hero with those of the exceptional blond Indian of traders' tales. The humour of the subplot (in which an entrepreneur tries to create a mountain haven named "Lucerne") elasticizes the powerful tension between the hero's prophetic vocation and his human impulses.

—**The Woman who got on at Jasper Station and other stories.** Chicago: Swallow Press, 1963. $1.65

Setting: Rocky Mountains

Of these eight stories, the most gripping affirm the value of adaptation to unexpected circumstances. Often the imagery, characters, and situations are reminiscent of *Tay John:* trappers, an absurd entrepreneur, hardy women, trees, horses, winter, mountains, violent death. Though written in a linear narrative style, the stories bring out the magical or mysterious aspects of missed or mismanaged opportunity.

OSTENSO, Martha 1900-1963

—**Wild geese.** 1925. NCL. Toronto: McClelland & Stewart, 1961. pb $2.95 [0-7710-9118-4]. Also published as **The Passionate flight.** London: Hodder, 1925. o/p

Setting: rural Manitoba

The tyranny of Caleb Gare over his wife and family is observed by a young schoolteacher, Lind Archer, who boards on his farm. Life on the land is sensitively depicted in this early attempt at realism in the Canadian novel.

—**The Dark dawn.** New York: Dodd Mead, 1926. o/p

—**The Mad carews.** New York: Dodd Mead, 1927. o/p

—**The Young May moon.** New York: Dodd Mead, 1929. o/p

—**The Waters under the earth.** New York: Dodd Mead, 1930. o/p

—**Prologue to love.** New York: Dodd Mead, 1932. o/p

—**There's always another year.** New York: Dodd Mead, 1933. o/p

—**The White reef.** New York: Dodd Mead, 1934. o/p

—**The Stone field.** New York: Dodd Mead, 1937. o/p

—**The Mandrake root.** New York: Dodd Mead, 1938. o/p

—**Love passed this way.** New York: Dodd Mead, 1942. o/p

—**O river remember.** New York: Dodd Mead, 1943. o/p

—**Milk route.** New York: Dodd Mead, 1948. o/p

—**The Sunset tree.** New York: Dodd Mead, 1949. o/p

—**A Man had tall sons.** New York: Dodd Mead, 1958. o/p

CB CL CW ON OX

PACEY, Desmond 1917-1975

—**The Picnic and other stories.** Toronto: Ryerson, 1958. o/p

—**Waken, lords and ladies gay: selected writings of Desmond Pacey.** Ed. and intro., Frank M. Tierney. Ottawa: University of Ottawa Press, 1974. pb $4.80 [0-7766-4334-7]

Pacey's stories radiate a simple country freshness. A straightforward story line, uncomplicated plots, and open characters reflect the outlook of the children who often narrate them.

OX

PACKARD, Pearl

—**The Reluctant pioneer.** Dorval, P.Q.: Palm, 1968. cl $6.50 [0-919366-27-9]

Setting: northern Ontario

Based on the life of the author's grandmother, this is the story of a pioneer woman's struggle to cope with life in the far northern woods in the mid-nineteenth century.

PAGE, P.K. 1916—

—**The Sun and the moon and other fictions.**
By Judith Cape (pseud.). 1944. Toronto:
Anansi, 1974. cl $7.95 [0-88784-429-4];
pb $3.50 [0-88784-327-1]

This book combines Page's short early
novel *The Sun and the moon* and a small
collection of short stories. The novel tells
the strange story of a girl, born during a
lunar eclipse, who has the power to take
over the identity of inanimate objects and
also of people, thus robbing them of their
being or souls. It focuses on the tragedy of
her love for a painter, for she soon realizes
that she cannot love him without absorbing
him and taking over his talent and his soul.
The strange, tragic ending seems inevitable.
The short stories have a more powerful
thrust and are compelling in their morbid
humour and bizarre insights.

CB CW ON2 OX OX2

PANNETON, Phillippe see Ringuet

PARKER, Gilbert 1862-1932

—**The Chief factor: a tale of the Hudson's
Bay Company.** New York: Trow Directory
Co., 1892. o/p

—**Pierre and his people. Tales of the far
north.*** 1892. Short Story Index Reprint
Series. Plainview, N.Y.: Books for Libraries.
cl $11.00

—**Mrs. Falchion. A novel.** London, Eng.:
Methuen, 1893. o/p

—**The Translation of a savage.** New York:
Appleton, 1893. o/p

—**The Trespasser.** New York: Appleton,
1893. o/p

—**A Lover's diary. Songs in sequence.** London, Eng.: Methuen, 1894. o/p

—**The Trail of the sword.** New York: Appleton, 1894. o/p

—**An Adventurer of the north. Being a con-
tinuation of Pierre and his people.*** 1895.
Story Reprint Series. Plainview, N.Y.:
Books for Libraries. cl $8.95

—**When Valmond came to Pontiac. The
story of a lost Napoleon.** London, Eng.:
Methuen, 1895. o/p

—**The Pomp of the Lavilettes.** Boston: Lamson Wolffe, 1896. o/p

—**A Romany of the snows.*** 1896.
Short Story Index Reprint Series. Plainview,
N.Y.: Books for Libraries, cl $8.95

*Setting: the Canadian north
These books are collections of stories focusing on Pretty Pierre—a half-breed voyageur,
gambler, and all-round adventurer, at the
height of the Hudson's Bay Company's
power. Men are killed, women are kidnapped
all sorts of crimes are committed, but justice
and honour prevail due to Pierre's basic
honesty. Despite a rather antiquated style,
and somewhat suspect factual content,
these stories bring to life northern Canada's
colourful history.

—**The Seats of the mighty. Being the memoirs of Captain Robert Moray, some time
an officer, in the Virginia Regiment and
afterwards of Amherst's Regiment.** 1896.
abr. NCL. Toronto: McClelland & Stewart, 1971. pb $2.95 [0-7710-9175-3]

Setting: New France
An historical romance of great popularity
at the turn of the century, this novel tells
of the escapades of Captain Robert Moray
who was held hostage in Quebec City prior
to 1759. Some of the episodes involve a
woman threatened with incarceration in a
nunnery, a man conversant with the great
men of the century and Québécois peasants
threatened with starvation due to a rapacious nobility. The book's original leisurely
pace has been stepped up by twentieth-
century editing.

—**The Battle of the strong. A romance of two
kingdoms.** London, Eng.: Methuen, 1898. o/p

—**Born with a golden spoon.** New York:
Doubleday, 1899. o/p

—**The Liar.** Boston: Brown, 1899. o/p

—**The Hill of pains.** Boston: Badger, 1899.
o/p (authorship disputed)

—**The Lane that had no turning, and other
associated tales.** New York: Doubleday,
1900. o/p

—**An Unpardonable liar.** Chicago: Sergel,
1900. (See The Liar.) o/p

—**The March of the White Guard.** New
York: Fenno, 1901. (Repr. from *Tavistock
tales*, by Gilbert Parker and others. London,
Eng.: Isbister, 1893.) o/p

—**The Right of way. Being the story of
Charley Steele and another.** London, Eng.:
Heinemann, 1901. o/p

—**Donovan Pasha and some people of Egypt**
London, Eng.: Heinemann, 1902. o/p

—A Ladder of swords. A tale of love, laughter, and tears. London, Eng.: Heinemann, 1904. Also published as **Michel and Angèle**. New York: Scribner, 1923. o/p

—The Weavers. A tale of England and Egypt of fifty years ago. New York: Harper, 1907. o/p

—Northern lights. Toronto: Copp Clark, 1909. o/p

—Cumner's son and other South Sea folk. London, Eng.: Heinemann, 1910. o/p

—The Going of the white swan. New York: Appleton, 1912. excpt. from **An Adventurer of the north**. o/p

—The Works of Gilbert Parker. Imperial Ed. New York: Scribner, 1912-23. 23 vol. o/p

—The Judgement house. A novel. Toronto: Copp Clark, 1913. o/p

—You never know your luck. Being the story of a matrimonial deserter. New York: Doran, 1914. o/p

—The Money master. Being the curious history of Jean Jacques Barville, his labours, his loves and ladies. New York: Harper, 1915. o/p

—The World for sale. New York: Harper, 1916. o/p

—Wild youth and another. Philadelphia: Lippincott, 1919. o/p

—No defence. Toronto: Copp Clark, 1920. o/p

—Carnac. Toronto: Copp Clark, 1922. o/p

—Carnac's Folly. Philadelphia: Lippincott, 1922. o/p

—The Power and the glory. A romance of the great La Salle. New York: Harper, 1925. o/p

—Tarboe. The story of a life. New York: Harper, 1927. o/p

—The Promised land. A story of David in Israel. London, Eng.; Cassell, 1928. o/p

———

Friden, George. *The Canadian novels of Gilbert Parker: historical elements and literary technique.* Copenhagen: Ejnar Munksgaard, 1953. o/p

CL CW OX

PARSONS, Nell Wilson 1898-1968

—The Curlew called. Seattle: Frank McCaffrey, 1947. o/p

—Upon a sagebrush harp. Saskatoon, Sask.: Prairie Books, 1969. cl $4.95 [0-919306-21-7]
Setting: Alberta

Presented as an autobiography, this book tells of a family that moved from Iowa to Alberta to take up homesteading. The parents' frustrated efforts to overcome climate, land, and a huge bank debt are barely compensated for by their children's modest successes. Land ownership is an important

PAYERLE, George 1945—

—The Afterpeople. Anansi Spiderline Editions. Toronto: Anansi, 1970. pb $2.50 [0-88784-312-3]
Setting: Vancouver

This experimental novel presents a highly disjointed account of the murder of a bank teller. The characters and their violently irrational actions blend until any semblance of a linear plot is obliterated.

PEATE, Mary

—Girl in a Red River coat. Toronto: Clarke, Irwin, 1973. pb $1.75 [0-7720-0595-8]
Setting: Montreal

A little girl grows up in the thirties—the time of the Depression, the Dionne quintuplets, Shirley Temple, polio epidemics and Duplessis. She and her best friends speculate about God, wonder where babies come from, send box tops away to get mail, turn in milk bottles to buy penny candy and suck ice wheedled from the ice man.

PENFIELD, Wilder 1891—

—No other gods. Toronto: Little, Brown, 1954. cl $5.95; [0-361-69836-9] ; CBL. Toronto: McClelland & Stewart, 1960. pb 95¢ [0-7710-6984-7]
Setting: Biblical

This religious novel traces the story of Abraham and Sarah.

—The Torch. CBL. Toronto: McClelland & Stewart, 1960. pb 95¢ [0-7710-6988-X]
Setting: Cos (an Aegean island)

This is an historical novel about Hippocrates, the famous Greek doctor. He is shown as a young man struggling to overcome the prejudices and superstitions surrounding the practice of medicine at that time, and also as a man in love.

OX

PERRAULT, Ernest G.

—The Kingdom carvers. Toronto: Doubleday, 1968. o/p

—The Twelfth mile. Toronto: Doubleday, 1972. $6.50 [no ISBN] ; London, Eng.: W. Collins.

Setting: the Pacific coast of Canada

When Christy Westholme is called out unexpectedly on a Pacific tugboat, he is immersed in adventures that include a hurricane and international intrigue. In the midst of his work, he must also find a way to save his foundering marriage.

PETER, John

—Along that coast. Garden City, N.Y.: Doubleday, 1964. o/p

—Take hands at winter. 1967. Garden City, N.Y.: Doubleday, 1969. pb 75¢.

Setting: a large Prairie city

Two cultured British immigrants gradually exchange places in the affections of a young Canadian wife.

—Runaway. Garden City, N.Y.: Doubleday, 1969. cl $5.95

Setting: South Africa

Runaway begins with the assassination of a white politician. Mark Dorstiger, an American who has returned to South Africa on his father's death, is caught up in the aftermath. He learns about the consequences of impetuosity when he tries to help a black fugitive and encounters a woman he once loved.

PINSENT, Gordon

—The Rowdyman. Scarborough, Ont.: McGraw-Hill Ryerson, 1973. cl. $6.95
[0-07-077663-6]

Setting: Grand Falls and St. John's, Nfld.

Will Cole laughs, drinks, curses and wenches his way through life, apparently frozen in a permanent, endearing youth. Those who knew him best give their versions of Will's rampage through life. Stan, the old drunk Will visits in an old age home becomes an image of Will's future. Will refuses to let Stan be old, refuses to accept he is dying, because as long as he lives Will can stay young. Stan dies; Will's best friend and drinking partner is killed in an accident which is partly Will's fault; even the old town constable who arrested Will so often, dies. Will is left, deserted but still defiant,

yelling in the street.

—John and the missus. Scarborough, Ont.: McGraw-Hill Ryerson, 1974. cl $7.95
[0-07-082201-8]

Setting: a mining town in Newfoundland

John Munn, near-patriarch of a small mining community in Newfoundland, is injured in a mining disaster. Suddenly with his head bandaged, his thoughts confused, his life begins to change. His son Matt marries and begins to talk of leaving the island, and so, incredibly, does John's wife, the Missus. The novel revolves around the relationship between John and the Missus which is expressed in a complex interplay between brief sections of dialogue and long inner musings. John, who might seem a simple man to those who do not know him well, is revealed in this relationship as complicated, wise and dignified.

———

The Rowdyman. Film.
Canada, Peter Carter, 1972.
col 92 min prod. Can-Art Films
16/35mm English: dist. New Cinema

PORTAL, Ellis see Bruce Powe

POWE, Bruce

—Killing ground: the Canadian civil war.
By Ellis Portal (pseud.). 1968. Toronto: Peter Martin, 1972. pb $3.95
[0-88778-066-0]

Setting: Quebec and Ontario

This novel projects the outbreak of civil war in Quebec as the governing party there votes for secession and simultaneously unleashes a reign of terror. The author describes *Killing ground* as a " 'war game novel' . . . an examination of what could happen given extreme assumptions."

—The Last days of the American empire.
Toronto: Macmillan, 1974. cl $8.95
[0-7705-1190-2]

Setting: West Africa and the eastern United States

One of the epigraphs of this twenty-first century science fiction satire is taken from Will Durant's *Age of faith:*

> The higher birth rates outside the empire and the higher standard of living within it, made immigration or invasion a manifest destiny for the Roman Empire then, as for North America today.

The events of this novel verge on the incredible, but black humour pushes home a valid point: all empires fall when they get too fat. The élite class of this society is hormone-fed to grotesque size. The Harvard professor, Harry Kornwire, tells half the story; the poet, Major Ofuru of the Euro-African invasion force, the other. Old cruise ships bear a malnourished and wretched army into the garden-like Manhatten; from then on old rules hold: greater desperation and numbers win over superior, but over-confident technology.

RADDALL, Thomas Head 1903–

—**The Pied piper of Dipper Creek and other stories.** Edinburgh: Blackwood, 1938. o/p

—**His Majesty's Yankees.** New York: Popular Library, 1942. pb 95¢
Setting: Nova Scotia
The divided loyalties of New England settlers in Nova Scotia are shown during their confrontation with incompetent British administration in Halifax during the American Revolution.

—**Roger Sudden.** 1944. NCL. Toronto: Mc-Clelland & Stewart, 1972. pb $2.95 [0-7710-9185-0]
Setting: Nova Scotia, eighteenth century
Roger Sudden, a young Englishman, makes his fortune and grows to maturity as a trader and Indian fighter in the eighteenth-century Maritimes. His picaresque progress includes imprisonment in Louisberg, giving Raddall an opportunity to explore the history of both sides of the English-French conflict. Sudden is the most convincing example of Raddall's favourite character—the prosperous and shrewd Nova Scotian merchant.

—**Tambour and other stories.** Toronto: Mc-Clelland & Stewart, 1945. o/p

—**Pride's fancy.** 1946. NCL. Toronto: Mc-Clelland & Stewart, 1974. pb $2.75 [0-7710-9198-2]
Setting: small Nova Scotian seaport, late eighteenth century
The adopted son of a Nova Scotian merchant sails a brigantine, "Pride's Fancy", as a privateer for the British in the West Indies. In classic historical romance fashion, the hero's adventures include encounters with storms, ghosts, mutiny, stowaways and a meeting with Toussaint L'Ouverture, the native rebel of Haiti. The portrait of Nova Scotian shipbuilding is vivid, the style melodramatic.

—**The Wedding gift and other stories.** Toronto: McClelland & Stewart, 1947. o/p

—**The Nymph and the lamp.** 1950. NCL. Toronto: McClelland & Stewart, 1963. pb $2.95 [0-7710-9138-9]
Setting: Sable Island
The mature romance of a wireless operator on Sable Island and a Nova Scotian woman provides Raddall with a vehicle for evocative description of the history and importance of radio communication at sea.

—**The Son of the hawk.** Philadelphia: Winston, 1950. o/p

—**Tidefall.** Toronto: McClelland & Stewart, 1953. o/p

—**A Muster of arms and other stories.** Toronto: McClelland & Stewart, 1954. o/p

—**Wings of the night.** New York: Doubleday, 1956. o/p

—**At the tide's turn and other stories.** 1959. NCL. Toronto: McClelland & Stewart, 1968. pb $2.35 [0-7710-9109-5]
Setting: Nova Scotia
These historical tales are arranged chronologically, starting with the settlement of Oldport in the eighteenth century, and ending with the Halifax Explosion in 1917. Raddall's often humorous, stylized plots (especially in "The Passion show" and "The Wedding gift") exploit the tension between collective history and individual resourcefulness.

—**The Governor's lady.** 1960. Eagle Series. New York: Popular Library, 1969. pb $1.25
Setting: Portsmouth, N.H., England, Halifax
The ambitious governor of New Hampshire and his frivolous wife face a severe decline in fortune during the American Revolution. However, political favouritism finally wins him the governorship of Nova Scotia. The novel depicts the events of the American revolt from the American viewpoint, forming a companion volume to *His Majesty's Yankees.*

—**Hangman's Beach.** 1966. New York: Popular Library, 1969. pb 95¢
Setting: Halifax
A love affair between a Scottish girl, adopted by a wealthy merchant, and a French prisoner-of-war is the focal point

of this novel. Raddall's description of Halifax just prior to the war of 1812 is lively, and the Napoleonic wars serve as an intrigue-filled background. Many of the characters reappear from his other novels.

CL CW OX OX2

REID, John

—**Horses with blindfolds.** Don Mills, Ont.: Longman, 1968. cl $5.95 [no ISBN] ; London, Eng.: M. Dent

Setting: Spain, Canada

Harold Windsor, a gentle, middle-aged businessman with an ulcer, spends some time in a Spanish coastal town. His second wife has recently died and he begins to come to terms with their past together and his love for her.

—**The Faithless Mirror: an historical novel.** Toronto: Darkwood, 1974. $24.00. Not seen.

RENAUD, Jacques 1943—

—**Flat broke and beat / Le Cassé.** 1964. Tr., Gerald Robitaille. Montreal: Les éditions de Belier, 1964. o/p

Setting: Montreal

In the first story a young worker kills a drug pusher whom he believes to have seduced his mistress. The eight stories which follow exploit the same situation of a young worker living in Montreal, always broke and resenting it. The author takes a radical stand in his exploration of the reasons behind the political violence in Quebec during the early sixties.

OX2

RICHARDS, David Adams

—**The Coming of winter.** Ottawa: Oberon Press, 1974. cl $8.95 [0-88750-128-1] ; pb $4.95 [0-88750-169-9].

Setting: Miramichi, N.B.

A boy grows up in an isolated community which seems to sap youth of its imagination. The book outlines the various forces which operate in the boy's development.

RICHARDSON, Evelyn M. 1902—

—**We keep a light.** 1947. Scarborough, Ont.: McGraw-Hill Ryerson, 1961. pb $3.95 [0-7700-0221-8]

Setting: Nova Scotia

This autobiographical novel tells how the author, her husband and family get along on an isolated island off the coast of Nova Scotia where they keep a lighthouse.

—**Desired haven.** Toronto: Ryerson Press, 1953. o/p

—**No small tempest.** Toronto: Ryerson Press, 1957. o/p

OX

RICHARDSON, John 1796-1852

—**Ecarté: or, the salons of Paris.** (Anon.) London, Eng.: Colburn, 1829. 3 vol. o/p

—**Wacousta: or, the prophecy.** 1832. abr. NCL. Toronto: McClelland & Stewart, 1967. pb $2.95 [0-7710-9158-3]

Setting: Detroit, 1763

The seige of Detroit by Pontiac is the historical background for this romance of beautiful maidens and their soldier lovers. Despite a melodramatic style, *Wacousta* was in part based on the stories of Richardson's grandmother and on the author's own observations of Indians living around Detroit. The mystery of the hero's origins and his hate for the commander of Detroit gives the story further interest.

—**The Canadian brothers: or the prophecy fulfilled. A tale of the late American war.** Montreal: Armour & Ramsay, 1840. 2 vol. Also published as **Matilda Montgomerie.** New York: Dewitt and Davenport, 1851. o/p

—**The Monk knight of St. John. A tale of the Crusades.** New York: Dewitt, 1850. o/p

—**Wau-Nan-Gee: or, the massacre at Chicago. A romance.** New York: Long, 1852. o/p

—**Hardscrabble: or, the fall of Chicago. A tale of Indian warfare.** New York: Dewitt and Davenport, 1856. o/p

—**Westbrooke the outlaw: or, the avenging wolf.** 1867. Montreal: Woolmer, 1973. cl $25.00; Montreal: Osiris, 1973. cl $25.00

Setting: the American border, during the war of 1812

This novel, once thought to be lost, was discovered serialized in seven issues of the *New York Sunday Mercury* (1851). Westbrooke is the personification of pure evil. In search of vengeance for a trifling insult, he kills a man and rapes his wife. The outlaw is finally killed by a wolf, but only after three good people have died. Richardson, writing in the lurid style popular with newspaper readers then, produced a story with a certain nightmare force.

Ballstadt, Carl, ed. *Major John Richardson: a selection of reviews and criticism.* Montreal: The Lawrence M. Lande Foundation at McGill, 1972. pb $6.00

Riddell, W.R. *John Richardson.* Toronto: Ryerson Press, 1926. o/p

Reviews and criticism from Richardson's time make up a large part of this work. There is also a biography of Richardson and short articles on his work by W.R. Riddell, Ray Palmer Baker and Ida Burwash. His obituary is reproduced. The introduction outlines the various critical opinions on Richardson's major works, particularly *Wacousta.* (Bibliography.)

CB CW ON OX

RICHLER, Mordecai 1931—

—**The Acrobats.** London, Eng.: Deutsch, 1954. o/p. Also published as **Wicked we love**

—**Son of a smaller hero.** 1955. NCL. Toronto: McClelland & Stewart, 1966. pb $1.75 [0-7710-9145-1] ; Panther Books. St. Albans, Eng.: Granada

Setting: Montreal

Noah, a sensitive but weak and sometimes cruel personality, attempts to leave the ghetto by getting a university education. However, he is dragged back to his oppressive family by his father's death. He then attempts to flee the trap by going to Europe.

—**A Choice of enemies.** 1957. Paper Jacks. Don Mills, Ont.: General Publishing, 1973. pb $1.50 [0-7737-7036-4]

Setting: Munich and London

Ernst, a young German, flees to England, where he becomes involved with the brother of a man he has killed, the brother's girlfriend, and his Jewish friends.

—**The Apprenticeship of Duddy Kravitz.** 1959. NCL. Toronto: McClelland & Stewart, 1969. pb $1.95 [0-7710-9166-4] ; Toronto: McClelland & Stewart, 1974. Uniform ed. $10.00 [0-7710-7497-2] ; pb (including stills, cast list and production details from the film) $2.95 [0-7710-7498-0]

Setting: Montreal

This story of a self-willed boy who substitutes hustling for his humanity is a portrait of compulsion and fear. The more obsessed Duddy becomes with buying land, the more ruthless he is in his manipulation of people. His attempt to break out of the ghetto is

chronicled in fast-paced, colloquial language.

—**The Incomparable Atuk.** 1963. NCL. Toronto: McClelland & Stewart, 1971. pb $1.95 [0-7710-9179-6] ; Panther Books. St. Albans, Eng.: Granada. Also published as **Stick your neck out.** New York: Simon & Schuster, 1963

Setting: Toronto

Similar to *Cocksure* in its excesses of black humour, this short novel satirizes just about everything Canadian: national identity, Eskimo culture, department store monopolies, the media, the RCMP, Canada's intelligentsia. Atuk, the "innocent savage", or would-be Eskimo poet, starts up an enterprise called Esky Products using his family as slave labour to mass produce Eskimo sculptures. He becomes a millionaire, and comes to a gruesome end in a program to stir up anti-American sentiment in Canada.

—**Cocksure.** Toronto: McClelland & Stewart, 1968. cl $5.95; New York: Simon & Schuster; London, Eng.: Weidenfeld and Nicholson; Panther Books. St. Albans, Eng.: Granada

Setting: London, Eng. and Los Angeles

In this satire of the publishing and film industries, Mortimer, a normal middle-aged WASP, discovers that the hermaphroditic Star Maker is attempting to kill him as he has so many others. Both the Establishment and its revolutionary replacement are attacked by Richler's double-edged sword.

—**The Street.** Toronto: McClelland & Stewart, 1969. cl $4.95 [0-7710-7494-8].

Fact and fiction mix in this collection of sketches which give insight into Richler's past.

—**St. Urbain's Horseman.** Toronto: McClelland & Stewart, 1971. cl $7.95 [0-7710-7486-7]; New York: Knopf; New York: Bantam; London, Eng.: Weidenfeld and Nicholson; Panther Books. St. Albans, Eng.: Granada

Setting: London, Eng., Montreal, Israel

Jake Hersh is a successful television director, happily married, rich and guilt-ridden. He considers his cousin Joey, the Horseman, as a defender of oppressed Jewry, and tries to find him, paying off a string of Joey's gambling debts and disgruntled women. In the spirit of the Horseman, he befriends the unscrupulous Harry Klein, who promptly involves him in a trial for sexual offences. Finally, the Horseman is reported dead. Jake at last has to come to terms with his own conscience and his own guilt, since they have led him to jeopardize both his happiness and success.

Fulford, Robert. *Mordecai Richler.* CWW.
Rexdale, Ont.: Forum House, 1969. o/p

Sheps, G.D. *Mordecai Richler.* Ed., Michael
Gnarowski. CVCW. Scarborough, Ont.:
McGraw-Hill Ryerson, 1971. pb $3.25
[0-7700-0321-4]
This collection of essays by such critics
as William H. New, Leslie Fiedler, Larry
Zolf and George Bowering contains con-
traversial interpretations of Richler's
work, and of his best-known character,
Duddy Kravitz.

Woodcock, George. *Mordecai Richler.* CWS.
NCL. Toronto: McClelland & Stewart,
1970. pb $1.25 [0-7710-9606-2].
This chronological series of eight-page commentaries on Richler's novels attempts to
show his stylistic shift from experiential
realism to fantasy and satire, but was published before *St. Urbain's Horseman.* It reveals the source of *Cocksure* as a short story
written ten years earlier—an interesting insight into Richler's compositional method.
It contains a succinct biographical introduction. (Bibliography.)

The Apprenticeship of Duddy Kravitz. Film.
Canada, Ted Kotcheff, 1973.
col 120 min 16/35mm English: dist.
Astral Communications

CB CL CW ON OX OX2

RINGUET (pseud. for Philippe Panneton)
1895-1960

—Thirty acres / Trente arpents. 1938. NCL.
Tr., Felix Walker and Dorothea Walker.
Toronto: McClelland & Stewart, 1970. pb
$1.95 [0-7710-9112-5]
Setting: rural Quebec, the United States.

Eucharist Moisan, a farmer, is tied to his
land by tradition, heredity and love. He
moves with the seasons and prospers. But
times change, his sons grow up and he refuses to bend to their pleas to modernize.
Finally he is defeated by one son and goes
to live with another in the United States,
forced to desert his beloved land. The realism of Panneton's approach to the subject
of "the land" broke with a long tradition
which saw only virtue and felicity in rural
life. The translation is generally satisfactory,
but there are occasional errors.

CW OX

ROBB, Wallace Havelock 1888—

—**Thunderbird: epic of the Mohawks of the
Kenté.** Kingston, Ont.: Abbey Dawn Press,
1949. o/p

—**Tecumtha.** Kingston, Ont.: Abbey Dawn
Press, 1958. cl $5.00
Setting: the area around Kingston

A eulogistic account of the native chief,
Tecumseh, which purports to contain much
authentic Indian lore.

—**Arrayed In wampum.** Kingston, Ont.:
Abbey Dawn Press, 1966. cl $2.50. Not
seen.

ROBERT, Marika

—**A Stranger and afraid.** Toronto: McClelland & Stewart, 1964. cl $5.95 [0-7110-7602-4]
pb 95¢ [0-7710-7603-7].
Setting: Paris and Toronto

A young Hungarian refugee meets André, a
sadistic but urbane black marketeer, in
Paris. She fights her attraction to him, but
finally accepts it just before he is killed.
She emigrates to Canada and marries Neil,
a man of quite different character from
André. Problems result and again she must
come to terms with her "strangeness".

ROBERTS, Charles G.D. 1860-1943

—**The Raid from Beauséjour, and how the
Carter boys lifted the mortgage: two
stories of Acadie.** New York: Hunt & Eaton,
1894. (First story later published as **The
Young Acadian; or, the raid from Beauséjour.** Boston: Page, 1907.) o/p

—**Reube Dare's shad boat: a tale of the
tide country.** New York: Hunt & Eaton,
1895. (Reprinted as **The Cruise of the
yacht "Dido".** Boston: Page, 1906.) o/p

—**Around the campfire.** New York: Crowell,
1896. o/p

—**Earth's enigmas: a book of animal and
nature life.*** 1896. Short Story Index
Reprint Series. Plainview, N.Y.: Books
for Libraries. cl $10.50

—**The Forge in the forest: being the narrative of the Acadian ranger, Jean de Mer.**
New York: Lamson Wolffe, 1896. o/p

—**A Sister to Evangeline: being the story
of Yvonne de Lamourie.** Boston: Lamson
Wolffe, 1898. Reprinted as **Lovers in
Acadie.** London: Dent, 1924. o/p

—By the marshes of Minas.* 1900. Short Story Index Reprint Series. Plainview, N.Y.: Books for Libraries. cl $11.00

—The Heart of the ancient wood. 1900. NCL. Toronto: McClelland & Stewart, 1974. pb $2.95 [0-7710-9210-5]
Setting: a wilderness clearing in the Maritimes
This romantic nature tale describes the maturing of a young girl, Miranda Craig. To escape gossip about her missing husband, the girl's mother moves to a remote clearing to start a new life with her daughter. Miranda has a special gift which allows her to see the animals in the woods when no one else can, and she establishes a friendly relationship with them. The latter part of the book concentrates on the conflict among animals and between animals and man, a conflict which is reflected in the tension arising from Miranda's attraction to a young hunter and trapper.

—Barbara Ladd. Boston: Page, 1902. o/p

—The Kindred of the wild.* 1902. Short Story Index Reprint Series. Plainview, N.Y.: Books for Libraries. cl $17.50

—The Prisoner of mademoiselle: a love story. Boston: Page, 1904. o/p

—The Watchers of the trails: a book of animal life. Boston: Page, 1904. o/p

—The Haunter of the pine gloom. Boston: Page, 1905. (Also included in the earlier book, The Kindred of the wild.) o/p

—The King of the Mamozekel. Boston: Page, 1905. (Also included in the earlier book, The Kindred of the wild.) o/p

—The Lord of the air. Boston: Page, 1905. (Also included in the earlier book, The Kindred of the wild.) o/p

—Red fox.* 1905. Scarborough, Ont.: McGraw-Hill Ryerson, 1948. cl $5.95 [0-7700-0163-7] ; New York: Dell; Boston & New York: Houghton Mifflin

—The Watchers of the camp-fire. Boston: Page, 1905. (Also included in the earlier book, The Kindred of the wild.) o/p

—The Heart that knows. Boston: Page, 1906. o/p

—The Little people of the sycamore. Boston: Page, 1906. (Also included in the earlier book The Kindred of the wild.) o/p

—The Return to the trails. Boston: Page, 1906. (Also included in the earlier book The Watchers of the trails.) o/p

—The Haunters of the silences: a book of animal life. Boston: Page, 1907. o/p

—In the deep of the snow. New York: Crowell, 1907. (Also included in the later book, The Backwoodsmen.) o/p

—The House in the water: a book of animal life. Boston: Page, 1908. o/p

—The Red oxen of Bonval. New York: Dodd Mead, 1908. o/p

—The Backwoodsmen. New York: Macmillan, 1909. o/p

—Kings in exile.* 1909. Scarborough, Ont.: McGraw-Hill. 1947. cl $5.20 [0-7700-0106-8]

—More kindred of the wild. London: Ward Lock, 1911. o/p

—Neighbours unknown.* 1911. SMC. Toronto: Macmillan, 1924. cl $1.15 [0-7705-0685-2]

—Babes of the wild. New York: Cassell, 1912. (Reprinted as Children of the wild. New York: Macmillan, 1913.) o/p

—The Feet of the furtive.* 1912. Scarborough, Ont.: McGraw-Hill, 1947. cl $5.95 [0-7700-0062-2]

—A Balkan prince. London: Everett, 1913. o/p

—Hoof and claw. London: Ward Lock, 1913. o/p

—Cock-Crow. New York: Federal Print, 1916. (Also included in the later book, The Secret trails.) o/p

—The Ledge on Bald Face. London: Ward Lock, 1916. (Reprinted as Jim: the story of a backwoods police dog. New York: Macmillan, 1924.) o/p

—The Morning of the silver frost. New York: Federal Print., 1916. (Also included in the later book, The Secret trails.) o/p

—The Secret trails. New York: Macmillan, 1916. o/p

—In the morning of time. London: Hutchinson, 1919. o/p

—Some animal stories. London: Dent, 1921. o/p

—More animal stories. London: Dent, 1922. o/p

—Wisdom of the wilderness.* 1922. Scarborough, Ont.: McGraw-Hill, 1948. cl $5.95 [0-7700-0224-2]

—They who walk in the wild. New York:

Macmillan, 1924. (Published in England as **They that walk in the wild**. London: Dent, 1924.) o/p

—**Eyes of the wilderness**. New York: Macmillan, 1933. o/p

—**Further animal stories**. London: Dent, 1935. o/p

—**Thirteen bears**. Ed., Ethel Hume Bennett. Toronto: Ryerson, 1947. o/p

—**Forest folk**. Ed., Ethel Hume Bennett. Toronto: Ryerson, 1949. o/p

—**The Last barrier, and other stories**.* NCL. Toronto: McClelland & Stewart, 1958. pb $1.95 [0-7710-9107-9]

—**King of beasts**.* Ed., Joseph Gold. Scarborough, Ont.: McGraw-Hill, 1967. cl $5.95 [0-7000-0104-1]

*Settings: the wilderness

All of Roberts' fiction in print, with the exception of *The Heart of the ancient wood*, which is discussed in a separate annotation, are stories about animals. Most of these works are collections of short stories, although one, *Red Fox*, is a complete novel. Roberts's fiction is in the same nature story tradition as the work of Kipling and Ernest Thompson Seton. However, he is far more a creative writer than a naturalist. He invests his animal characters with personalities by describing the world through their eyes.

––––––

Cappon, James. *Charles G.D. Roberts*. Toronto: Ryerson, 1925. o/p

Cappon, James. *Roberts and the influences of his time*. Toronto: Briggs, 1905. o/p

Keith, W.J. *Charles G.D. Roberts*. SCL. Toronto: Copp Clark, 1969. pb $2.35 [0-7730-3007-7]
Beginning with a biographical outline of Roberts's life, Keith provides a general overview of his poetry, novels and short stories. Keith deals in a straightforward manner with the author's deficiencies and strengths in each of these genres. His conclusion is that the "stories of the wild" are Roberts's best work. A bibliography includes important critical texts.

Pomeroy, E.M. *Sir Charles G.D. Roberts*. Toronto: Ryerson, 1943. o/p

Roberts, Lloyd. *The Book of Roberts*. Toronto: Ryerson, 1923. o/p

See also Grey Owl, *Wilderness Writers*, by James Polk.

CB CL CW ON OX

ROBERTS, Theodore Goodridge 1877-1953

—**The House of Isstens**. Boston: Page, 1900. o/p

—**Hemming, the adventurer**. Boston: Page, 1904. o/p

—**Brothers of peril. A story of old Newfoundland**. Boston: Page, 1905. o/p

—**The Red feathers**. Boston: Page, 1907. o/p

—**Captain Love**. Boston: Page, 1908. o/p

—**Flying Plover, his stories. Told him by Squat-by-the-fire**. Boston: Page, 1909. o/p

—**A Cavalier of Virginia**. Boston: Page, 1910. o/p

—**Comrades of the trails**. Boston: Page, 1910. o/p

—**A Captain of Raleigh's**. Boston: Page, 1911. o/p

—**Soldier of Valley Forge**. With Robert Neilson Stephens. Boston: Page, 1911. o/p

—**Rayton. A backwoods mystery**. Boston: Page, 1912. o/p

—**The Harbour master**. 1913. NCL. Toronto: McClelland & Stewart, 1968. pb $1.95 [0-7710-9163-X]; Also published as **The Toll of the tides**. London, Eng.: Laurie,1912
Setting: a small sea-coast village in Newfoundland
The violence and charisma of Black Dennis Nolan convert a community of poor fishermen into "wreckers" who live off what can be salvaged from the many ships driven or lured onto the dangerous coast.

—**Love on Smoky River**. London, Eng.: Long, 1913. o/p

—**Two shall be born**. New York: Cassell, 1913. o/p

—**Blessington's folly**. London, Eng.: Long. 1914. o/p

—**Jess of the river**. New York: Dillingham, 1914. o/p

—**The Wasp**. New York: Killingham, 1914. o/p

—**In the high woods**. London, Eng.: Long, 1916. o/p

—**Forest fugitives**. Toronto: McClelland & Stewart, 1917. o/p

—**The Islands of adventure**. New York: Hodder, 1918. o/p

—**The Exiled lover**. London, Eng.: Long, 1919. o/p

—The Master of the moose horn and other back-country stories. London, Eng.: Hodder, 1919. o/p

—Moonshine. London, Eng.: Hodder, 1920. o/p

—The Lure of Piper's Glen. New York: Doubleday, 1921. o/p

—The Fighting Starkleys. Boston: Page, 1922. o/p

—Musket house. New York: Doubleday, 1922. o/p

—Tom Akerley. His adventures in the tall timber and at Gaspard's Clearing. Boston: Page, 1923. o/p

—Green timber thoroughbreds. Garden City, N.Y.: Garden City Publishing Co., 1924. o/p

—The Oxbow wizard. Garden City, N.Y.: Garden City Publishing Co., 1924. o/p

—The Red pirogue. A tale of adventure in the Canadian wilds. Boston: Page, 1924. o/p

—The Stranger from up-along. Toronto: Gundy, 1924. o/p

—Honest fool. London, Eng.: Hodder, 1925. o/p

—Prize money. Boston: Page, 1926. o/p

—The Golden Highlanders; or, the romantic adventures of Alastair Mac-Iver. Boston: Page, 1929. o/p
CW OX

ROBERTS, George see Scott Young

ROHMER, Richard
—Ultimatum: oil or war? Toronto: Clarke, Irwin, 1973. cl $7.25 [0-7720-0618-0]; Markham, Ont.: Simon & Schuster, 1974. pb $1.50 [0-671-787855-1]
Setting: Ottawa
This novel portrays a sudden confrontation between Canada and the United States on the issue of energy resources. Obviously capitalizing on the recent energy crisis, Rohmer has set his story in 1980, and opens it with a phone call from the American president to the prime minister: Canada is magnanimously given thirty-six hours to accept or reject U.S. demands for total rights to natural gas on the Canadian Arctic islands.

—Exxoneration. Toronto: McClelland & Stewart, 1974. cl $8.95 [0-7710-7702-5]
Setting: Washington, Toronto, Vancouver, Calgary, Zurich, Ottawa, St. Pierre et Miquelon, and London
American armies invade Canada to secure much needed oil supplies for their industries

after Ottawa refuses to agree to the Alaska Pipeline route.

ROSS, Sinclair 1908—
—As for me and my house. 1941. NCL. Toronto: McClelland & Stewart, 1958. pb $1.75 [0-7710-9104-4]
Setting: a small Prairie town
This novel examines life in the bleak and rain-starved Prairie town of Horizon. The town's new preacher, a failed artist, is described by his wife in her journal. She writes in detail of the tensions in their childless marriage. Both natural and spiritual droughts are finally relieved, but not without pain.

—The Well. Toronto: Macmillan, 1958. o/p

—The Lamp at noon and other stories. NCL. Toronto: McClelland & Stewart, 1968. pb $1.95 [0-7710-9162-1]
Setting: the Prairies
The men in these stories are dedicated to the land—inevitably a harsh and loveless mistress. Their women are left without comfort, seeing the futility of the men's struggle, but unable whole-heartedly to share in it or to escape from it. Love and hope gradually fail with the crops.

—A Whir of gold. Toronto: McClelland & Stewart, 1970. cl $6.95 [0-7710-7745-9]
Setting: Montreal
A sense of degradation pushes a hard-up clarinet player into partnering a robbery. Helped by a warm-hearted ex-stripper, he is unable to respond to her need for love. Ross describes with clarity the ways men and women injure one another.

—Sawbones memorial. Toronto: McClelland & Stewart, 1974. cl $7.95 [0-7710-7747-5]
Setting: a small town in Saskatchewan
The small town of Upward has finally built its first hospital. The old doctor is retiring and the gossipy conversation at his farewell party forms the basis of the novel. A picture develops of the defects, petty feuds and prejudices of the townspeople, mellowed somewhat by their years of closeness. They feel they know everything about each other, but the doctor's private musings on his past reveal events that would profoundly shock his former patients if they had been aware of them.

Cornet at night. Film.
A dramatization of Ross's short story.
NFB b&w 15min. 16mm· dist. CFI
CB CL CW ON OX OX2

ROY, Gabrielle 1909—

—The Tin flute / Bonheur d'occasion. 1945. NCL. Tr., Hannah Josephson. Toronto: McClelland & Stewart, 1969. pb $1.95 [0-7710-9105-2]

Setting: Montreal

Set at the end of the Depression and at the beginning of World War II, this novel presents in stark detail the lives of city-dwelling French-Canadians who have been almost defeated by poverty. The central female characters, Florentine Lacasse and her mother, Rose-Anna, deal with poverty in different ways: Florentine refuses to be trapped by it and becomes hardened; Rose-Anna survives through love of her family. The male characters deal with their situation by manipulating others or by choosing in desperation to go to war. The author plays on the paradox that only war could bring a modicum of prosperity to the poor of Montreal. There is a glaring error in translation (p. 15) which has *moité peuple* translated as "half slut". This is completely inaccurate and falsifies the reader's perception of Florentine. There are other inadequacies. This novel merits a translation worthy of it.

—Where nests the water hen / La Petite poule d'eau. 1950. NCL. Tr., Harry Binsse. Toronto: McClelland & Stewart, 1961. pb $1.95 [0-7710-9125-9]; text $1.70

Setting: northern Manitoba

Roy depicts the life of a small community bound together by its isolation. The central characters are the mother of a large French-Canadian family, Luzina Tousignant, and a Capuchin monk, Father Joseph-Marie. In his contact with the northern land and its people, Father Joseph-Marie learns the same love that is almost innate in Luzina. The translation is good.

—The Cashier / Alexandre Chênevert. 1954. Tr., Harry Binsse. Toronto: McClelland & Stewart, 1955. cl $5.00 [0-7710-7749-1]; NCL. Toronto: McClelland & Stewart, 1963. pb $1.95 [0-7710-9140-0]

Setting: Montreal and Lac Vert

Alexendre Chênevert, a cashier in a bank, is a hyperanxious man who worries about the world's problems while barely able to cope with his own. His personality is composed of extremes and inconsistencies. Roy, by describing the cashier's introspection, reveals the character of a seemingly insignificant man in all its ambiguity. Through him she criticizes and satirizes the Roman

Catholic church, aspects of the Cold War and other political and social phenomena, thus anticipating the Quiet Revolution. The translation is good.

—Street of riches / Rue Deschambault. 1955. NCL. Tr., Harry Binsse. Toronto: McClelland & Stewart, 1967. pb $1.95

Setting: St. Boniface, Man.

A plain little girl called Christine narrates these eighteen self-contained sketches. They are partially autobiographical and deal with the childhood of this youngest girl in a large French-Canadian family. Nicknamed *"Petite Misère"* by her father, because of her large capacity for grief, she has an equally large capacity for joy and wonder. The novel creates a sensuous impression of the riches of childhood, the most important being the imagination, which in Roy was transformed into art.

—The Hidden mountain / La Montagne secrète. 1961. NCL. Tr., Harry Binsse. Toronto: McClelland & Stewart, 1974. pb $2.75 [0-7710-9209-1]

Setting: northern Canada and Paris

A young man travels through the Canadian north, trying though the medium of his art to come to terms with himself and with an environment which is both generous and hostile. He becomes a legend in the north and eventually, with the aid of a scholarship, goes to Paris to study painting. In a slow-moving but interesting story, Gabrielle Roy traces the artist's never-ending search for perfection. The translation is a good one.

—The Road past Altamont / La Route d'Altamont. 1966. Tr., Joyce Marshall. Toronto: McClelland & Stewart, 1966. pb $2.95

Setting: Manitoba

The narrator, Christine, describes several central experiences of her childhood, including the lessons in life that she learned from her mother, her grandmother and an old man. The experience which affects her most is the discovery of an unexpected group of hills near Altamont when she is out driving with her mother. In this simple story the road comes to represent the possibilities for discovery that one makes throughout life, as well as one's inability to recapture the past completely. The translation is good.

—Windflower / La Rivière sans repos. 1970. Tr., Joyce Marshall. Toronto: McClelland & Stewart, 1970. cl $5.95

Setting: The Canadian Arctic

When Elsa Kumachuk, an Eskimo girl at Fort Chimo, has a single swift encounter with an American GI stationed at the fort, the result is a blonde-haired, blue-eyed son, Jimmy, who becomes the centre of her life. This story traces the changes, not always for the better, that take place in Elsa's life because of her ambitions for the child. In Elsa's story can be seen the conflicts between generations, not only of the changing Eskimo culture, but of all cultures. The original French contained several short stories not reproduced in the English text. The translation is very good.

Grosskurth, Phyllis. *Gabrielle Roy.* CWW. Rexdale, Ont.: Forum House, 1969. pb $1.25

Grosskurth devotes a chapter to each of Roy's novels from *The Tin flute* to *The Road past Altamont.* She identifies the dominant maternal figure as central to Roy's vision and links to this the childlike simplicity of most of her characters. Grosskurth sees a certain failure in Roy's omission of any internal struggle with evil in her characters' lives, although she praises her ability to create convincing characters whose striving for humanity is played out in a circumscribed and impersonal world.

CL CW FC OX OX2

ROY, Katharine 1907–

—**Lise.** 1954. CBL. Toronto: McClelland & Stewart, 1967. pb 95¢ [0-7710-7752-1]

Setting: Paris, London, Montreal

Lise is a light romance about the marriage of a beautiful but naïve girl to a rich Parisian playboy and her subsequent unhappiness.

—**The Gentle fraud.** Toronto: McClelland & Stewart, 1959. o/p

RULE, Jane 1931–

—**The Desert of the heart.** Toronto: Macmillan, 1964. pb $1.95 [0-7705-1120-1]

Setting: Reno

Evelyn Hall, an English professor at Berkeley, goes to Reno to obtain a quick divorce. Confronted with the prospect of the necessary six-week residency, she soon becomes involved with the people in her boarding house—in particular, a young woman who bears a striking resemblance to her. This book provides its intriguing descriptions of the desert and gambling casinos as well as giving an account of a woman's sexual reawakening.

—**This is not for you.** 1970. New York: Popular Library, 1972. pb 95¢

Setting: various cities in the United States and Europe

In the form of a long monologue addressed to her friend Esther, Kate George goes over the past ten years of their lives. She describes their college years, graduate work in London, travels, mutual friends, and finally, Esther's decision to enter a convent. Dominating these memories is Kate's unfulfilled love for Esther.

—**Against the season.** 1971. London, Eng.: P. Davies, 1972

Setting: a small, seaside American town

Jane Rule has created a "typical" small American town in this book about the problems of love and loneliness encountered by all the members of the community. The intricate relationships are explored with insight. Of noteworthy interest is Rule's portrayal of several people who are old but very much alive.

—**Theme for diverse instruments.** Vancouver: Talonbooks, 1974. cl $8.50 [0-88922-060-3]; pb $4.50 [0-88922-062-X]

Setting: North America, England

The subject of female sexuality is studied in a series of interior monologues. The book is of interest from a stylistic point of view for its manipulation of tempo and frequently epigrammatic phrasing.

OX2

RYGA, George 1932–

—**Hungry hills.** 1963. Vancouver: Talonbooks, 1974. cl $8.50 [0-88922-061-1]; pb $4.50 [0-88922-078-6]

Setting: Alberta

Snit Mandolin, born of an incestuous relationship, runs away from the orphanage to which he is sent, and eventually returns to the drought-ridden farm where his supposedly insane aunt lives. The illegal whisky business he gets involved in ends violently. Ryga's account of Prairie farm life during the Depression is written in a compact, objective style that heightens the turbulently emotional aspects of the story.

—**Ballad of a stone picker.** Toronto: Macmillan, 1966. o/p

CB OX2

ST. PIERRE, Paul

—**Boss of the Namko Drive.** Scarborough: McGraw-Hill Ryerson, 1965. cl $5.95 [0-7700-0027-4] ; school ed. 1968. $2.25 [0-7700-3024-6]
Setting: British Columbia ranching country
In a simple, humorous manner, Paul St. Pierre's adaptation of his original television drama describes the frustrations of a rancher who contends with a casual old Indian and a murder trial while trying to get one of his horses broken.

—**The Chilcotin holiday.** Toronto: McClelland & Stewart, 1970. cl $5.95 [0-7710-8276-2]
Setting: British Columbia
Chosen from columns written for the *Vancouver Sun,* these short pieces are mainly anecdotes about interesting or unusual people. Also included are some "tall stories" which, as St. Pierre says in the prologue, "nobody except an Easterner would be likely to swallow unsalted".

SANDMAN, John

—**Eating out.** Anansi Spiderline Editions. Toronto: Anansi, 1969. pb $1.95 [0-88784-307-7]
Setting: New York
A street bum finds himself in a restaurant which is being held up by a bungling robber pulling his first job. The situation takes on a comic aspect as everyone but the bum ignores the robber's threats. The tragic qualities of this scene are also expressed through the revelation of the hero's thoughts and emotions.

—**Fords eat Chevs.** Ottawa: Oberon Press, 1973. cl $5.95 [0-88750-092-7] ; pb $2.95 [0-88750-093-5]
Setting: Trans-Canada Highway
A young man decides to hitch-hike to Vancouver to find work. The description of his bizarre adventures along the way is interwoven with the revelation of his personal anxieties and prejudices. The character study is both sympathetic and comic.

SCHROEDER, Andreas 1946—

—**The Late man.** Delta, B.C.: Sono Nis Press, 1971. cl $6.95; Red Bluff, Calif.: Kanchenjunga Press
Setting: mostly sea-coast
In these surrealistic fables, Schroeder trans-

lates aesthetic and philosophic paradoxes into characters, landscapes and incidents. Though fantastic, the events described are comprehensible: men turn into mannequins or trees, are run over by cars and yet remain human and uninjured. The recurrent motif is that of a man left outside the natural/ social mainstream because of his exceptional thoughtfulness or inventiveness.

SCHULL, Joseph 1910—

—**The Jinker.** Toronto: Macmillan, 1968. pb $2.50 [0-7705-0278-4]
Setting: Newfoundland
Coming from divergent backgrounds, Tim Mahan and Robbie Torrance become captains of ships on seal-hunting expeditions. Brutal animal slaughter serves as a background for the destructive fascination the two men, once boyhood friends, have for each other. Suspense is maintained as Torrance's latent homosexuality jeopardizes his marriage and the lives of his crewmen.

CW OX OX2

SCOTT, Chris

—**Bartleby.** Toronto: Anansi, 1971. cl $8.50 [0-88784-415-4]
Setting: indeterminate
In a captivating but perplexing stylistic union of eighteenth-century bawdiness and twentieth-century subjectivity, the author relates what happens when two manuscripts in his drawer become intermingled. Unfortunately, he is overwhelmed by the narrative power of De'Ath, perverted hermit and author-within-the-novel. In its *nouveau roman* structural and thematic preoccupations and its witty play on various styles of language, the book provides esoteric entertainment.

SCOTT, Duncan Campbell 1862-1947

—**In the village of Viger and other stories.** 1896. NCL. Toronto: McClelland & Stewart 1973. pb $2.95 [0-7710-9192-3]
Setting: Quebec, Alberta, N.W.T.

These nineteenth-century stories are still lively and suspenseful, and sustain a mood of high adventure and mystery. Elopers, swindlers, murderers, gypsies, lumberjacks, fur traders and noble savages are the characters involved in fast-paced accounts of life in Victorian Canada.

—**The Witching of Elspie.** 1923. Short Story Index Reprint Series. New York: Books For Libraries. cl $9.50

Setting: Quebec and the north

Half of these stories are to be found in later paperback collections. Two stories which are in print in the collection only, "The Vain shadow" and "A Legend of Welly Legrave", are both of mythic proportions; events and discoveries border convincingly on the supernatural. The lives of trappers and marginally genteel villagers provide the centres for mysterious or passionate legends.

—**Selected stories.** Ed., Glenn Clever. Ottawa: University of Ottawa Press, 1972. pb $3.50 [0-7766-4331-2]

Setting: northern and western Canada

These tales of simple events among Québécois peasants, traders and Indians reflect their nineteenth-century origin. With few exceptions, the stories Clever has collected are to be found in the more comprehensive edition, *In the village of Viger and other stories.* The book is valuable for its inclusion of a select bibliography.

Bourinot, Arthur Stanley, ed. *Some letters of D.C. Scott, Archibald Lampman and others.* Ottawa: Bourinot, 1959. o/p

_____ . *More letters of Duncan Campbell Scott.* 2nd Series. Ottawa: Bourinot, 1960. o/p

CB CW ON OX

SEARS, Dennis T. Patrick 1925—

—**The Lark in the clear air.** Toronto: McClelland & Stewart, 1974. cl $6.95 [0-7710-8027-1]

Setting: rural Ontario, the thirties

Danny Mulcahy tells the story of his abrupt initiation into adulthood. The book begins in Alberta with his parents' macabre deaths, and covers the period Danny spends with his flamboyant Irish uncle in Ontario. First-person narration and an emphasis on action make this novel an energetic study of social forces. The theme of the love triangle recurs throughout.

SEERS, Eugène see Louis Dantin

SETON, Ernest Thompson 1860-1946

—**Wild animals I have known.*** 1898.

Tempo. New York: Grosset & Dunlap, 1967. pb 60¢; New York: McGraw-Hill Ryerson, 1962. pb $2.00; New York: Scribner's. $4.50

—**The trail of the Sandhill stag.*** 1899. New York: Dutton. $3.95

—**The Biography of a grizzly.*** 1900. New York: Schocken. $2.69. Also published as **King of the grizzlies**; London, Eng.: Dent

—**Two little savages.*** 1903. New York: Dover. pb $2.50

—**Monarch, the big bear of Tallac.** New York: Scribner's, 1904. o/p

—**Animal heroes.** New York: Scribner's, 1905. o/p

—**Woodmyth and fable.** Toronto: Briggs, 1905. o/p

—**The Natural history of the Ten Commandments.** New York: Scribner's, 1907. o/p

—**The Biography of a silver fox.** New York: Century, 1909. o/p

—**Rolf in the woods.** New York: Doubleday, 1911. o/p

—**Wild animals at home.** Toronto: Briggs, 1913. o/p

—**Wild animal ways.** Garden City, N.Y.: Doubleday, 1916. o/p

—**The Preacher of Cedar Mountain. A tale of the open country.** New York: Doubleday, 1916. o/p

—**Woodland tales.** New York: Doubleday, 1921. o/p

—**Bannertail; the story of a gray squirrel.** New York: Scribner's, 1922. o/p

—**Famous animal stories . . . myths, fables, fairy tales. Stories of real animals.** New York: Brentano, 1932. o/p

—**Johnny Bear, Lobo and other stories.** New York: Scribner's, 1935. o/p

—**The Biography of an arctic fox.** New York: Appleton-Century, 1937. o/p

—**Great historic animals: mainly about wolves.** London: Methuen, 1937. o/p

—**The Buffalo wind.** Santa Fe, N.M.: Seton Village Press, 1938. o/p

—**Ernest Thompson Seton's trail and camp-fire stories.** Ed., Julia M. Seton. New York: Appleton-Century, 1940. o/p

—Trail of an artist naturalist: the autobiography of Ernest Thompson Seton.
New York: Scribner's, 1940. o/p

—Santana, the hero dog of France. Los
Angeles: Phoenix Press, 1945. o/p

—The Best of Ernest Thompson Seton.*
Selected by W. Kay Robinson. London,
Eng.: Hodder, 1949

*Seton was educated as an animal illustrator
at the Ontario School of Art and the Royal
School of Painting and Sculpture in London,
England. He was also a respected and expert
self-taught woodsman and naturalist. Each
of his stories was based on a specific animal
whose personality he had observed closely,
usually in the wild. Unlike many other
"animal writers", he made no attempt to
draw a moral from the lives of these
animals—he was a naturalist, not a fabulist.
Two little savages, subtitled "The adventures of two boys who lived as Indians
and what they learned", is concerned
mainly with woodlore, while the other
four titles emphasize descriptions of
animal life.

See also Grey Owl, *Wilderness Writers,*
by James Polk.
CW ON OX

SHAFFER, Ivan

—The Midas compulsion. Toronto: McClelland & Stewart, 1969. o/p

—Business is business? Thirty days in the
life of Richard Rash, entrepreneur. Toronto:
Lester and Orpen, 1974. cl $8.95
[0-919630-59-6]
Setting: Toronto
Richard Rash, a dedicated entrepreneur,
has a cash flow problem and thirty days
to save his skin. He and his upper-crust
partner D'Arcy Macdonald Brown set in
motion an elaborate fraud to generate
$12,000 out of thin air. After all, business
is business, and the fact that Rash's business is PR (intrinsically absurd if not
actually evil) adds to the humour of his
sexual, social and financial machinations.

SHARP, Edith Lambert

—Nkwala. Toronto: McClelland & Stewart,
1958. pb $2.79 [0-7710-8124-3] ; Boston:
Little, Brown
Setting: British Columbia

Nkwala is the name of a Spokane Indian boy
whose initiation to adult life coincides with
a period of great hardship for his people.
Drought forces the tribe to leave their
territory, and during their exile, they encounter many signs of violence. With its
sparse style and suspenseful story, this
book would appeal to an adolescent audience.

SHELDON, (Frank) Michael

—The Gilded rule. Toronto: Nelson, Foster
and Scott, 1963. o/p

—The Unmelting pot. London, Eng.:
Hutchinson, 1965. o/p

—The Personnel man. Toronto: McClelland
& Stewart, 1966. o/p

—Death of a leader. Toronto: McClelland
& Stewart, 1972. $4.95 [0-7710-8141-3] ;
London, Eng.: Robert Hale
Setting: Quebec
In the tense setting of political confronta-
tion in Quebec, the leader of an organiza-
tion called Quebec Libre is murdered. Marc
Demontigny, a diplomat/undercover agent,
is asked to track down the killer.

SHERWOOD, Roland 1902—

—Story parade. Sackville, N.B.: Tribune
Press, 1948. o/p

—Atlantic harbours. Windsor, N.S.: Lancelot
1972. pb $2.50
Setting: Nova Scotia
Local legends, mostly involving shipwrecks,
are offset by accounts of the first tran-
atlantic flights and of the laying of the
transatlantic cable. Sherwood's historical
anecdotes are no less mythic for their
factual basis.

—Tall tales of the Maritimes. Windsor, N.S.:
Lancelot, 1972. pb $1.00
Setting: Nova Scotia and Newfoundland
Sherwood has gathered together several
fantastic anecdotes from Maritime story-
tellers. Along with the standard exaggera-
tions of fishing and hunting feats, there are
unusual accounts of weather conditions,
over-sized vegetables, animals, and mosquitoes.

SHIPLEY, Nancy

—Anna and the Indians. Toronto: Ryerson,
1955. o/p

—The Scarlet lily. New York: F. Fell,
1959. o/p

—**Whistle on the wind.** New York: F. Fell, 1961. o/p

—**Return to the river.** Toronto: Ryerson, 1964. o/p

—**The Railway builders.** Canadian Careers Library. Scarborough, Ont.: McGraw-Hill Ryerson, 1965. cl $5.95 [0-7700-0162-9]
Setting: a northwestern Ontario village
The discovery of important mineral deposits changes the lives of railwaymen and their families. A sixteen-year-old boy is affected when the time comes for him to decide whether or not to go to university. The story is aimed at an unsophisticated, adolescent male audience.

—**Almighty Voice and the Red Coats.** Don Mills, Ont.: Burns & McEachern, 1967. pb $1.00 [0-88768-035-6]
Setting: an Indian reserve on the Prairies
When Almighty Voice, a young brave, is arrested by the RCMP for killing a deer without permission, he is told as a joke that his punishment will be death. The rest of this short novel recounts his escape and subsequent shoot-out with the Mounties.

—**The Blonde voyageur.** Don Mills, Ont.: Burns & McEachern, 1971. cl $4.95 [0-88768-026-7]
Setting: Manitoba
Disguised as a poor boy, Jo Ness travels from Britain to Manitoba in 1807. Unsuccessful in her search for her fiancé, Jo maintains the disguise until she becomes pregnant. This fictionalized account of the first white woman to visit the Canadian west is both short and simple.

—**Wild drums: tales and legends of the Plains Indians.** With Alex Grisdale. Winnipeg: Peguis, 1972. cl $4.95 [0-919566-11-1]; 1974. pb $2.50 [0-919566-35-9]
Setting: Manitoba
These tales of Plains Indian life were told to the author by an Indian named Alex Grisdale. Accounts of Indian women's courage, strength and cunning figure prominently; the "story" of Grisdale's life stands out as well, as a factual contemporary reference point. History and mythology blend in these stories of Prairie life prior to European settlement.

SIMPSON, Jonathan

—**No Virgin Mary.** Dorann Publishing, Toronto: Saanes, 1973. pb $2.50
Setting: northern Ontario, Toronto

This is the story of an Indian woman who loses her son and her soul because of meddling white men.

SIMPSON, Leo

—**Arkwright.** Toronto: Macmillan, 1971. cl $9.95 [0-7705-0775-1]; 1974. pb $4.95 [0-7705-1211-9]
Setting: New York and Toronto
This novel satirizes contemporary Canadian culture, particularly the greed of big business and the madnesses of the technological society. The narrator and protagonist, Addison Arkwright, finds himself in the position of promoting the very evils to which he objects. The story follows his encounters with the strange characters who try to control society and his attempts to escape his negative existence.

—**The Peacock papers.** Toronto: Macmillan 1973. cl $6.95 [0-7705-1047-7]
Setting: a small Ontario city
This story of a middle-aged man's breakdown combines nightmarish sequences with straightforward narration and the techniques of the nineteenth-century satirist, Thomas Love Peacock. The protagonist, Jeffrey Anchyr, finds that he can no longer separate reality from fantasy in a disintegrating world of one-dimensional people. Simpson's depiction of this world induces in the reader both laughter and terror.

SLATER, Patrick (pseud. for John Mitchell) **1882-1951**

—**The Yellow briar. A story of the Irish on the Canadian countryside.** 1933. SMC. Toronto: Macmillan, 1966. $1.75 [0-7705-0707-7]; Toronto: Macmillan, 1970. cl $7.95 [0-7705-0285-7]; pb $2.95 [0-7705-0284-9]; quality pb $3.95 [0-7705-1100-7]
Setting: Toronto, Mono Mills, Port Credit
This simple account of a young Irish boy thrown on his own resources in Canada during the 1840s provides many interesting details of rural life and of historic events such as the Rebellion of 1837, the Irish potato famine, the rise of Methodism and the American Civil War.

—**Robert Harding. A story of every day life.** Toronto: Thomas Allen, 1938. o/p
OX

SLUMAN, Norma Pauline 1924—

—**Blackfoot crossing.** Toronto: Ryerson, 1959. o/p

—**Poundmaker.** Scarborough, Ont.: McGraw-Hill Ryerson, 1967. cl $7.95 [0-770-0159-9]

Setting: Prairies

Poundmaker was one of the Indian chiefs held responsible for the violence that resulted when treaty promises were broken in the 1880s. Respected by his own and rival bands, Poundmaker was humiliated and finally destroyed by the machinery of white politics. Though her prose style is more conventional, Sluman's fictionalized account of the rebellions and trials bears many similarities to Wiebe's novel *The Temptations of Big Bear.* The book will be of great interest to students of Canadian history.

SMITH, Ray

—**Cape Breton is the thought control centre of Canada.** Toronto: Anansi, 1969. o/p

—**Lord Nelson tavern.** Toronto: McClelland & Stewart, 1974. $6.95 [0-7710-8195-2]

Setting: a city port

This novel follows the activities of a group of individuals loosely connected by the fact that they all attended the same university in their youth and drank at the same tavern. The book is subdivided into intricately interwoven sections each dealing with one of the characters (often in the form of a journal). A large time span is covered as each character develops a sense of identity. The setting is never explicitly given; this combined with the characters' strange names (Paleologue, Ti-Paulo, Grilse) adds to the novel's mysterious and compelling qualities.

SOUSTER, Raymond 1921—

—**The Winter of time.** By Raymond Holmes (pseud.). New Toronto: Export Publishing Enterprises, 1949. o/p

—**On target.** By John Holmes (pseud.). Toronto: Village Bookstore Press, 1973. cl $7.50 [0-919621-01-5]

Setting: Yorkshire, England

One aircrew of the RCAF's Six Bomber Group of the RAF Bomber Command represents the many Canadians who flew in this group in World War II. The happy, slangy, drunken off-duty hours of the men contrast with the tense raids made over a retreating Germany. Souster gives not only a detailed picture of the Handley Halifax Bomber, but also of the twenty-year-olds

who flew her and died in her.

CB CW ON2 OX OX2

STEAD, Robert James Campbell 1880-1959

—**The Bail jumper.** Toronto: Briggs, 1914 o/p

—**The Homesteaders.** 1916. Literature of Canada: Poetry and Prose in Reprint. Toronto: University of Toronto Press, 1973. cl $12.50 [0-8020-2067-4]; pb $4.50 [0-8020-6196-6]

Setting: Manitoba and Alberta

Only after the loss of his hired man and the near loss of his own family does John Harris realize that land ownership is not life's ultimate purpose. With dastardly intrigues and shoot-outs, this story of pioneer farm life has the suspenseful pace of a western.

—**Dennison Grant.** Toronto: Musson, 1920. o/p

—**Neighbours.** Toronto: Hodder, 1922. o/p

—**The Smoking flax.** Toronto: McClelland & Stewart, 1924. o/p

—**Zen of the Y.D.** London: Hodder, 1925. o/p (a rev. ed. of **Dennison Grant**)

—**Grain.** 1926. NCL. Toronto: McClelland & Stewart, 1963. pb $1.95 [0-7710-9136-0]

Setting: Manitoba

This novel traces Gander Stake's development from childhood on the farm around the turn of the century to a vaguely troubled single-minded adulthood. His main problem is deciding how to act with courage and integrity when two alternative courses seem equally possible but only partially appropriate. His relationships with the land, with his family and neighbours, and with the women he loves are related in linear style.

—**The Copper disc.** New York: Doubleday, 1931. o/p

CB CW OX

STEIN, David Lewis

—**Scratch one dreamer.** Toronto: McClelland & Stewart, 1967. cl $5.00 [0-7710-8345-9]; pb $2.50 [0-7710-8346-7]

Setting: Toronto and northern Ontario

Joe Fried, returning to Toronto after four years of travelling, finds himself enmeshed in the problems of the people he had tried to escape. He becomes involved again with the girl he had deserted, and gets caught up in demonstrations against nuclear weapons in a mining town. In the end Joe finds that he must come to terms with the past and the future.

—**My sexual and other revolutions.** Don Mills, Ont.: New Press, 1971. cl $4.95 [0-88770-096-9] ; pb $1.50 [0-88770-097-7]
Setting: Big Town, a city closely resembling Toronto
In this grotesque, sometimes humorous satire, Stein attacks contemporary pre-occupations with sex, violence, race and other issues. The book abounds in scenes which are often repellent, but which usually make a point. The novel centres on a young man with a strange curse growing up in Stein's fantastic world, a world in which time, space and matter are out of joint.

STENSON, Fred
—**Lonesome hero.** Toronto: Macmillan, 1974. cl $7.95 [0-7705-1173-2]
Setting: Alberta and England
Tyrone Lock is born into a farming community where virility is expected of men; he is a disappointment to his parents who regard him as weak. He wants to be left alone, but his girl friend tricks him into going to Europe. His comic attempts to resist fail and the trip results in unexpected consequences. However reluctant Tyrone may be to plunge into life, he manages to keep afloat.

STERN, Karl 1906—
—**Through dooms of love.** New York: Farrar Straus & Giroux, 1960. cl $4.95
Setting: Chicago
Marianne Radbert is the devoted daughter of a cultured but impoverished European refugee from fascism. The novel charts her confused progress through a maze of mental illness to freedom from her father and her background.

STILMAN, Abram 1903—
—**Healer of all flesh.** Don Mills, Ont.: Burns & McEachern, 1959. o/p
—**Mariette.** Don Mills, Ont.: Greywood, 1961. pb 95¢ [0-7745-0106-5]
Setting: Montreal
The novel focuses on the tragic romance of a French Catholic and an English Jew.
—**Doctor in court.** New York: Fountainhead Publishers, 1967. o/p

—**Levy.** Toronto: Saanes, 1971. pb $4.95 [0-88904-072-9]
Setting: Montreal and Israel
The son of a wealthy Jewish businessman goes through a series of religious and psychological counselling sessions in an attempt to understand his place in society. Torn between lonely fanaticism and his father's materialistic nationalism, Levy opts for life on an Israeli kibbutz. Told in an episodic style, the story ends at Jerusalem's Wailing Wall with the betrothal of Levy to his gentile girl friend, Virginia.

STRINGER, Arthur J.A. 1874-1950
—**The Loom of destiny.** 1899. Short Story Index Reprint Series. Plainview, N.Y.: Books For Libraries. cl $8.75
Setting: urban slums
This series of sketches concentrates on the struggles of Cockney and New York street brats. Each story is prefaced by a rhyme in lower-class dialect. The stories portray hunger, young love, and neighbourhood bullies.
—**The Silver poppy.** New York: Appleton, 1903. o/p
—**Lonely O'Malley.** Boston: Little, Brown, 1905. o/p
—**The Wire tappers.** Boston: Little, Brown, 1906. o/p
—**Phantom wires.** Boston: Little, Brown, 1907. o/p
—**The Under groove.** New York: McClure, 1908. o/p
—**The Gun-runner.** New York: Dodge, 1909. o/p
—**The Shadow.** New York: Century, 1913. Also published as **Never-fail Blake.** 1924
—**The Hand of peril.** New York: Macmillan, 1915. o/p
—**The Prairie wife.** Indianapolis: Bobbs-Merrill, 1915. o/p
—**The Door of dread.** Indianapolis: Bobbs-Merrill, 1916. o/p
—**The House of intrigue.** Indianapolis: Bobbs-Merrill, 1918. o/p
—**The Man who couldn't sleep.** Indianapolis: Bobbs-Merrill, 1919. o/p
—**The Stranger.** Toronto: Dominion Publicity Com. Victory Loan, 1919. o/p
—**The Prairie mother.** Toronto: McClelland & Stewart, 1920. o/p

—Twin tales: Are all men alike? and The Lost Titian. Indianapolis: Bobbs-Merrill, 1921. o/p

—The Wine of life. New York: Knopf, 1921. o/p

—The Prairie child. Indianapolis: Bobbs-Merrill, 1922. o/p

—The City of peril. New York: Knopf, 1923. o/p

—The Diamond thieves. Indianapolis: Bobbs-Merrill, 1923. o/p

—Empty hands. Indianapolis: Bobbs-Merrill, 1924. o/p

—Manhandled. With Russell Holmes. New York: Bobbs-Merrill, 1924. o/p

—The Story without a name. With Russell Holmes. New York: Grosset, 1924. o/p

—Power. Indianapolis: Bobbs-Merrill, 1925. o/p

—In bad with Sinbad. Indianapolis: Bobbs-Merrill, 1926. o/p

—Night hawk. New York: Burt, 1926. o/p

—White hands. Indianapolis: Bobbs-Merrill, 1927. o/p

—The Wolf woman. Indianapolis: Bobbs-Merrill, 1928. o/p

—Christina and I. Indianapolis: Bobbs-Merrill, 1929. o/p

—The Woman who couldn't die. Indianapolis: Bobbs-Merrill, 1929. o/p

—A Lady quite lost. Indianapolis: Bobbs-Merrill, 1931. o/p

—The Mud lark. Indianapolis: Bobbs-Merrill, 1932. o/p

—Marriage by capture. Indianapolis: Bobbs-Merrill, 1933. o/p

—Man lost. Indianapolis: Bobbs-Merrill, 1934. o/p

—Prairie stories. (Containing The Prairie wife, The Prairie mother, The Prairie child.) New York: Burt, 1936. o/p

—Tooloona. London: Methuen, 1936. o/p

—The Wife traders. Indianapolis: Bobbs-Merrill, 1936. o/p

—Heather of the high hand. New York: Bobbs-Merrill, 1937. o/p

—The Lamp in the valley. New York: Bobbs-Merrill, 1938. o/p

—The Dark wing. New York: Bobb-Merrill, 1939. o/p

—The Ghost plane. Indianapolis: Bobbs-Merrill, 1940. o/p

—Intruders in Eden. Indianapolis: Bobbs-Merrill, 1942. o/p

—Star in a mist. Indianapolis: Bobbs-Merrill, 1943. o/p

—The Devastator. Toronto: McClelland & Stewart, 1944. o/p

Lauriston, Victor. *Arthur Stringer, son of the north.* Biography and anthology. Toronto: Ryerson Press, 1941. o/p

CB CW OX

SUCH, Peter

—Fallout. Toronto: Clarke, Irwin, 1969. o/p
Setting: Blind River, Elliot Lake, Espanola
A man returns to Elliot Lake, once booming, now a ghost town. He meets an Indian sculptor who welds his art from the scrap left by the mines. Like this artist, he creates an artistic whole out of the disconnected memories of his past. Elliot Lake becomes a microcosm of civilization, the artist, a glimmer of light in a dark age.

—Riverrun. Toronto: Clarke, Irwin, 1973. cl $5.95 [0-7720-0620-2]
Setting: Newfoundland and Labrador
This poetic lament for the extinction of the Beothuk Indians of Newfoundland is reinforced by documentary and archaeological sources. In 1829 the last of the Beothuk died, but before that disease, starvation and indiscriminate killing by the white man and their Micmac allies had reduced them to scavengers. Their use of red ochre on their bodies led the European explorers to call them Red Indians; it is thought that they were the last of the original archaic Indian group from whom all the distinct tribes of North America evolved.

SULLIVAN, Alan 1868-1947

—The Passing of Oul-i-but and other tales. Toronto: Dent, 1913. o/p

—Blantyre-alien. London, Eng.: Dent, 1914. o/p

—The Inner door. New York: Century, 1917. o/p

—Brother Eskimo. Toronto: McClelland, 1921. o/p

—The Rapids. 1922. SHC. Toronto: University of Toronto Press, 1972. cl $12.50 [0-8020-1890-4]; pb $3.95 [0-8020-6148-6]

Setting: Sault Ste. Marie, Ontario

The hero of this fictionalized account of the industrialization of Sault Ste. Marie is a charismatic American entrepreneur. More interesting from a historic than from a literary point of view, the book describes how a multi-million dollar energy and mining complex was conceived and developed. Sullivan's sympathy for his hero's thwarted intentions appears sinister in modern economic and ecological contexts.

—The Birthmark. London, Eng.: Arnold, 1924. o/p

—The Jade god. London, Eng.: Bles, 1924. o/p

—The Crucible. By Sinclair Murray (pseud.) London, Eng.: Bles, 1925. o/p

—The Days of their youth. New York: Century, 1926. o/p

—Human clay. By Sinclair Murray (pseud.) and B.V. Shann. London, Eng.: J. Murray, 1926. o/p

—In the beginning. London, Eng.: Hurst & Blackett, 1926. o/p

—Under the northern lights. 1926. Kings Treasury of Literature Series. London, Eng.: Dent.

Setting: northern Canada

This is a collection of short stories set in Canada's wilderness. The concerns are simple and elemental: survival, the beauty of the North, the ways of the tundra's inhabitants—animals, natives and settlers. Many of the stories are written in the tradition of folk tales.

—Brother Blackfoot. New York: Century, 1927. o/p

—The Verdict of the sea. London, Eng.: Hurst & Blackett, 1927. o/p

—Whispering Lodge. By Sinclair Murray (pseud.). Toronto: Ryerson, 1927. o/p

—John Frensham, K.C. By Sinclair Murray (pseud.). New York: Dutton, 1928. o/p

—Sands of fortune. By Sinclair Murray (pseud.). New York: Dutton, 1928. o/p

—The Broken marriage. By Sinclair Murray (pseud.) New York: Dutton, 1929. o/p

—Double lives. By Sinclair Murray (pseud.). Toronto: Macmillan, 1929. o/p

—The Splendid silence. New York: Dutton, 1929. o/p

—The Story of One-Ear. London, Eng.: Philip, 1929. o/p

—The Training of the sea. London, Eng.: Philip, 1929. o/p

—A Little way ahead. Toronto: Macmillan, 1930. o/p

—The Magic makers. London, Eng.: J. Murray, 1930. o/p

—Mr. Absolom. London, Eng.: Murray, 1930. o/p

—Queer partners. By Sinclair Murray (pseud.). Toronto: Macmillan, 1930. o/p

—Golden foundling. By Sinclair Murray (pseud.). Toronto: Macmillan, 1931. o/p

—The Ironmaster. London, Eng.: J. Murray, 1931. o/p

—No Secrets Island. London, Eng.: Murray, 1931. o/p

—Antidote. By Sinclair Murray (pseud.). London, Eng.: J. Murray, 1932. o/p

—Colonel Pluckett. London, Eng.: Ward Lock, 1932. o/p

—Cornish interlude. By Sinclair Murray (pseud.). London, Eng.: J. Murray, 1932. o/p

—Man at Lone Tree. London, Eng.: Ward Lock, 1933. o/p

—What fools men are! By Sinclair Murray (pseud.). London, Eng.: Sampson Low, 1933. o/p

—The Obstinate virgin. London, Eng.: Low Marston, 1934. o/p

—The Great divide. Toronto: Macmillan, 1935. o/p

—The Money spinners. By Sinclair Murray (pseud.). London, Eng.: Low Marston, 1936. o/p

—The Fur masters. London, Eng.: Murray, 1938. o/p

—With love from Rachel. By Sinclair Murray (pseud.). Toronto: Oxford University Press, 1938. o/p

—Three came to Ville Marie. Toronto: Oxford University Press, 1941. o/p

—"And from that day". Toronto: Ryerson, 1944. o/p

—The Cariboo Road. Toronto: Nelson, 1946. o/p

CW OX

SUMMERS, Merna 1933—

—The Skating party. Ottawa: Oberon Press, 1974. cl $5.95 [0-88750-122-?]; pb $2.95 [0-88750 129-0].

Setting: rural Alberta

With one exception, these stories are about middle-aged or older people. Often the characters are unmarried or widowed, and their stories involve explorations of loneliness, pathos or remorse. Most stories move from a conversational opening to the triggering of a reminiscence.

SUTHERLAND, Ronald 1933–

—**Lark des neiges.** Don Mills, Ont.: New Press, 1971. cl $5.50 [0-88770-088-8]

Setting: Montreal

This novel embodies in fiction the thesis of Sutherland's critical work, *Second image*: that Canada's "two solitudes" are not as far apart as they think. Part English, part French, speaking in both languages, Suzanne Laflamme (formerly Susy Macdonald) remembers her past in a bilingual monologue to her cat. Once the toast of the East End, receiving "hot" jewels from her boyfriend, she now is married with four children. The French is introduced into the text in such a way that even someone who knows nothing of the language can understand the novel.

SYMONS, R.D. 1898-1973

—**Hours and the birds: a Saskatchewan record.** Toronto: University of Toronto Press, 1967. o/p

—**The Broken snare.** 1970. New York: Curtis, 1972. pb 95¢; London, Eng.: Robert Hale

Setting: British Columbia

Based on Symons's own experiences after staking a claim and building a ranch in the Rockies, this novel shows in interesting detail both the positive and negative aspects of the battle between man and nature. In the end man's delicate relationship with nature is totally disrupted by the coming of hunters and oil drillers.

—**Many trails.** Windjammer Books. Don Mills: Longman, 1971. pb $1.75 [0-7747-0121-8]

Setting: the Canadian west

This book clearly demonstrates the author's great love for and knowledge of the country to which he first came at age sixteen. He describes his discoveries and adventures during the first thirty years of his life in Canada. His concern for the land, the native people and their legends, and the animals he has encountered is conveyed through various episodes.

—**Still the wind blows. A historical novel of the Canadian northwest 1860-1916.** Saskatoon: Prairie Books, 1971. cl $9.50 [0-919306-29-2]

Setting: the Canadian northwest

This work of historical fiction is based on life in the Canadian northwest from 1860 to 1916. Included are such historical figures as Father Lacombe, Poundmaker and Big Bear. The central story concerns the final defeat of the western Indians and the destruction of their way of life. The book is illustrated with drawings by the author.

—**North by west.** Toronto & Garden City, N.J.: Doubleday, 1973. cl $5.95 [0-385-07475-1]; Paper Jacks. Markham, Ont.: General Publishing, 1974. pb $1.50 [0-7737-7073-9]

Setting: British Columbia and Northwest Territories

Two very different stories are linked by the idea of man's collective memory. The first is a retelling of a Cree legend about the establishment of the Indian in North America; the second the story of a lost white baby raised by Eskimos, and his arduous journey back to the land of his white ancestors.

—**Where the wagon led: one man's memories of the cowboy's life in the old west.** Toronto & Garden City, N.J.: Doubleday, 1973. cl. $8.95 [0-385-07503-0]

Setting: the Canadian west

As Symons indicates, the book is a personal history of the cowboy in the Canadian west from 1906 to the sixties. Symons combines anecdote with factual information about the cowboys' life.

SYMONS, Scott

—**Place d'Armes.** Toronto: McClelland & Stewart, 1967. cl. $6.00 [0-7710-8375-0]. pb $2.50 [0-7710-8376-9]

Setting: Montreal

The author describes *Place d'Armes* as "at once a first novel, a meticulously tangled diary, an insanely indiscreet autobiography, an existential Canadian allegory". It is written as the journal of a snobbish young Toronto intellectual, a descendant of the Upper Canada WASP élite, who goes to Montreal to revitalize his spirit through the beauty and vitality of French Canada. He feels that English Canadians are defeated souls who have lost the ability to love, and it is only through his admiration for Quebec culture that he will save himself. The book is structured as a novel within a novel.

—**Civic Square**. Toronto: McClelland & Stewart, 1969. cl $17.50 [0-7710-8374-2]

Setting: Toronto and Montreal

Like *Place d'Armes*, this massive journal is a largely autobiographical account of the author's obsessions. He monologues repetitiously on Canadians' lack of sensuality, their "constipated souls", their fear of touching, Rosedale as a bastion of smugness and "deadness". He eulogizes sex as a salvation, and describes his homosexual encounters and contacts with Toronto's gay world.

The Novel. Audiotape.
Discussions with Hugh Garner and Yves Thériault. Three tapes.
CBC Cat. Nos. 837-839 30 min.

OX2

TEMPLETON, Charles

—**The Kidnapping of the president**. Toronto: McClelland & Stewart, 1974. cl $8.95. [0-7710-8458-7]

Setting: New York

This is a suspenseful account of a presidential kidnapping, concentrating on the details of secret service protection work.

THERIAULT, Yves 1916

—**Agaguk / Agaguk**. 1958. Tr., Miriam Chapine. Scarborough, Ont.: McGraw-Hill Ryerson, 1967. pb $3.15 [0-7700-6016-1]

Setting: northern Quebec

Thériault exploits the contrast between the beauty of northern landscape and the harsh realities faced by the people who must survive in it. Agaguk finds himself in conflict with the white traders who control him economically, with his family and tribe, and finally with nature. His personality, formed by brutal confrontations, is slowly tamed by his wife's love. She saves his life after he is mauled by a wolf and helps him escape the police who want him for the murder of a white bootlegger and thief. Finally, he comes into conflict with her as well when she wants to keep an infant daughter, going against a tradition that de-

mands such burdens on survival be killed. Many aspects of the alleged "Eskimo" setting of this novel are questionable. The translation is a good one.

—**Ashini / Ashini**. 1968. FWCS. Tr., Gwendolyn Moore. Montreal: Harvest House, 1972. pb $2.50 [0-88772-119-2].

Setting: northern Quebec

Ashini is a solitary sixty-year-old Montagnais Indian who feels his people are dying as they go to live on reserves. He decides to talk to the prime minister about this. Suspense builds as his plan unfolds and it becomes clear that Ashini's sense of humour and politics differs from that of the white man. The author uses animal stories to make his points about the ill-treatment and betrayal of the Indians in this simply written novel. The translation is good.

—**N'Tsuk / N'Tsuk**. 1968. FWCS. Tr., Gwendolyn Moore. Montreal: Harvest House, 1972. pb $2.00 [0-88772-124-9]

Setting: northern Quebec

N'Tsuk is a one-hundred-year-old Montagnais Indian woman. She tells of her past happiness living a traditional way of life in tune with nature. At times her story is moving and poetic as she mourns the passing of old ways and the destruction of nature, at times explicit when she describes day-to-day life. The translation is a good one.

The Novel. Audiotape.
Discussions with Hugh Garner and Scott Symons. Three tapes.
CBC Cat. Nos. 837-839 30 min.

CW FC OX OX2

THOMAS, Audrey Grace 1935—

—**Ten green bottles**. Indianapolis, Ia.: Bobbs-Merrill, 1967. o/p

—**Mrs. Blood**. 1970. Vancouver: Talonbooks, 1974. pb $4.50 [0-88922-063-8]

Setting: Ghana

A white woman lies in a hospital, weakened by fear and the threat of a miscarriage. Continually forced to think of death and loss, she remembers the pain of her past—her lost lover, her unhappy childhood and her uncertain marriage. She observes both the expatriate and African societies around her with the eyes of an outsider.

—Munchmeyer and Prospero on the island.
New York: Bobbs-Merrill, 1972. cl $5.95

Setting: an island off the B.C. coast

This book consists of two diaries: one is Munchmeyer's, a writer who has just left his wife, and the other is Miranda Archer's, who is writing a novel on an island in British Columbia. Miranda's delight in her children, husband and friend Prospero seem totally unconnected with Munchmeyer's unhappiness and egoism. Gradually, however, it becomes clear that Munchmeyer is a fictional character created by Miranda. Beneath the simple narrative lies a concern for the relationship between art and life, fantasy and reality.

—Songs my mother taught me. Vancouver: Talonbooks, 1973. cl $8.50 [0-88922-044-1]; pb $4.50 [0-88922-054-9]; New York: Bobbs-Merrill; New York: Ballantine

Setting: northern New York State

As she grows up Isobel becomes aware of her parents' weaknesses—her father fears both death and life, her mother tries to live through her daughters. Somehow, despite the quarrels, the unpaid bills, the unpopularity at school, and her interfering mother, Isobel emerges as a strong and alive person.

—Blown figures. Vancouver: Talonbooks, 1974. cl $8.50 [0-88922-074-3]; pb $4.50 [0-88922-079-4]

Isobel, feeling she has abandoned the body of her still-born child in a West African hospital, is compelled by guilt to return. She meets Delilah, who is seeking an abortion, and who miscarries in the same hospital without regret. Fragments of nursery rhymes, advertisements and children's stories interrupt the narrative. An African purification ceremony fails to cleanse Isobel and the final surrealistic scenes raise the possibility that this voyage to Africa may be a psychological one.

ON2 OX2

THOMPSON, Kent

–The Tenants were Corrie and Tennie.
Toronto: Macmillan, 1973. cl $6.95
[0-7705-1001-9]

Setting: Fredericton, N.B.

William A. Boyd, a solitary man, resigns his job as a teacher, buys a duplex and plans to live on the rent paid him by his tenants, Corrie and Tennie. Despite his conservative views, the reader is attracted by his air of common sense and self-reliance. Gradually his behaviour becomes peculiar. He spies shamelessly on his neighbours, whose marriage is in trouble, and finally sleeps with Corrie. His moral collapse, and theirs, (which may also be self-deception, or a lapse into insanity) is made to seem both surprising and inevitable.

—Across from the Floral Park. New York: St. Martin's Press, 1974. cl $7.95

Setting: indeterminate

A man buys a large house. He finds a woman living in it who cannot be evicted. He marries her. The man narrates their strange and disturbing life together in such a matter-of-fact manner that the reader is almost compelled to accept it as normal. The woman takes a lover, they are blackmailed, they have a child. The man, a near recluse, becomes an actor, then a politician. One day he comes home to find all the locks changed. He cannot get in and goes away.

THOMSON, Edward William 1849-1924

—Old Man Savarin, and other stories.
Toronto: Briggs, 1895. o/p

—Smoky days. New York: Crowell, 1896. o/p

—Walter Gibbs, the young boss and other stories. Toronto: Briggs, 1896. o/p

—Between earth and sky and other strange stories of deliverance. Toronto: Briggs, 1897. o/p

—Old Man Savarin stories: tales of Canada and Canadians. 1917. Toronto: University of Toronto Press, 1974. cl $15.00 [0-8020-2077-1]; pb $4.50 [0-8020-6207-5]

Setting: Glengarry, the Ottawa Valley

Thomson reprinted here twelve of the fourteen stories in *Old Man Savarin, and other stories* (1895) and added five others. His stories often have the reminiscent focus of an old story-teller talking to a young listener. They have the immediacy, simplicity and casual quality of the spoken as opposed to the written word, attributes which are reinforced by Thomson's use of dialect. Thomson depicts a primarily male world of *habitants*, store-keepers, farmers and lumbermen, perhaps because he wrote most often for boys. His style was much more realistic than was common in his romantic and sentimental time, although like Dickens, he thought of the "young person" and provided happy endings.

CB

—Selected stories of E.W. Thomson. Ed., Lorraine McMullen. Ottawa: University of Ottawa Press, 1973. pb $3.75 [0-7766-4333-9] These stories are selected from **Old Man Savarin Stories.**

Bourinot, Arthur S., ed. *The Letters of Edward William Thomson to Archibald Lampman. 1891-1897.* Ottawa: Bourinot, 1957. $3.50

TORGOV, Morley

—**A good place to come from.** Toronto: Lester and Orpen, 1974. $7.95 [0-919630-66-9]
Setting: Sault Ste. Marie
This book consists of a series of vignettes about a boy growing up in a small Jewish community in Sault Ste. Marie during the late thirties and early forties. Of particular interest are the author's use of dialogue and his portrayal of life in a small-town environment.

TRAILL, Catherine Parr 1802-1899

—**Reformation; or, the cousin.** London, Eng., 1819. o/p

—**Prejudice reproved.** London, Eng.: Harvey & Darton, 1826. o/p

—**The Backwoods of Canada.** 1836. abr. NCL. Toronto: McClelland & Stewart, 1966. pb $1.75 [0-7710-9151-6] ; Coles Canadiana Collection. Toronto: Coles, 1971. cl $10.95; pb $4.50 [no ISBN]
Setting: Upper Canada

*Part household compendium, part almanac, part diary, part settler's guide, *The Backwoods of Canada* includes among its wealth of information recipes for making maple sugar, candles and soap, statistics on emigration to Canada, and advice on how to raise livestock and build a log cabin. Much of it is composed of letters written by Traill to her family in the early 1830s, supplemented by a diary written during the year of the Rebellions, 1837-38. She describes the trip to Canada, the area around the farm near Peterborough, the native people who lived nearby, and the local flora.

—**Adventures of Little Downy; The field mouse; and The little princess, or Passion and patience.** London, Eng.: Dean, 1844. o/p

—**The Canadian Crusoes.** Ed., Agnes Strickland. London, Eng.: Hall, 1850. Also published as **Lost in the backwoods.** 1882. o/p

—**The Canadian settler's guide.** 1855. NCL. Toronto: McClelland & Stewart, 1969. pb $2.95 [0-7710-9164-8]
Subtitled "A Manual of Canadian housewifery" this book is an expansion of *The Backwoods of Canada.* In her introduction to the New Canadian Library edition Clara Thomas suggests the useful exercise of comparing it with Mrs. Beeton's famous *Book of household management* (published five years later in England) which would reveal the enormous problems women faced in adapting to the bush.

—**Afar in the forest.** London, Eng.: Nelson, 1869. Also published as **Lady Mary and her nurse.** 1856; **Little Mary and her nurse: stories of the Canadian forest.** 1861; **In the forest.** 1886. o/p

—**Cot and cradle stories.** Ed., Mary Agnes Fitzgibbon. Toronto: Briggs, 1895. o/p

---

Eaton, Sara. *Lady of the backwoods: a biography of Catherine Parr Traill.* Toronto: McClelland & Stewart, 1969 cl $6.95 [0-7710-3015-0]
This biography covers the life of Catherine Parr Traill from early childhood to her death at the age of ninety-seven. The author has used available documentation to create scenes of realistic dialogue concerning various important events in Mrs. Traill's life.

Hume, Blanche. *The Strickland sisters.* Toronto: Ryerson Press, 1928. o/p

Needler, G.H. *Otonabee pioneers: the story of the Stewarts, the Stricklands, the Traills and the Moodies.* Toronto: Burns & MacEachern, 1953. o/p

See also Susanna Moodie.

CB CW ON OX

TRUEMAN, Stuart 1911–

—**Cousin Elva.** Toronto: McClelland & Stewart, 1955. o/p

—**The Ordeal of John Gyles.** 1963. Toronto: McClelland & Stewart, 1973. cl $5.95 [0-7710-8605-9] ; pb $2.95 [0-7710-8604-0]
Setting: seventeenth century New England
The diary of a boy captured in an Indian raid and traded to the French has been converted into an exciting historical novel. John Gyles loses his family's Puritan dogmatism during nine years of captivity, as he learns to understand the languages and beliefs of his captors.

TRUSS, Jan

—**Bird at the window.** Toronto: Macmillan, 1974. cl $7.95 [0-7705-1175-9]

Setting: Alberta and England

Angela, an intelligent eighteen-year-old, discovers she is pregnant and is unable to tell her parents or hope for sympathy in her small Alberta farming community. She leaves to visit her grandparents in England. Her fears and dilemmas are well expressed as she tries to decide on a course of action— abortion, adoption or marriage. Finally she comes home and begins to come to terms with her parents, her past and her future as a writer.

UNDERWOOD, Miles see John Glassco

VACZEK, Louis Charles 1913—

—**River and empty sea. A novel.** 1950. New York: Popular Library, 1971. pb 95¢.

Setting: New France, around 1671

An aristocrat, in New France against his will, is sent by the Intendant Jean Talon to claim Hudson's Bay for New France. The gruelling trip by canoe in the company of a Jesuit and several Indians transforms him into a wanderer and a lover of the wilds and its people. The historical information concerning the conflict between the interests of the Intendants, the habitants and the Jesuits provides the framework for this adventure based on a real journey by Father Charles Albanel.

—**The Frightened dove.** By Peter Harden (pseud.). New York: Scribner, 1951. o/p

—**The Hidden grave.** By Peter Harden (pseud.). New York: Dell, 1955. o/p

—**The Golden calf.** New York: Sloane, 1956. o/p

VALGARDSON, W.D.

—**Bloodflowers.** Ottawa: Oberon Press, 1973. pb $3.50 [0-88750-086-2]

Setting: Maritimes and northern Manitoba

Each of these ten thematically linked stories is concerned with isolation and its psychological, spiritual, and physical effects on the protagonists. Combining elements of drama, mystery, and adventure, Valgardson displays a variety of forms.

VIGNEAULT, Gilles 1928—

—**Tales sur la pointe des pieds.** (Bilingual ed.) Tr., Paul Allard. Erin, Ont.: Press Porcépic, 1972. cl $7.95 [0-88878-004-4]

In these tales one finds such themes as the beauty and sorrow of life, the destruction of nature by civilization, nostalgia for the purity and simplicity of childhood and the search for true love. Vigneault's style is simple and poetic. He is very conscious of how difficult it is to find words to translate deep feelings and this becomes one of his themes.

CW FC OX2

VIZINCZEY, Stephen

—**In praise of older women: the amorous recollections of Andrus Vajda.** 1965. New York: Ballantine, 1971. pb 95¢; London, Eng.: Barrie and Jenkins, 1966

Setting: Budapest, Rome, Vienna, Toronto, Saskatchewan

Each chapter presents a different woman with whom Andrus becomes involved. The book takes him from boyhood to manhood, from World War II to a decade after the Hungarian uprising, in a series of separate episodes.

WALKER, David Harry 1911—

—**The Storm and the silence.** Boston: Houghton Mifflin, 1949. cl $3.95; New York: Belmont-Tower, 1971. pb 95¢; London, Eng.: Collins

Setting: Scotland

When Tam Diamond is fired from his truck-driving job, he leaves town on foot. Stopping for a meal, he loses his temper and accidentally kills a farm wife. The account of Diamond's unsuccessful evasion of police is padded out with flashbacks and fantasized scenes.

—**Geordie.** Boston & New York: Houghton Mifflin, 1950. cl $5.95; Laurel & Gold Series. London, Eng.: Collins

Setting: Scotland and Boston

Sensitive about his small size, Geordie takes a muscle-building course, going on to win an Olympic medal for shot-putting.

—**The Pillar.** 1952. Don Mills, Ont. and London, Eng.: Collins, 1972. cl $6.50 [0-00221656-6]; New York: Popular Library. Also published as **The Wire.** Garden City, N.Y.: Permabooks, 1953. o/p

Setting: Germany

This symmetrically-structured novel is about the lives of six British men who spend most of the war in a prisoner of war camp. The leisurely pace Walker uses to describe the men's past lives is offset by the excitement of the many escape attempts.

—**Digby.** 1953. New York: Popular Library, 1968. pb 75¢
Setting: New York City and Scotland
Digby P. Ross, an American tycoon, goes to Scotland to escape business and marital pressures.

—**Harry Black.** 1956. Don Mills, Ont. and London, Eng.: Collins, 1970. cl $4.95 [0-00221317-6]
Setting: India
Between a dangerous tiger hunt and a precarious romance with his best friend's wife, Harry Black finds how debilitating is his isolation as a human being. An ex-colonel and a veteran of the tea industry, Harry blusters and commands with the flair of a 1940s war movie hero. The pace of military flashbacks and hunting scenes is impeded by literary effects intended to make Harry seem complex and tragic.

—**Sandy was a soldier's boy.** London, Eng.: Collins, 1957
Setting: Scotland
This short novel is about a mischievous Scottish boy who performs a courageous act during an enemy invasion.

—**Where the high winds blow.** Boston: Houghton Mifflin, 1960. o/p

—**Dragon Hill.** Boston & New York: Houghton Mifflin, 1962. o/p

—**Storms of our journey.** Boston: Houghton Mifflin, 1962. cl $4.95
Setting: Canadian wilderness, India, Scotland
All of these stories in some way involve man and the outdoors. Walker is at his best when describing an adventure such as tiger hunting in India or fishing in the Scottish Highlands.

—**Mallabec.** 1965. New York: Belmont-Tower, 1971. pb 95¢
Setting: New Brunswick
John and Moira Hyde return to their fishing lodge on the Mallabec River after an absence of twenty-three years. When their son Robin joins them, old memories are stirred up by the romance which develops between him and a married woman.

—**Come back, Geordie.** Boston & New York: Houghton Mifflin, 1966. cl $4.95
Setting: Scotland
In this sequel to *Geordie*, Geordie's son Charlie goes through a turbulent adolescence, attends university in New Brunswick,

and like Geordie, enters the Olympics. Also like his father, Charlie falls in love with a hot-tempered Scottish girl, and the book ends with a marriage.

—**Devil's Plunge.** Don Mills, Ont. and London, Eng.: Collins, 1968. cl $4.95. Also published as **CAB-Intersec.** Boston: Houghton Mifflin; New York: Belmont-Tower
Setting: Switzerland
Assuming his assignment requires only the retrieval of a stolen diamond, Harry Ambler gets dangerously caught between big-time criminals and the police. With the wizardry of a James Bond, Ambler is saved from nuclear destruction just in time to shoot the arch-fiend.

—**Big Ben.** Boston & New York: Houghton Mifflin, 1969. cl $3.95. o/p

—**Pirate Rock.** Don Mills, Ont. and London, Eng.: Collins, 1969. cl $3.95; Boston and New York: Houghton Mifflin
Setting: a New Brunswick town on the Bay of Fundy
Two brothers are drawn into the exciting world of international espionage when they ignore parental warnings and accept summer jobs from a mysterious neighbour. The emphasis is on suspense and humour.

—**The Lord's pink ocean.** Don Mills, Ont. and London, Eng.: Collins, 1972. cl $5.95 [0-00221478-4]; Boston: Houghton Mifflin; New York: Daw Books
Setting: rural United States, in the future
This science fiction novel is about survivors isolated after ecological disaster. The book also deals with racial tension and its mitigation by love.

—**Black Dougal.** Don Mills, Ont.: Collins, 1973. cl $6.95 [0-00-221095-9]; Boston: Houghton Mifflin
Setting: Montreal and Scotland
Sir Dougal Trocher of Drin, a poverty-stricken young nobleman, decides to rescue his estate through illegitimate means. His successful escapades in Montreal's high society allow him to save his land and salvage the love of Tirene, daughter of Lord Tarquin.

—**Winter of madness.** Don Mills, Ont.: Collins, 1973. cl $5.95 [0-00221910-7]; Boston & New York: Houghton Mifflin
Setting: rural Scotland
A bemused and often amusing Scottish Lord Tarquin relates the extraordinary results when he rented to an American million-

aire for the winter. The satire of Tiger Clyde, the double-O colleague of James Bond, is somewhat forced but not inaccurate.

CW OX OX2

WARWICK, Jarvis see Hugh Garner

WATSON, Patrick

—Zero to airtime. Don Mills, Ont.: Fitzhenry & Whiteside, 1974. cl $6.95 [0-88902-015-9]; New York: Warner Paperback Library
Setting: Ottawa, the James Bay area
Environmental Commando is a guerrilla group whose frightening record of terrorist acts is not consistent with their stated idealistic mission to save the ecology. Tough, rude and bad-tempered Joe Ireton, a news filmmaker who works from his own plane, tangles with them when he covers a conference on the James Bay hydro-electric project. The plausibility of this thriller is enhanced by the author's intimate knowledge of planes and the world of TV and film.

WATSON, Scott

—Stories. Vancouver: Talonbooks, 1974. pb $4.00 [0-88922-064-6]
Setting: Vancouver, B.C.
Set in a milieu of poetry readings, Tarot cards and gay bars, each of these five stories culminates in the consummation of a homosexual encounter.

WATSON, Sheila 1919—

—The Double hook. 1959. NCL. Toronto: McClelland & Stewart, 1966. pb $1.50; text $1.50 [0-7710-9154-0]
Setting: a valley
The death of an old woman touches the families of a small, remote ranch community. The author examines the disorientation man feels when death reminds him of his unaccomodated hopes and passions. The stark prose, bizarre imagery, desert-like landscape and anonymous location create a strange atmosphere and a universal perspective.

CW ON OX

WEATHERBY, Hugh 1908—

—Tales the totems tell. 1944. Toronto: Macmillan, 1951. cl $4.95 [0-7705-0306-3]
Setting: British Columbia
These brief tales explain the origin of the totem-pole and the significance of particular animal emblems. Written simply enough to be understood by children, the book will also appeal to those interested in the art and beliefs of Canada's native people.

—Fir forest fun. Toronto: Ryerson, 1947. o/p

—Teddy, Dappy, and Joe. Toronto: Ryerson, 1948. o/p

—How the fir forest was saved. Victoria: British Columbia Forest Service, 1949. o/p

WEINTRAUB, William

—Why rock the boat? 1961. CBL. Toronto: McClelland & Stewart, 1968. pb 95¢ [0-7710-8990-2]
Setting: Montreal.
A comic view of the ideosyncrasies of the daily press is presented through the eyes of a cynical but love-stricken cub reporter.

_____

Why rock the boat? Film.
Canada, John Howe, 1974.
col 112 min
35mm English: dist. Astral/Columbia

WEINZWEIG, Helen

—Passing ceremony. Toronto: Anansi, 1973. cl $6.95 [0-88784-424-3]; pb $2.95 [0-88784-325-5].
Setting: indeterminate
The skeletal base of this *nouveau roman* is a wedding: ceremony, reception, and following night. A series of very short sections flesh out into the bizarre nightmares of each character. A deflating and biting humour surfaces, emphasizing the dissociation of each character from the others, including the bride and groom.

WIEBE, Rudy 1934—

—Peace shall destroy many. Toronto: McClelland & Stewart, 1962. cl $6.95 [0-7710-8988-0]; 1972 NCL pb $1.95 [0-7710-9182-6]; Grand Rapids, Mich.: Eerdmans
Setting: Saskatchewan
A young man is torn between Mennonite tradition and his own conscience when the reality of world war forces him to justify pacifist "non-resistance". He becomes increasingly critical of the community's treatment of its non-conforming members and its Métis neighbours. This portrait of Mennonite life and beliefs is complex and slow-moving.

—First and vital candle. Toronto: McClelland & Stewart, 1966. o/p

—The Blue mountains of China. Grand Rapids, Mich.: Eerdman, 1970. pb $5.95.

Setting: Russia, Paraguay, Viet Nam, Alberta

This novel about Mennonite resettlement after the Russian Revolution suggests that search for a homeland is ultimately a religious quest. Throughout, Wiebe explores various forms of faith, from materialism to the fanaticism of a man who decides in 1967 to carry a wooden cross along the Trans-Canada highway. The fragmentation of several families is revealed by the bizarre reunion of surviving relatives half a century after their emigration. The final scenes of recognition reveal an intricate pattern of historical and philosophical discoveries.

—The Temptations of Big Bear. Toronto: McClelland & Stewart, 1973. cl $8.95 [0-7710-8985-6]

Setting: the Prairies

Big Bear, the imposing chief of a band of Cree Indians, originally opposed the 1876 treaty promising food in exchange for land. Later he signed, hoping to alleviate the starvation that resulted from white interference with the prairies' natural balance. Treaty provisions proved inadequate, and Big Bear's people participated in violent rebellions. Wiebe's fictional account of Big Bear's role in the rebellions and his punishment by a white court makes frequent use of interior monologue and historical documents.

—Where is the voice coming from? Toronto: McClelland & Stewart, 1974. pb $4.95 [0-7710-8987-2]

Setting: Edmonton, Montana, Prairies, Yukon

These thirteen stories are about desperate men or men reconstructing the past: their actions often follow a pattern of search for bearings in unfamiliar situations. With few exceptions, Wiebe's heroes participate in ritualistic encounters with strange or hostile environments. The stylistic innovations, like those in The Temptations of Big Bear, involve abrupt juxtapositions of fantasy and document.

CB ON2 OX2

WILLER, Jim

—Paramind. Toronto: McClelland & Stewart, 1973. cl $7.95 [0-7710-8999-6]

Setting: the future

The computer moves from its role as man's tool to the role of man's rival. Paramind is the computer's account of its inventor, Kasgar, and of the evolutionary step that follows man on the earth. The idea of a computer takeover is not as chilling as Willer's picture of the society that precedes it: a society where the ruling class has become so super-rational, so machine-like, that all emotional life of importance is dead. Willer creates a convincing model, not only of this society, but of its language and technology.

WILSON, Ethel Davis 1890—

—Hetty Dorval. 1947. Richmond, B.C.: Alcuin, 1967. cl $18.50 [0-919026-01-X]; LL. Toronto: Macmillan, 1967. pb $1.95 [0-7705-0251-2]

Setting: the Prairies and England

A young girl's acquaintance with an insidiously irresponsible woman named Hetty Dorval, and their eventual rivalry is the focus of this novel. Hetty is undone when her disillusioned protégée exposes proof of the older woman's scandalous past. The triumph of propriety over deceit satisfies the requirements of the novel's simple plot.

—The Innocent traveller. Toronto: Macmillan, 1949. o/p

—Equations of love: Tuesday and Wednesday / Lilly's story. 1952. LL. Toronto: Macmillan, 1974. pb $2.95 [0-7705-1171-6]

Setting: British Columbia

Tuesday and Wednesday, the first novelette in the book, deals with a lower class couple, their friends and relatives, ending with the death of the husband. The author emphasizes her dislike of the characters. Lilly's story is the romantic but simple story of an orphan girl who, in the course of manufacturing a respectable life for her illegitimate daughter, herself finds dignity and happiness.

—Swamp angel. 1954. NCL. Toronto: McClelland & Stewart, 1962. pb $1.95 [0-7710-9129-X]

Setting: Vancouver and central B.C.

Maggie Vardoe, seeking independence, leaves her claustrophobic marriage to work as cook in a fishing lodge in the interior of B.C. She runs into more domestic problems as the lodge owner's wife becomes convinced that Maggie is squeezing her out of her roles as wife and mother. In her frustrated attempt to relocate herself in society, Maggie asks an old Vancouver friend for advice. The book's strong point is its characterization of women in various marital roles.

—**Love and salt water.** Toronto: Macmillan, 1956. o/p

—**Mrs. Golightly and other stories.** Toronto: Macmillan, 1961. cl $1.95 [0-7705-0312-8]
Setting: Vancouver
These stories explore the lives of middle-aged couples and spinsters. Mysterious appearances and disappearances force ordinary characters into extraordinary situations.

Pacey, Desmond. *Ethel Wilson.* World Author Series. New York: Twayne, 1968. cl $5.95
Declaring his "intense admiration" for Wilson's writing, Pacey proceeds from a general and biographical overview to a discussion of her books. Pacey's analysis concentrates on thematic patterns, symbolism and techniques of characterization. (Bibliography.)
CB CL CW ON OX

WILSON, Helen Dacey
—**Tales from Barrett's Landing: a childhood in Nova Scotia.** Toronto: McClelland & Stewart, 1964. o/p

—**More tales from Barrett's Landing.** Toronto: McClelland & Stewart, 1967. cl $4.95 [0-7710-9031-5]
Setting: Nova Scotia
Helen Wilson reminisces about the childhood escapades of a large family. Anecdotal in style, the stories look nostalgically at treasure hunts, circus gypsies, special occasions, romantic fantasies, and everyday life.

WIPER, David see David Fennario

WISEMAN, Adele 1928—
—**The Sacrifice.** 1956. LL. Toronto: Macmillan, 1968. pb $1.95 [0-7705-0253-9]
Setting: a city in Canada
The dreams and aspirations of a wise and proud Jewish father are crushed by death—two of his sons are murdered, a third has a heart attack, and his wife dies of a lung disease. He himself begins to feel rejected by his remaining relatives. Wiseman shows the pain that wisdom and pride can cause when a man is so entirely bereft of good fortune.

—**Crackpot.** Toronto: McClelland & Stewart, 1974. cl $10.00 [0-7710-9034-X]

Setting: a western Canadian city
This novel tells the story of Hoda, the daughter of a hunchbacked mother and a blind father. Both in childhood and in her adult life as a prostitute Hoda's actions are governed by her sensuous nature and her love of life. Wiseman draws on her knowledge of Jewish culture and on her insight into human tragedy and humour to paint a compelling portrait.
CW ON2

WOOD, Ted
—**Somebody else's summer.** Toronto: Clarke, Irwin, 1974. cl $6.95 [0-7720-0623-7]
Remarkably varied in plot, these fifteen stories are united by their insight into human emotions. One story is science fiction, another is narrated by a trout who lives in the fish tank of a fancy restaurant, several concern "backward" children and their families, others concern alcoholics. The trout's concern with survival is mirrored, more seriously perhaps, in several other stories.

WRIGHT, Richard
—**The Weekend man.** Toronto: Macmillan, 1970. cl $7.95 [0-7705-0321-7]. Scarborough, Ont. & New York: New American Library, 1972. pb $1.25; New York: Farrar, Straus & Giroux
Setting: a large Canadian city
Wes Wakenham lives a painstakingly routine life and worries about it. He describes his unhappy marriage and his Mongoloid son with ambiguous calm.

—**In the middle of a life.** Toronto & London, Eng.: Macmillan, 1973. cl $7.95 [0-7705-1049-3]; Paper Jacks. Don Mills, Ont.: General Publishing, 1974. pb $1.25 [0-7737-7081-X]; New York: Farrar, Straus & Giroux
Setting: a large Canadian city
A divorced, unemployed, middle-class, middle-aged man comes to terms with the broken dreams of his past life and begins again more realistically. Wright demonstrates an ability to make the lives of ordinary, even dull, people interesting.

WYATT, Rachel
—**The String box.** Toronto: Anansi, 1970. cl $6.00 [0-88784-409-X]; pb $2.95 [0-88784-309-3]
Setting: Toronto
Wyatt creates a society which, in its mad-

ness, startlingly resembles the society which most of us see as normal. One's status is measured by the amount of string saved in a special box and weighed in annually. The protagonist, John Bogden Smith, moves through this strange world trying to cope with its insanity.

YATES, J. Michael

—The Man in the glass octopus. Delta, B.C. Sono Nis, 1968. pb $2.95.
Setting: indeterminate
Sono Nis may be a god, a dee-jay, a gentleman, a hunter, a photographer; he is a composite being—a man obsessed with his own consciousness. He strays easily into danger, hunting the true north until he loses his human scent and his senses. He creates myths and parables of technology, of inquests, of examinations, of photography. His fears of apocalypse, entropy, and mass suicide are reflected in short fictions which seem to recount the nightmares and archetypal dreams of the human race. Despite the cruelty, alienation and fear in these stories, they hint at something of what it means to be human and alive.

—The Abstract beast. Delta, B.C.: Sono Nis, 1971. cl $9.95.

Seven short pieces of fiction alternate with eight radio dramas to make up this unusual and experimental collection. Many stories are internal musings, concerned with metamorphosis and disintegration. Many resemble dreams or fantasies related to art, disease, death, aphasia and sleep.

YORK, Thomas

—We, the wilderness. Scarborough, Ont. and New York: McGraw-Hill Ryerson, 1973. cl $6.95 [0-07-077628-8]
Setting: a small Indian village on the British Columbia coast
York names each chapter after its narrator. The result of the many first person accounts of the same events is a story that must finally be pieced together in the reader's mind; the truth reverberates *between* the accounts. The central focus of the story is the young white doctor's search for a solution to the mystery of the incredibly high suicide rate among the Indians in the village. He feels part of the answer lies in his own family background and especially with his father, the village doctor before him.

YOUNG, Egerton R. 1840-1909

—Stories from Indian wigwams and northern campfires. 1893. Coles Canadiana Collection. Rexdale, Ont.: Coles, 1970. cl $3.95 [no ISBN] ; Detroit: Gale
Setting: northern and western Canada
These stories are the fictionalized memoirs of a missionary in western Canada before the turn of the century. Young's attitude towards the Indians he worked with is self-satisfied and patronizing.

—Oowikapun; or how the gospel reached the Nelson River Indians. London, Eng.: Kelly, 1895. o/p

—Three boys in the wild north land, summer. New York: Eaton & Mains, 1896. o/p

—Winter adventures of three boys in Great Lone Land. New York: Eaton & Mains, 1899. o/p

—Algonquin Indian tales. New York: Eaton & Mains, 1903. o/p

—Children of the forest. New York: Revell, 1904. o/p

—Duck Lake. New York: Eaton & Mains, 1905. o/p

—Hector my dog. Boston: Wilde, 1905. o/p

—The Battle of the bears. London, Eng.: R. Culley, 1907. o/p

OX

YOUNG, Phyliis Brett

—Psyche. Don Mills, Ont.: Longman, 1959. cl $4.50 [no ISBN]
Setting: indeterminate
Kidnapped at the age of two from her rich and adoring parents, Psyche is left for dead by her abductor in a remote mining area. A kind but uneducated couple take her in, and she grows up in an environment which is the antithesis of the one in which she was born. She is vaguely aware that she does not fit in, and, in the end, she is reunited with her parents.

—The Ravine. Don Mills, Ont.: Longman, 1960. o/p

—The Torontonians. Don Mills, Ont.: Longman, 1960. o/p

—Undine. Don Mills, Ont.: Longman, 1964. cl $4.95 [no ISBN] ; Ulverscroft Large Print Series. Glenfield, Leicester, Eng.: F.A. Thorpe

Setting: a country house outside New York City

A highstrung actress marries a widower whose former wife she resembles. Her paranoid state of mind is aggravated by a superstitious neighbour and by the mad artist brother of the dead wife. This psychological thriller ends with a macabre fantasy.

—A Question of judgement. Don Mills, Ont.: Longman, 1969. cl $6.95 [no ISBN]; New York: Putnam

Setting: a New England town

A small town becomes the scene of scandal when a woman drowns. The local schoolteacher manages to piece together what really happened, but conceals this knowledge to protect five of her pupils. This murder mystery ends with an ambiguous triumph of justice.

YOUNG, Scott 1918—

—Scrubs on skates. Toronto: Little, Brown, 1952. cl $3.95 [0-316-97704-7]

Setting: Toronto

When star high school hockey player Pete Gordon is transferred to a new school, he is faced with a new team that lacks a tradition of good hockey. The story tells how Pete and the other boys build up the team.

—Boy on defense. Toronto & Boston: Little, Brown, 1953. cl $5.95 [0-316-977020-0]

Setting: Winnipeg

A young immigrant to Canada and newcomer to hockey, Bill Spunska quickly adapts to both. Young extols the virtues of team spirit, fair play, hard work and respect for one's parents.

—The Flood. 1956. CBL. Toronto: McClelland & Stewart, 1967. pb 95¢ [0-7710-9060-9]

Setting: Winnipeg

Depressed by the death of his wife, Martin Stewart eventually regains self-confidence and his son's respect by helping an emergency crew when Winnipeg is flooded. Harmony is threatened when Martin's son sees him making love to another man's wife. This study of natural disaster and human feelings is more dynamic than Young's other novels.

—Big city office junior. With Astrid Young. Canadian Careers Library. Scarborough, Ont.: McGraw-Hill Ryerson, 1964. o/p

—Boy at the Leafs' camp. Toronto: Little, Brown, 1963. cl $3.95 [0-316-97701-2]

Setting: Peterborough, Ont.

At the Maple Leafs' hockey training camp, Bill Spunska antagonizes a notoriously rough player. After they become friends, Bill unintentionally injures the other boy. Ending happily for all, the novel is simple in plot and style.

—We won't be needing you, Al. Toronto: Ryerson, 1968. o/p

—Face-Off. With George Robertson. Toronto: Macmillan, 1971. cl $6.95 [0-7705-0766-2]

Setting: Toronto

The much-publicized romance of a hockey celebrity and a rock star is the subject of this novel. Sherri's career is ruined when she begins experimenting with hard drugs and breaks up with her clean-cut, violent boyfriend. Ending with Sherri's drug-crazed death, the story pays dubious tribute to the world of hockey.

Title Index

Subject Guide

History:
Early Canada—pioneers
The Depression
World War I
World War II

Nature:
Animals
Terrain

Political life:
Canadian identity
Politics
U.S. influence

Regions:
Atlantic provinces
British Columbia
North
Ontario
Quebec

Prairies
Rural
Small town
Urban

Social life:
Crime
Death
Expatriates
Human sexuality
Immigrants
Jews
Magic
Marriage
Native people
Poverty
Religion
Social class
Technology
Women

EARLY CANADA — PIONEERS

Aubert de Gaspé, Phillippe
Canadians of old

Bird, Will
An Earl must have a wife

Brooke, Frances
The History of Emily Montague

Coburn, Kathleen
The Grandmothers

Conan, Laure
Angéline de Montbrun

Connor, Ralph
Glengarry school days
The man from Glengarry

Cormack, Barbara
Westward ho: 1903

de la Roche, Mazo
Possession

Dunham, (Bertha) Mabel
The Trail of the Conestoga

Green, Henry
A Time to pass over

Grove, Frederick Philip
Fruits of the earth
Settlers of the marsh

Holmes, Abraham S.
Belinda; or, the rivals

Jameson, Anna
Winter studies and summer rambles in Canada

Joliffe, Edward B.
The First hundred

Kirby, William
The Golden dog

Leprohon, Rosanna
Antoinette de Mirecourt

McNamee, James
Them damned Canadians hanged Louis Riel!

Moodie, Susanna
Roughing it in the bush

Packard, Pearl
The Reluctant pioneer

Parker, Gilbert
An Adventurer of the north
Pierre and his people
A Romany of the snows
The Seats of the mighty

Parsons, Nell
Upon a sagebrush harp

Raddall, Thomas
At the tide's turn
His Majesty's Yankees

Roberts, Theodore Goodridge
The Harbour master

Scott, Duncan Campbell
In the village of Viger and other stories
Selected stories
The Witching of Elspie

Shipley, Nancy
The Blonde voyageur
Wild drums

Slater, Patrick
The Yellow briar

Sluman, Norma
Poundmaker

Stead, Robert
The Homesteaders

Sullivan, Alan
Under the northern lights

Traill, Catherine Parr
The Backwoods of Canada
Canadian settler's guide

Trueman, Stuart
The Ordeal of John Gyles

Vaczek, Louis
River and empty sea

Wiebe, Rudy
The Temptations of Big Bear

THE DEPRESSION

Baird, Irene
Waste heritage

Boyle, Harry
Homebrew and patches

Braithwaite, Max
The Night we stole the Mountie's car
Why shoot the teacher?

Brewster, Elizabeth
The Sisters

Callaghan, Morley
Such is my beloved

Craig, John
How far back can you get?

Dewdney, Selwyn
Wind without rain

Frey, Cecelia
Breakaway

Garner, Hugh
Cabbagetown

Glassco, John
Memoirs of Montparnasse

Kroetsch, Robert
The Words of my roaring

Laurence, Margaret
A Bird in the house

McCourt, Edward
Music at the close

Marlyn, John
Under the ribs of death

Ross, Sinclair
As for me and my house

Roy, Gabrielle
The Tin flute

Ryga, George
Hungry hills

WORLD WAR I

Durkin, Douglas
The Magpie

Harrison, Charles Yale
Generals die in bed

Jack, Donald
Three cheers for me

McCourt, Edward
Music at the close

MacLennan, Hugh
Barometer rising
Two Solitudes

Raddall, Thomas
The Nymph and the lamp

Stead, Robert J.C.
Grain

WORLD WAR II

Birney, Earle
Turvey

Buckler, Ernest
The Mountain and the valley

Carrier, Roch
La Guerre, yes sir!

Charney, Ann
Dobryd

Childerhose, R.J.
Splash one tiger

Gallant, Mavis
The Pegnitz Junction

Garner, Hugh
Storm below

Gotlieb, Phyllis
Why should I have all the grief?

Hardy, W.G.
The Unfulfilled

Jacot, Michael
The Last butterfly

Repan, Douglas
The Deserter

Levine, Norman
I don't want to know anyone too well

McCourt, Edward
Music at the close

McDougall, Colin
Execution

MacLennan, Hugh
Two solitudes

Meade, E.
Remember me

O'Connell, A.
The Loveliest and the best

Roy, Gabrielle
The Cashier

Walker, David
The Pillar
Sandy was a soldier's boy

Wiebe, Rudy
Peace shall destroy many

Wilson, Ethel
Hetty Dorval

ANIMALS

Bodsworth, Fred
The Last of the curlews
The Sparrow's fall
The Strange one

Burnford, Sheila
The Incredible journey

Carr, Emily
The House of all sorts
Klee Wyck

Heath, Terence
The Truth and other stories

Markoosie
The Harpoon of the hunter

Grey Owl
A Book of Grey Owl
Sajo and her beaver people
Tales of an empty cabin

Mowat, Farley
The Dog who wouldn't he

Never cry wolf
Owls in the family
A Whale for the killing

O'Hagan, Howard
Tay John
The Woman who got on at Jasper Station

Roberts, Charles G. (See his animal stories)

Schull, Joseph
The Jinker

Seton, Ernest Thompson
The Best of Ernest Thompson Seton
The Biography of a grizzly
The Trail of the Sandhill stag
Wild animals I have known

Sherwood, Roland
Tall tales of the Maritimes

Sullivan, Alan
Under the northern lights

Symons, R.D.
The Broken snare

Thériault, Yves
Ashini

Weatherby, Hugh
Tales the totems tell

TERRAIN

Atwood, Margaret
Surfacing

Bodsworth, Fred
The Sparrow's fall
The Strange one

Buckler, Ernest
The Mountain and the valley

Burnford, Sheila
Mr. Noah and the second flood
One woman's Arctic
Without reserve

Carr, Emily
Klee Wyck

Drew, Wayland
The Wabeno feast

Evans, Hubert
Mist on the river

Fry, Alan
The Revenge of Annie Charlie

Grey Owl
Pilgrims of the wild
Tales from an empty cabin

Grove, Frederick Philip
Fruits of the earth
Over prairie trails

Horwood, Harold
White Eskimo

Houston, James
The White dawn

Jameson, Anna
Winter studies and summer rambles in Canada

Knister, Raymond
Selected stories of Raymond Knister
White narcissus

Moodie, Susanna
Roughing it in the bush

O'Hagan, Howard
Tay John
The Woman who got on at Jasper station

Parsons, Nell
Upon a sagebrush harp

Richardson, E.M.
We keep a light

Roberts, Charles G.D.
The Heart of the ancient wood

Ross, Sinclair
As for me and my house

Roy, Gabrielle
The Cashier
The Hidden mountain
Where nests the water hen

Ryga, George
Hungry Hills

Scott, Duncan Campbell
The Witching of Elpsie

Sharp, Edith
Nkwala

Sherwood, Roland
Tall tales of the Maritimes

Sullivan, Alan
The Rapids

Summers, Merna
The Skating party

Symons, R.D.
Many trails
Where the wagon led

Thériault, Yves
Agaguk
Ashini
N'Tsuk

Trueman, Stuart
The Ordeal of John Gyles

Vaczek, Louis
River and empty sea

Walker, David
Mallabec
Storms of our journey

Wiebe, Rudy
Where is the voice coming from?

Young, Scott
The Flood

CANADIAN IDENTITY

Adams, Ian
The Trudeau papers

Atwood, Margaret
Surfacing

Boyle, Harry
The Great Canadian novel

Carrier, Roch
Floralie, where are you?

Duncan, Sara Jeanette
Cousin Cinderella

Fancott, Edmund
The Shell game

Grove, Frederick Philip
A Search for America

Haliburton, Thomas Chandler
The Old judge
The Sam Slick anthology

Harlow, Robert
Scann

Lee, Robert
Goddamn gypsy

MacLennan, Hugh
Barometer rising
Two solitudes

Powe, Bruce
Killing ground

Richler, Mordecai
The Incomparable Atuk
St. Urbain's horseman

Rohmer, Richard
Ultimatum

Stilman, Abram
Levy

Sullivan, Alan
The Rapids
Under the northern lights

Symons, Scott
Civic Square

POLITICS

Adams, Ian
The Trudeau papers

Aquin, Hubert
Blackout
Prochain épisode

Ardies, Tom
Kosygin is coming
Pandemic
Their man in the White House
This suitcase is going to explode

Baird, Irene
The Climate of power
Waste heritage

Ballem, John
The Dirty scenario

Brennan, Anthony
The Carbon copy

Buller, Herman
Days of rage

Butler, Juan
The Garbageman

Connor, Ralph
The Foreigner

DeMille, James
*A Strange manuscript found in a copper
    cylinder*

Duncan, Sara Jeanette
The Imperialist

Fancott, Edmund
The Shell game

Garner, Hugh
Cabbagetown

Godbout, Jacques
Knife on the table

Godfrey, Dave
The New ancestors

Grey, Francis W.
The Curé of St. Philippe

Haliburton, Thomas Chandler
The Clockmaker
The Letter bag of the Great Western

The Old judge
The Sam Slick anthology
The Season ticket

Hood, Hugh
You can't get there from here

Jasmin, Claude
Ethel and the terrorist

Jolliffe, Edward B.
The First hundred

Koch, Eric
The Leisure riots

McClung, Nellie
The Stream runs fast

MacLennan, Hugh
Return of the sphinx
Two Solitudes
The Watch that ends the night

Mills, John
The October men

Moore, Brian
The Revolution script

Newman, C.J.
A Russian novel

Raddall, Thomas
Roger Sudden

Richler, Mordecai
A Choice of enemies

Rohmer, Richard
Exxoneration
Ultimatum

Stein, David Lewis
Scratch one dreamer

Templeton, Charles
The Kidnapping of the president

Thériault, Yves
Ashini

U.S. INFLUENCE

Adams, Ian
The Trudeau papers

Ballem, John
The Dirty scenario

Blaise, Clarke
A North American education

Boyle, Harry
The Great Canadian novel

De la Roche, Mazo
The Two saplings

Farmiloe, Dorothy
And some in fire

Grove, Frederick Philip
A Search for America

Haliburton, T.C.
The Clockmaker
The Old judge
The Sam Slick anthology
The Season ticket

Hardy, W.G.
The Unfulfilled

Hémon, Louis
Maria Chapdelaine

Koch, Eric
The Leisure riots

Lemelin, Roger
The Town below

Raddall, Thomas
At the tide's turn
Governor's lady
Hangman's Beach
His Majesty's Yankees
Roger Sudden

Rohmer, Richard
Exxoneration
Ultimatum

Sullivan, Alan
The Rapids

ATLANTIC PROVINCES

Bird, Will
Angel Cove
An Earl must have a wife

Brewster, Elizabeth
The Sisters

Buckler, Ernest
The Mountain and the valley
Ox bells and fireflies

Day, Frank Parker
Rockbound

Haliburton, Thomas Chandler
The Clockmaker
The Old judge

Janes, Percy
House of hate

McCulloch, T.
The Stepsure letters

MacLennan, Hugh
Barometer rising
Each man's son

MacPhail, Margaret
Loch Bras d'Or

Nowlan, Alden
Miracle at Indian River

Pinsent, Gordon
John and the missus
The Rowdyman

Raddall, Thomas
At the tide's turn
Hangman's Beach
His Majesty's Yankees
Pride's fancy
Roger Sudden

Richards, David
The Coming of winter

Robert, Theodore Goodridge
The Harbour master

Schull, Joseph
The Jinker

Sherwood, Roland
Atlantic Harbours
Tall tales of the Maritimes

Wilson, Helen Dacey
More tales from Barrett's Landing

BRITISH COLUMBIA

Carr, Emily
The Book of Small
Growing pains
The House of all sorts
Hundreds and thousands
Klee Wyck

Connor, Ralph
Black rock

Glynn-Ward, Hilda
The Writing on the wall

Grainger, M. Allerdale
Woodsmen of the west

Lowry, Malcolm
October ferry to Gabriola

Mills, John
The Land of Is

Symons, R.D.
The Broken snare
Many trails
Where the wagon led

Thomas, Audrey
Munchmeyer and Prospero on the island

Wilson, Ethel
Mrs. Golightly and other stories
Swamp angel

NORTH

Bodsworth, Fred
The Sparrow's fall
The Strange one

Burnford, Sheila
One woman's Arctic

Drew, Wayland
The Wabeno feast

Fry, Alan
Come a long journey

Grey Owl
A Book of Grey Owl
Tales from an empty cabin

Harlow, Robert
Scann

Horwood, Harold
White Eskimo

Houston, James
The White dawn

Kroetsch, Robert
But we are exiles
Gone Indian

Markoosie
The Harpoon of the hunter

Mowat, Farley
The Desperate people
Lost in the Barrens
People of the deer

Richler, Mordecai
The Incomparable Atuk

Sullivan, Alan
Under the northern lights

Symons, R.D.
North by west

Thériault, Yves
Agaguk
Ashini

Wiebe, Rudy
Where is the voice coming from?

ONTARIO

Beattie, Jessie L.
A Season past

Callaghan, Morley
An Autumn penitent

Davies, Robertson
Leaven of malice
A Mixture of Frailties

Moodie, Susanna
Roughing it in the bush

Slater, Patrick
The Yellow briar

QUEBEC

Aquin, Hubert
Blackout
Prochain Episode

Aubert de Gaspé, Phillippe
Canadians of old

Bacque, James
The Lonely ones

Beaulieu, Victor-Lévy
The Grandfathers

Bessette, Gérard
Not for every eye

Blais, Marie-Claire
St. Lawrence blues
A Season in the life of Emmanuel

Blaise, Clarke
A North American education
Tribal justice

Buller, Herman
Days of rage

Carrier, Jean-Guy
My father's house

Carrier, Roch
Floralie where are you?
La Guerre, yes sir!
Is it the sun, Philibert?
They won't demolish me!

Conan, Laure
Angéline de Montbrun

Ferron, Jacques
Dr. Cotnoir
The Juneberry tree
The St. Elias

Godbout, Jacques
Hail Galarneau!
Knife on the table

Hébert, Jacques
The Temple on the river

Hémon, Louis
Maria Chapdelaine

Hood, Hugh
Around the mountain

*The Fruit man, the meat man and the
manager*

Jasmin, Claude
Ethel and the terrorist

Kirby, William
The Golden dog

Lemelin, Roger
The Town below

MacLennan, Hugh
Return of the sphinx
Two solitudes

Mills, John
The October men

Parker, Gilbert
The Seats of the mighty

Peate, Mary
The Girl in the Red River coat

Powe, Bruce
Killing ground

Renaud, Jacques
Flat broke and beat

Scott, Duncan Campbell
In the village of Viger and other stories
Selected stories

Sutherland, Ronald
Lark des neiges

Symons, Scott
Place d'Armes

Thériault, Yves
Agaguk
Ashini
N'Tsuk

PRAIRIES

Bhatia, Jamunadeui
The Latchkey kid

Braithwaite, Max
Why shoot the teacher?

Cormack, Barbara
Westward ho! 1903

Durkin, Douglas
The Magpie

Grove, Frederick Philip
Fruits of the earth
Over prairie trails
Settlers of the marsh
Tales from the margin

Hiebert, Paul
Sarah Binks

Kroetsch, Robert
Gone Indian
Studhorse man
The Words of my roaring

Laurence, Margaret
The Diviners

Livesay, Dorothy
A Winnipeg childhood

McCourt, Edward
Music at the close

McNamee, James
*Them damn Canadians hanged Louis
Riel!*

Mitchell, W.O.
Jake and the kid
The Kite
Who has seen the wind

Ostenso, Martha
Wild Geese

Parsons, Nell
Upon a sagebrush harp

Ross, Sinclair
As for me and my house
The Lamp at noon
Sawbones memorial

Sluman, Norma
Poundmaker

Stead, Robert J.C.
Grain
The Homesteaders

Symons, R.D.
Many trails
Still the wind blows
Where the wagon led

Wiebe, Rudy
Peace shall destroy many
The temptations of Big Bear
Where is the voice coming from?

RURAL

Boyle, Harry J.
Mostly in clover
A Summer burning
With a pinch of sin

Braithwaite, Max
The Night we stole the Mountie's car
Why shoot the teacher?

Bruce, Charles
The Channel shore

Buckler, Ernest
The Mountain and the valley
Ox bells and fireflies

Carrier, Roch
Floralie, where are you?

Coburn, Kathleen
The Grandmothers

Cohen, Matt
The Disinherited

Dantin, Louis
Fanny

Dunham, (Bertha) Mabel
The Trial of the Conestoga

Ferron, Jacques
The Saint Elias

Green, Henry
Diary of a dirty old man
The Praying mantis

Grove, Frederick Philip
Fruits of the earth
Tales from the margin

Hémon, Louis
Maria Chapdelaine

Hughes, (Aubrey) Dean
Along the sideroad

Jolliffe, Edward B.
The First hundred

Kiriak, Illia
Sons of the soil

Knister, Raymond
Selected stories of Raymond Knister

McCulloch, T.
The Stepsure letters

Marquis, Helen
The Longest day of the year

Mitchell, W.O.
Jake and the kid

Montgomery, L.M.
The Golden road
The Story girl

Ostenso, Martha
Wild geese

Ringuet
Thirty acres

Roy, Gabrielle
Where nests the water hen

Ryga, George
Hungry hills

Slater, Patrick
The Yellow briar

Stead, Robert J.C.
Grain
The Homesteaders

Summers, Merna
The Skating party

Symons, R.D.
The Broken snare

SMALL TOWN

Bessette, Gérard
Not for every eye

Bhatia, Jamunadeui
The Latchkey kid

Boyle, Harry J.
A Summer burning
With a pinch of sin

Braithwaite, Max
The Night we stole the Mountie's car
A Privilege and a pleasure

Buckler, Ernest
The Mountain and the valley

Callaghan, Morley
An Autumn penitent

Craig, John
How far back can you get?

Creighton, Luella
Turn east, turn west

Davies, Robertson
Fifth business
Leaven of malice
The Manticore
A mixture of frailties
Tempest-tost

Dobbs, Kildare
Running to paradise

Earl, Lawrence
Risk

Elliott, George
The Kissing man

Epps, Bernard
Pilgarlic the death

Ferron, Jacques
Dr. Cotnoir

Grey, Francis
The Curé of St. Philippe

Harlow, Robert
Scann

Holmes, Abraham S.
Belinda; or, the rivals

Howard, Blanche
The Manipulator

Kroetsch, Robert
The Words of my roaring
Langevin, André
Dust over the city

Laurence, Margaret
A Bird in the house
A Jest of God
The Stone angel

Leacock, Stephen
Sunshine sketches of a little town
Lewis, David
A Lover needs a guitar
McClung, Nellie
Sowing seeds in Danny
Mitchell, W.O.
Who has seen the wind
Montgomery, L.M.
Chronicles of Avonlea
The Anne books
Further chronicles of Avonlea
Kilmeny of the orchard
Mistress Pat
Pat of Silver Bush
Rainbow Valley
Rilla of Ingleside
Munro, Alice
Lives of girls and women

Ross, Sinclair
As for me and my house
Sawbones memorial
Rule, Jane
Against the season
Sullivan, Alan
The Rapids
Torgov, Morley
A good place to come from

URBAN

Aquin, Hubert
The Antiphonary
Blais, Marie-Claire
St. Lawrence blues
Blicker, Seymour
Schmucks
Callaghan, Morley
The Loved and the lost
Carr, Emily
The Book of Small
Carrier, Roch
They won't demolish me!

Cohen, Matt
Columbus and the fat lady
The Disinherited

Ferron, Jacques
Dr. Cotnoir
Garner, Hugh
Silence on the shore
Grove, Frederick Philip
A Search for America
MacEwen, Gwendolyn
Noman
Moore, Brian
An Answer From limbo
Fergus
I am Mary Dunne
The Lonely passion of Judith Hearne
The Luck of Ginger Coffey

Richler, Mordecai
The Apprenticeship of Duddy Kravitz
The Incomparable Atuk
Sutherland, Ronald
Lark des neiges

CRIME

Aquin, Hubert
Blackout
Prochain épisode
Ardies, Tom
Kosygin is coming
Pandemic
Their man in the White House
This suitcase is going to explode
Bruce, John
Breathing space
Buell, John
The Pyx
The Shrewsdale exit
Butler, Juan
Cabbagetown diary: a documentary
Callaghan, Morley
It's never over
The Loved and the lost
The Many coloured coat
More joy in heaven
Morley Callaghan's stories
Strange fugitive
Craig, John
If you want to see your wife again
DeMille, James
The Cryptogram

Fry, Alan
The Revenge of Annie Charlie

Garner, Hugh
The Sin sniper

Godfrey, Dave
The New ancestors

Haliburton, T.C.
The Letter bag of the Great Western

Hébert, Anne
Kamouraska

Knight, David
Farquharson's physique

Miller, Orlo
The Donnellys must die

Mills, John
The Land of Is
The October men

Montrose, David
Gambling with fire

O'Hagan, Howard
The Woman who got on at Jasper Station

Richler, Mordecai
The Apprenticeship of Duddy Kravitz
A Choice of enemies
Cocksure
Saint Urbain's horseman

Ross, Sinclair
A Whir of gold

Ryga, George
Hungry hills

Sears, Dennis T. Patrick
The Lark in the clear air

Templeton, Charles
The Kidnapping of the president

Walker, David
Black Dougal
Devil's Plunge
Mallabec
Pirate Rock
Winter of madness

Young, Phyllis
A Question of judgment

DEATH

Aquin, Hubert
The Antiphonary

Beaulieu, Victor-Lévy
The Grandfathers

Blais, Marie-Claire
David Sterne
St. Lawrence blues

Brandis, Marianne
This spring's sowing

Buckler, Ernest
The Cruelest month
The Mountain and the valley
Ox bells and fireflies

Buell, John
The Pyx
The Shrewsdale exit

Callaghan, Morley
It's never over
Morley Callaghan's stories
They shall inherit the earth

Carrier, Roch
La Guerre, yes sir!

Cohen, Matt
The Disinherited

Craven, Margaret
I heard the owl call my name

DeMille, James
A Strange manuscript found in a copper cylinder

Earl, Lawrence
Risk

Elliott, George
The Kissing man

Epps, Bernard
Pilgarlic the death

Ferron, Jacques
Dr. Cotnoir

Gibson, Graeme
Five legs

Godfrey, Dave
Death goes better with Coca-Cola
The New ancestors

Green, Henry
A Time to pass over

Hébert, Anne
Kamouraska

Helwig, David
The Streets of summer

Hémon, Louis
Maria Chapdelaine

Hunter, Robert
Erebus

Jasmin, Claude
Ethel and the terrorist

Knight, David
Farquharson's physique

Kroetsch, Robert
But we are exiles

Langevin, Andre
Dust over the city

Laurence, Margaret
The Diviners
The Stone angel

Levine, Norman
I don't want to know anyone too well

Lowry, Malcolm
Dark as the grave wherein my friend is laid
Under the volcano

Ludwig, Jack
Above ground

MacEwen, Gwendolyn
King of Egypt, king of dreams

MacLennan, Hugh
The Watch that ends the night

McWhirter, George
Bodyworks

Markoosie
The Harpoon of the hunter

Mitchell, W.O.
Who has seen the wind

Moore, Brian
An Answer from limbo
Fergus
The Lonely passion of Judith Hearne
The Luck of Ginger Coffey

Munro, Alice
Lives of girls and women
Something I've been meaning to tell you

O'Hagan, Howard
The Woman who got on at Jasper Station

Richardson, John
Westbrooke the outlaw

Richler, Mordecai
Son of a smaller hero
St. Urbain's horseman

Rule, Jane
Against the season

Thomas, Audrey
Mrs. Blood

Watson, Sheila
The Double hook

Weinzweig, Helen
Passing ceremony

Wiseman, Adele
The Sacrifice

EXPATRIATES

Callaghan, Morley
That summer in Paris

Gallant, Mavis
The End of the world and other stories
A Fairly good time
My Heart is broken
The Other Paris

Garber, Lawrence
Garber's tales from the Quarter

Glassco, John
Memoirs of Montparnasse

Knight, David
Farquharson's physique

Levine, Norman
From a seaside town

Richler, Mordecai
A Choice of enemies
St. Urbain's horseman

Stilman, Abram
Levy

HUMAN SEXUALITY

Aquin, Hubert
The Antiphonary
Blackout

Ballem, John
The Devil's lighter
The Dirty scenario

Benoit, Jacques
Jos Carbone

Butler, Juan
Cabbagetown diary
The Garbageman

Callaghan, Morley
A Passion in Rome

Cohen, Leonard
The Favourite game

Drew, Wayland
The Wabeno feast

Garber, Lawrence
Garber's tales from the Quarter

Glassco, John
The Fatal woman

Hardy, W.G.
The City of libertines

Knight, David
Farquharson's physique

Knister, Raymond
White narcissus

Koch, Eric
The Leisure riots

Ludwig, Jack
Above ground

McWhirter, George
Bodyworks

Marois, Russell
The Telephone pole

Mosher, Jack
Some would call it adultery

Richler, Mordecai
Cocksure
St. Urbain's horseman

Rule, Jane
Against the season
Desert of the heart
This is not for you

Schull, Joseph
The Jinker

Stein, David Lewis
My sexual and other revolutions

Sutherland, Ronald
Lark des neiges

Symons, Scott
Place d'Armes
Civic Square

Weinzweig, Helen
Passing ceremony

Wiseman, Adele
Crackpot

IMMIGRANTS

Blaise, Clarke
A North American education
Tribal justice

Clarke, Austin
The Meeting point
Storm of fortune
*When he was free and young and he used
  to wear silks*

Coburn, Kathleen
The Grandmothers

Connor, Ralph
The Foreigner

Dobbs, Kildare
Running to paradise

Fielden, Charlotte
Crying as she ran

Glynn-Ward, Hilda
The Writing on the wall

Godfrey, Denis
No Englishman need apply

Grove, Frederick Philip
A Search for America
Tales from the margin

Kiriak, Illia
Sons of the soil

Kreisel, Henry
The Betrayal
The Rich man

Lee, Ronald
Goddam gypsy

MacLennan, Hugh
Each man's son

MacPhail, Margaret
Loch Bras d'Or

Maraville, Simon
Fool's gold

Marlyn, John
Under the ribs of death

Moodie, Susanna
Roughing it in the bush
Life in the clearing

Moore, Brian
An Answer from limbo
The Luck of Ginger Coffey

Robert, Marika
A Stranger and afraid

Stern, Karl
Through dooms of love

Wiebe, Rudy
The Blue mountains of China

JEWS

Bell, Don
Saturday night at the bagel factory

Charney, Ann
Dobryd

Cohen, Leonard
The Favourite game

Gotlieb, Phyllis
Why should I have all the grief?

Fielden Charlotte
Crying as she ran

Graham, Gwethalyn
Earth and high heaven

Jacot, Michael
The Last butterfly

Jasmin, Claude
Ethel and the terrorist

Klein, A.M.
The Second scroll

Kreisel, Henry
The Betrayal
The Rich man

Levine, Norman
From a seaside town
I don't want to know anyone too well

Ludwig, Jack
Confusions
A Woman of her age

Newman, C.J.
We always take care of our own

Richler, Mordecai
The Apprenticeship of Duddy Kravitz
A Choice of enemies
Cocksure
The Incomparable Atuk
St. Urbain's horseman
Son of a smaller hero

Roy, Gabrielle
The Cashier

Stilman, Abram
Levy
Mariette

Torgov, Morley
A Good place to come from

Wiseman, Adele
Crackpot
The Sacrifice

MAGIC

Cohen, Leonard
Beautiful losers

Cohen, Matt
Too bad Galahad

Davies, Robertson
Fifth business
The Manticore

MacEwen, Gwendolyn
King of Egypt, king of dreams
Noman

O'Hagan, Howard
Tay John

Sharp, Edith
Nkwala

Sherwood, Roland
Atlantic harbours

Shipley, Nancy
Wild drums

Symons, R.D.
North by west

Weatherby, Hugh
Tales the totems tell

MARRIAGE

Atwood, Margaret
The Edible woman

Beaulieu, Victor-Lévy
The Grandfathers

Beresford-Howe, Constance
The Book of Eve

Callaghan, Morley
An Autumn penitent
Strange fugitive

Carrier, Roch
Floralie, where are you?

De la Roche, Mazo
Delight
The *Jalna* series

Epps, Bernard
Pilgarlic the death

Grove, Frederick Philip
Settlers of the marsh

Hébert, Anne
Kamouraska

Hémon, Louis
Maria Chapdelaine

Janes, Percy
House of hate

Knight, David
Farquharson's physique

Knister, Raymond
White narcissus

Langevin, André
Dust over the city

Laurence, Margaret
The Fire-dwellers

Lowry, Malcolm
Dark as the grave wherein my friend is laid
October ferry to Gabriola

Ludwig, Jack
Confusions
A Woman of her age

Mirvish, Robert
Holy Loch

Munro, Alice
Lives of girls and women
Something I've been meaning to tell you

Raddall, Thomas
At the tide's turn

Reid, John
Horses with blindfolds

Ross, Sinclair
As for me and my house
The Lamp at noon

Roy, Gabrielle
The Cashier

Scott, Duncan Campbell
In the village of Viger and other stories

Sears, Dennis T. Patrick
The Lark in the clear air

Summers, Merna
The Skating party

Thériault, Yves
Agaguk
N'Tsuk

Thomas, Audrey
Mrs. Blood
Munchmeyer and Prospero on the island
Songs my mother taught me

Weinzweig, Helen
Passing ceremony

Wilson, Ethel
The Equations of love
Hetty Dorval
Swamp angel

NATIVE PEOPLE

Bacque, James
A Man of talent

Ballem, John
The Dirty scenario

Bodsworth, Fred
The Sparrow's fall
The Strange one

Burnford, Sheila
One woman's Arctic
Without reserve

Butler, Juan
Cabbagetown diary: a documentary

Carr, Emily
Klee Wyck

Cormack, Barbara
Westward ho! 1903

Craig, John
Zach

Craven, Margaret
I heard the owl call my name

Cutler, Ebbitt
The Last noble savage

Drew, Wayland
The Wabeno feast

Evans, Hubert
Mist on the river

Forer, Mort
The Humback

Fry, Alan
Come a long journey
How a people die
The Revenge of Annie Charlie

Grey Owl
A Book of Grey Owl
Tales of an empty cabin

Hepworth, R. Gordon
The Making of a chief

Horwood, Harold
White Eskimo

Houston, James
The White dawn

Jameson, Anna
*Winter studies and summer rambles in
    Canada*

McNamee, James
Them damn Canadians hanged Louis Riel!

Markoosie
Harpoon of the hunter

Mitchell, W.O.
The Vanishing point

Mosher, Jack
Some would call it adultery

O'Hagan, Howard
Tay John

Parker, Gilbert
An Adventurer of the north
Pierre and his people
A Romany of the snows

Raddall, Thomas
Roger Sudden

Richardson, John
Wacousta, or the prophecy

Richler, Mordecai
The Incomparable Atuk

Roy, Gabrielle
Windflower

Scott, Duncan Campbell
In the village of Viger and other stories
Selected stories

Sharp, Edith
Nkwala

Shipley, Nancy
Almighty voice and the red coats
The Railway builders
Wild drums

Sluman, Norma
Poundmaker

Such, Peter
Riverrun

Sullivan, Alan
Under the northern lights

Symons, R.D.
North by west
Still the wind blows

Thériault, Yves
Agaguk
Ashini
N'Tsuk

Trueman, Stuart
The Ordeal of John Gyles

Vaczek, Louis
River and empty sea

Weatherby, Hugh
Tales the totems tell

Wiebe, Rudy
Peace shall destroy many
The Temptations of Big Bear

York, Thomas
We, the wilderness

Young, Egerton R.
Stories from Indian wigwams and northern campfires

POVERTY

Baird, Irene
Waste heritage

Blais, Marie-Claire
The Manuscripts of Pauline Archange
A Season in the life of Emmanuel

Blaise, Clarke
Tribal justice

Butler, Juan
Cabbagetown diary: a documentary

Callaghan, Morley
Such is my beloved

Carrier, Roch
They won't demolish me!

Dantin, Louis
Fanny

Davies, Peter
Fly away Paul

Dickson, Barry
Home safely to me

Fennario, David
Without a parachute

Fry, Alan
How a people die

Garner, Hugh
Cabbagetown
The Sin sniper

Green, Henry
A Time to pass over

Ladoo, Harold
No pain like this body
Yesterdays

Laurence, Margaret
The Tomorrow-tamer

Lemelin, Roger
The Town below

Levine, Norman
From a seaside town

Moore, Brian
The Lonely passion of Judith Hearne
The Luck of Ginger Coffey

Nowlan, Alden
Miracle at Indian River

Richler, Mordecai
The Apprenticeship of Duddy Kravitz
Son of a smaller hero

Roberts, Theodore Goodridge
The Harbour master

Ross, Sinclair
Whir of gold

Sandman, John
Eating out

Stringer, Arthur
The Loom of destiny

Wilson, Ethel
The Equations of love

Wilson, Helen Dacey
More tales from Barrett's Landing

RELIGION

Aquin, Hubert

Peace shall destroy many
Wiseman, Adele
The Sacrifice
Young, Egerton
Stories from Indian wigwams and northern campfires

SOCIAL CLASS

Adams, Ian
The Trudeau papers
Aubert de Gaspé, Philippe
Canadians of old
Baird, Irene
Waste heritage
Blais, Marie-Claire
St. Lawrence blues
Buller, Herman
Days of rage
Butler, Juan
Cabbagetown diary
The Garbageman
Callaghan, Morley
The Loved and the lost
More joy in heaven
Such is my beloved
Carrier, Roch
They won't demolish me!
Clarke, Austin
The Meeting point
Storm of fortune
Garner, Hugh
Cabbagetown
Graham, Gwethalyn
Earth and high heaven
Hébert, Jacques
The Temple on the river
Jasmin, Claude
Ethel and the terrorist
Langevin, André
Dust over the city
Lemelin, Roger
The Town below
Ludwig, Jack
A Woman of her age
McCourt, E.A.
Music at the close
MacLennan, Hugh
Each man's son

Marcotte, Gilles
Burden of God
Mitchell, Ken
Wandering Rafferty
Renaud, Jacques
Flat broke and beat
Richler, Mordecai
The Apprenticeship of Duddy Kravitz
Schull, Joseph
The Jinker
Stein, David L.
My sexual and other revolutions
Symons, Scott
Place d'Armes
Civic Square

TECHNOLOGY

Adams, Ian
The Trudeau papers
Ballem, John
The Devil's lighter
Franklin, Stephen
Knowledge Park
Godfrey, Dave
The New ancestors
Grove, Frederick Philip
The Master of the mill
Koch, Eric
The Leisure riots
Powe, Bruce
The Last days of the American Empire
Schroeder, Andreas
The Late man
Shipley, Nan
The Railway builders
Simpson, Leo
Arkwright
The Peacock papers
Stead, Robert J.C.
Grain
Sullivan, Alan
The Rapids
Willer, Jim
Paramind

WOMEN

Atwood, Margaret
The Edible woman

Baird, Irene
Waste heritage

Ballem, John
The Devil's lighter
The Dirty scenario

Bhatia, Jamunadeui
The Latchkey kid

Blais, Marie-Claire
St. Lawrence blues

Butler, Juan
Cabbagetown diary

Callaghan, Morley
It's never over

Carrier, Roch
Floralie, where are you?

Dantin, Louis
Fanny

Davies, Robertson
A Mixture of frailties

Engel, Marian
The Honeyman Festival
Monodromos
Sarah Bastard's notebook

Farmiloe, Dorothy
And some in fire

Glassco, John
The Fatal woman

Harvor, Beth
Women and children

Hémon, Louis
Maria Chapdelaine

Laurence, Margaret
The Diviners
The Fire-dwellers
A Jest of God
The Stone angel

Ludwig, Jack
A Woman of her age

McClung, Nellie
The Stream runs fast

Moore, Brian
I am Mary Dunne
The Lonely passion of Judith Hearne

Munro, Alice
Dance of the happy shades
Lives of girls and women
Something I've been meaning to tell you

Newman, C.J.
A Russian novel

Rule, Jane
Desert of the heart
Theme for diverse instruments

Roy, Gabrielle
Windflower

Shipley, Nan
The Blonde voyageur
Wild drums

Thériault, Yves
N'Tsuk

Thomas, Audrey
Blown figures
Mrs. Blood

Wilson, Ethel
The Equations of love
Hetty Dorval
Swamp angel

Wiseman, Adele
Crackpot

In-print collections of short stories by more than one author are listed here by title and annotated. Collections of short stories written by one author are listed under that author's entry in the novels section. The contents of each anthology are listed after the annotation. There are indexes by short story title and by author at the end of the section. The author index does not include foreign authors appearing in the anthologies, and the title index does not include untitled excerpts from longer works, although these are listed in the main section.

ABCS	A Book of Canadian stories
BCP	The Book of Canadian prose, vol. 1 (The Colonial century)
CL	Canadian literature
CSS	Canadian short stories
CSS2	Canadian short stories, 2nd series
CSS(K)	The Canadian short story, Kilgallin, ed.
CWT	Canadian winter's tales
CV	Contemporary voices
FSH	Fourteen stories high
GCSS	Great Canadian short stories
K	Kaleidescope
KI	Klanak Islands
MCS	Modern Canadian stories
NV	The Narrative voice
72NCS	72: New Canadian stories
73NCS	73: New Canadian stories
74NCS	74: New Canadian stories
SBT	Sixteen by twelve
SFO	Stories from Ontario
SFAC	Stories from Atlantic Canada
SFPAC	Stories from Pacific and Arctic Canada
SFQ	Stories from Quebec
SFWC	Stories from western Canada
TCC	The Canadian century (The Book of Canadian Prose, vol. 2)
TCE	The Canadian experience (shortened version of the Book of Canadian prose, vols. 1 & 2)
TSM	The Story-makers
TSSF	The Story so far
TSSF2	The Story so far 2
TSSF3	The Story so far 3
TS	Tigers of the snow
WS	Winnipeg stories

Short Story Anthology Annotations

The Book of Canadian prose: volume I. Early beginnings to Confederation. A.J.M. Smith, ed. Toronto: W.J. Gage, 1965. cl $7.25 [0-7715-1175-2]; pb title: **The Colonial century: English-Canadian writing before Confederation.** 1973. pb $4.85 [0-7715-1174-4]

A survey of the early literature of Canada, this volume includes excerpts from the journals of explorers, fur-traders and travellers, selections from memoirs and letters of famous Canadians and pieces from the works of Frances Brooke, Susanna Moodie and the Nova Scotian humorist, Thomas Chandler Haliburton. The collection provides an interesting overview of the origins of Canadian literary interest. (The following list includes fiction titles only.)

Brooke, Frances Moore: from *The History of Emily Montague:* "Colonel Rivers' impressions of Canada", "An English belle in Quebec", "A British Tory on the Canadians, the Americans, and the savages"

Haliburton, Thomas Chandler: from *The Clockmaker* (First Series): "The Clockmaker's opinion of Halifax", "The American eagle", "Mr. Slick's opinion of the British", "The White Nigger"; from *The Clockmaker* (Second Series): "Canadian Politics", "English aristocracy and Yankee mobocracy"

Moodie, Susanna: from *Roughing it in the bush:* "The Fever of immigration" (from the Introduction), "Uncle Joe and his family"

The Book of Canadian prose: volume II. See **The Canadian century**

A Book of Canadian stories. Desmond Pacey, ed. 1947. Toronto: McGraw-Hill Ryerson, 1962. pb $3.95 [0-7700-6-18-8]

The revised edition of this established text omits the Indian stories in translation (though without a parallel revision of the Introduction), and some other early pieces, and includes several more contemporary stories. The time span of the thirty stories in this collection remains, however, early nineteenth century to the present. The selection focuses relentlessly on the land and, except in the most recent pieces, the dominant theme is man's struggle with nature, as though the stories had been chosen specifically for their theme rather than for literary merit or their illustration of an author's methods. Questions for discussion are included at the end.

Bird, Will R.: "The Movies come to Gull Point"

Buckler, Ernest: "The First born son"

Callaghan, Morley: "The Blue kimono"

de la Roche, Mazo: "Come fly with me"

Duncan, Norman: "The Fruits of toil"

Garner, Hugh: "One, two, three little Indians"

Grove, F.P.: "Snow"

Gustafson, Ralph: "The Pigeon"

Haliburton, Thomas Chandler: "Sam Slick the clockmaker"

Howe, Joseph: "The Locksmith of Philadelphia"

Knister, Raymond: "The Strawstack"

Kreisel, Henry: "Two Sisters in Geneva"

Layton, Irving: "A Plausible story"

Leacock, Stephen: "The Speculations of Jefferson Thorpe"

Ludwig, Jack: "Requiem for Bibul"

Moodie, Susanna: "Old Woodruff and his three wives"

Moore, Brian: "Lion of the afternoon"

Munro, Alice: "Sunday afternoon"

Nowlan, Alden: "True confession"

Pacey, Desmond: "The Boat"

Pickthall, Marjorie: "The Worker in sandalwood"

Raddall, Thomas H.: "The Amulet"

Richler, Mordecai: "Benny"

Roberts, Charles G.D.: " 'The Young ravens that call upon him' "

Ross, Sinclair: "The Lamp at noon"

Scott, Duncan Campbell: "Paul Farlotte"

Thomson, Edward W.: "The Privilege of the limits"

Walker, David: "Storms of our journey"

Wilson, Ethel: "Hurry, hurry!"

The Canadian century. English-Canadian writing since Confederation. Also known as **The Book of Canadian prose, volume II.** A.J.M. Smith, ed. Toronto: W.J. Gage, 1973. cl $12.95 [0-7715-1176-0]; pb $6.95 [0-7715-1178-9]

A.J.M. Smith has divided his material into two major historical periods: 1816-1914 and 1914 to the present. In the introduction, he argues that the spirit of the earlier period is best reflected in the prose and fiction concerned with the new political and social institutions. The second period, being one of simultaneous world change and national maturation, has produced a literature that is growing more analytic, symbolic and experimental. Biographical information prefaces each selection, and an appendix of selected critical bibliographies for each author is included. Smith's scope allows for a general picture of the context in which stylistic trends have developed. (The following list includes fiction titles only.)

Callaghan, Morley: from *A Native argosy:* "Ancient Lineage"; "Predicament"; excerpt from *That summer in Paris*

Cohen, Leonard: excerpt from *The Favourite game*

Davies, Robertson: excerpt from *A Mixture of frailties*

Garner, Hugh: "One, two, three little Indians"

Glassco, John: "A Season in limbo"

Godfrey, Dave: "The Hard-headed collector"

Grove, F.P.: from *A Search for America:* "I come in contact with humanity again"

Hood, Hugh: "The End of it"

Klein, A.M.: from *The Second scroll:* "On first seeing the ceiling of the Sistine Chapel

Laurence, Margaret: "A Queen in Thebes"

Leacock, Stephen: "The Great election in Missinaba County"; "The Candidacy of Mr. Smith"; "The Rival churches of St. Asaph and St. Osoph"

Lowry, Malcolm: "Through the Panama"

Ludwig, Jack: "Requiem for Bibul"

MacLennan, Hugh: excerpt from *The Watch that ends the night*

Mitchell, W.O.: from *Who has seen the wind:* "Saint Sammy"

Munro, Alice: "The Dance of the happy shades"

O'Hagan, Howard: from *Tay John:* "The Fight with the bear"

Raddall, Thomas: "Bald eagle"

Richler, Mordecai: "Mortimer Griffin, Shalinsky, and how they settled the Jewish question"

Roberts, Charles G.D.: "The Watchers in the swamp"

Ross, Sinclair: "The Painted door"

Watson, Sheila: "Antigone"

Whalley, George: "The Legend of John Hornby"

Wilson, Ethel: from *The Innocent traveller:* "The Innumerable laughter"

The Canadian experience: a brief survey of English-Canadian prose. Toronto: W.J. Gage, 1973. pb $2.95 [0-7715-1177-9]

This is a slightly shortened, one-volume version of *The Book of Canadian prose* (see above). It is a chronological view of Canadian prose as represented by outstanding writers from Haliburton to Alice Munro. (The following list includes fiction titles only.)

Brooke, Frances Moore: from *The History of Emily Montague:* "Colonel Rivers' impressions of Canada", "An English belle in Quebec"

Callaghan, Morley: from *A Native argosy:* "Ancient lineage"; "A Predicament"

Duncan, Sara Jeannette: from *The Imperialist:* "The Orator from England"

Garner, Hugh: "One, two, three little Indians"

Grove, F.P.: from *A Search for America:* "I come in contact with humanity again"

Haliburton, Thomas Chandler: from *The Clockmaker* (First Series): "The American eagle", "The White Nigger"

Laurence, Margaret: "A Queen in Thebes"

Leacock, Stephen: from *Sunshine sketches of a little town:* "The Great election in Missinaba County", "The Candidacy of Mr. Smith"

Ludwig, Jack: "Requiem for Bibul"

MacLennan, Hugh: excerpt from *The Watch that ends the night*

Mitchell, W.O.: from *Who has seen the wind:* "Saint Sammy"

Moodie, Susanna: from *Roughing it in the bush:* "Uncle Joe and his family"

Munro, Alice: "The Dance of the happy shades"

O'Hagan, Howard: from *Tay John:* "The Fight with the bear"

Radall, Thomas H.: "Bald Eagle"

Richler, Mordecai: "Mortimer Griffin, Shalinsky, and how they settled the Jewish question"

Roberts, Charles G.D.: from *Wisdom of the Wilderness*: "The Watchers of the swamp"

Whalley, George: "The Legend of John Hornby"

Wilson, Ethel: from *The Innocent traveller:* "The Innumerable laughter"

Canadian literature: two centuries in prose.
Brita Mickleburgh, ed. Toronto: McClelland & Stewart, 1973. pb $3.95 [0-7710-5823-3]

(See Secondary Sources section for a full annotation.) Much of this book consists of excerpts from well-known novels which are annotated in the Novel Annotations section. Authors so excerpted are Frances Brooke, Susanna Moodie, James de Mille, Ralph Connor, Lucy M. Montgomery, Martha Ostenso, Mazo de la Roche, Emily Carr, Hugh MacLennan, Sinclair Ross, Gabrielle Roy, Robertson Davies, Marie-Claire Blais, Mordecai Richler, Brian Moore, Morley Callaghan, Leonard Cohen, Farley Mowat, Margaret Laurence and Percy Janes. The following is a list of the short stories included:

Garner, Hugh: "E equals MC squared"

Grove, F.P.: "The Desert"

Haliburton, Thomas Chandler: "The Wrong room"

Johnson, E. Pauline: "The Two sisters"

Leacock, Stephen: "Bass fishing on Lake Simcoe"

Lowry, Malcolm: "The Present state of Pompeii"

Parker, Gilbert: "The Stone"

Raddall, Thomas: "The Wedding gift"

The Canadian short story. Anthony Raymond Kilgallin, ed. Toronto: Holt Rinehart and Winston, 1971. pb $1.75 [0-03-923380-4]

Clearly designed as a teaching guide, this anthology contains five stories by Hugh Hood, David Helwig, John Metcalf, Mordecai Richler and Malcolm Lowry. The introduction discusses the nature of Canadian literature and of the short story genre. Kilgallin also outlines the history of the Canadian short story and speculates on its future. Each story is preceded by a brief biographical and critical introduction.

Helwig, David: "Something for Olivia's scrapbook I guess"

Hood, Hugh: "Flying a red kite"

Lowry, Malcolm: "Strange comfort afforded by the profession"

Metcalf, John: "The Happiest days"

Richler, Mordecai: "Some grist for Mervyn's mill"

Canadian short stories. Robert Weaver, ed. 1960. Toronto: Oxford University Press, 1966. pb $2.95 [0-19-540134-X]

Including three French-Canadian stories in translation, the twenty-seven stories in this anthology represent an attempt at a comprehensive survey of Canadian short fiction. Certainly two-thirds of these stories have been extensively anthologized since the first appearance of Robert Weaver's collection, which seems to have become a milestone in Canadian short story publishing.

Callaghan, Morley: "Last spring they came over"; "A Sick call"

Gallant, Mavis: "The Legacy"

Garner, Hugh: "One, two, three little Indians"

Grove, F.P.: "Snow"

Gustafson, Ralph: "The Pigeon"

Hébert, Anne: "The House on the esplanade"

Kennedy, Leo: "A Priest in the family"

Knister, Raymond: "Mist-green oats"

Layton, Irving: "Vacation in La Voiselle"

Leacock, Stephen: "The Marine excursion of the Knights of Pythias"

Lemelin, Roger: "The Stations of the Cross"

Lowry, Malcolm: "The Bravest boat"

Marshall, Joyce: "The Old woman"

Mitchell, W

Mitchell, W.O. : "The Owl and the Bens"

Munro, Alice: "The Time of death"

Page, P.K.: "The Green bird"

Raddall, Thomas H.: "Blind MacNair"

Reaney, James: "The Bully"

Richler, Mordecai: "Benny, the war in Europe and Myerson's daughter Bella"

Ringuet: "The Heritage"

Ross, Sinclair: "The Painted door"

Roberts, Charles G.D.: "Strayed"

Scott, Duncan Campbell: "Paul Farlotte"

Spettigue, Douglas: "The Haying"

Thomson, E.W.: "The Privilege of the limits"

Wilson, Ethel: "Mrs. Golightly and the first convention"

Canadian short stories. Second series.
Robert Weaver, ed. Toronto: Oxford University Press, 1968. cl $6.50 [0-19-540133-6] ; pb $3.25 [0-19-540134-4]

This selection of stories mainly by younger writers popular in the 1950s and 1960s complements Weaver's *Canadian short stories* (1960). Included are several longer pieces which do not usually find their way into anthologies.

Callaghan, Morley: from *A Native argosy:* "Ancient lineage"

Faessler, Shirley: "Maybe later it will come back to my mind"

Gallant, Mavis: "Bernadette"; "My heart is broken"

Garner, Hugh: "E equals MC squared"; "Hunky"

Godfrey, Dave: "River Two Blind Jacks"; "Newfoundland night"

Helwig, David: "Something for Olivia's scrapbook I guess"

Hood, Hugh: "Flying a red kite"; "Getting to Williamstown"

Laurence, Margaret: "A Gourdful of glory"

Ludwig, Jack: "A Woman of her age"

Munro, Alice: "The Dance of the happy shades"; "The Peace of Utrecht"

Richler Mordecai: "Some grist for Mervyn's mill"; "This year at the Arabian Nights Hotel"

Wilson, Ethel: "Haply the soul of my grandmother"

Canadian winter's tales. Norman Levine, ed. Toronto: Macmillan, 1968. cl $4.95 [0-7705-0784-0] ; 1973 pb $2.50 [0-7705-0998-3]

Nine stories, chiefly from the sixties, include the original short story, "Under the volcano", by Malcolm Lowry, "A Bird in the house", by Margaret Laurence, and Mordecai Richler's "Playing ball on Hampstead Heath". Other established fiction writers complete this basic collection of good Canadian short stories.

Callaghan, Morley: "It must be different"

Gallant, Mavis: "The End of the world"

Hood, Hugh: "The End of it"

Laurence, Margaret: "A Bird in the house"

Levine, Norman: "I'll bring you back something nice"

Lowry, Malcolm: "Under the volcano"

Moore, Brian: "Uncle T"

Richler, Mordecai: "Playing ball on Hampstead Heath"

Wilson, Ethel: "Mr. Sleepwalker" .

Contemporary voices. The short story in Canada. Donald Stephens, ed. Toronto: Prentice Hall, 1972. cl $5.00 [0-13-171314-0]; pb $2.95 [0-13-171306-X]

Less contemporary than its title suggests, this collection of fifteen strong, and in many cases familiar stories, incorporates a wide variety of styles. Malcolm Lowry's "The Forest path to the spring" is in fine contrast to Dave Godfrey's "Kwame bird lady day", while Mordecai Richler's "This year at the Arabian Nights Hotel" adds to the rather cosmopolitan flavour of this anthology.

Callaghan, Morley: "Let me promise you"

Gallant, Mavis: "My heart is broken"

Garner, Hugh: "Red racer"

Godfrey, Dave: "Kwame bird lady day"

Helwig, David: "Something for Olivia's scrapbook I guess"

Hood, Hugh: "After the sirens"

Laurence, Margaret: "Horses of the night"

Levine, Norman: "A True story"

Lowry, Malcolm: "The Forest path to the spring"

Munro, Alice: "The Time of death"

Nowlan, Alden: "There was an old woman from Wexford"

Richler, Mordecai: "This year at the Arabian Nights Hotel"

Rule, Jane: "Theme for diverse instruments"

Thomas, Audrey: "Aquarius"

Wilson, Ethel: "Haply the soul of my grandmother"

Fourteen stories high: best Canadian stories of 1971. David Helwig and Tom Marshall, eds. Ottawa: Oberon Press, 1971. pb $2.95 [0-88750-047-1]

The authors of this exciting group of stories are among Canada's best. All areas of the country are represented and a variety of styles employed.

Bailey, Don: "A Few notes for Orpheus"

Bowering, George: "Apples"

Engel, Marian: "Amaryllis"

Garner, Hugh: "The Happiest man in the world"

Gotlieb, Phyllis: "The Military hospital"

Keeling, Nora: "Agathe"

Levine, Norman: "In Quebec City"

MacEwen, Gwendolyn: "House of the whale"

Nowlan, Alden: "The Coming of age"

Schroeder, Andreas: "The Late man"

Scobie, Stephen: "The White sky"

Spettigue, D.O.: "Pity the poor piper"

Thompson, Kent: "Still life composition: woman's clothes"

Wiebe, Rudy: "Where is the voice coming from?"

Great Canadian Short Stories. Alec Lucas, ed. New York: Dell, 1971. pb 95¢

This selection is drawn from the work of Canada's best-known writers of the past 150 years. The stories encompass a wide variety of settings and themes, and except for an experiment in verbal association by Ray Smith represent the mainstream in Canadian writing.

Blaise, Clark: "Notes beyond a history"

Callaghan, Morley: "One spring night"
Gallant, Mavis: "Acceptance of their ways"
Garner, Hugh: "A Trip for Mrs. Taylor"
Godfrey, Dave: "The Hard-headed collector"
Grove, F.P.: "Snow"
Haliburton, Thomas Chandler: excerpt
from "How many fins has a cod?"
Hébert, Anne: "The House on the esplanade"
Hood, Hugh: "Three halves of a house"
Laurence, Margaret: "A Gourdful of glory"
Layton, Irving: "Unemployed"
Leacock, Stephen: "The Speculations of
Jefferson Thorpe"
Lowry, Malcolm: "Under the volcano"
Ludwig, Jack: "Requiem for Bibul"
McConnell, William C.: "Love in the park"
Metcalf, John: "Keys and watercress"
Moore, Brian: "Uncle T."
Munro, Alice: "The Office"
Richler, Mordecai: "Playing ball on Hamp-
stead Heath"
Roberts, Charles G.D.: "When twilight falls
on the stump lots"
Ross, Sinclair: "The Painted door"
Roy, Gabrielle: "Wilhelm"
Scott, Duncan Campbell: "Labrie's wife"
Smith, Ray: "The Dwarf in his valley ate
codfish"
Thériault, Yves: "Anguish of God"
Thomson, Edward William: "The Privilege
of the limits"
Wilson, Ethel: "Mrs. Golightly and the first
convention"

Kaleidoscope. John Metcalf, ed. Toronto:
Van Nostrand Reinhold, 1972. pb $3.50;
school text $2.50 [0-442-25319-2]

Illustrated with striking photographs by
John de Visser, these short stories vary
widely in subject and setting. They provide
a useful introduction to the many variations
on the conventional form of the short story
and are good examples of the writing of
some of the best fiction writers in Canada.
Included are pieces by Margaret Laurence,
Hugh Garner, Sinclair Ross, Morley Callaghan and Mordecai Richler. Biographical
information and a selected bibliography
are provided for each author.

Callaghan, Morley: "An old quarrel"
Garner, Hugh: "The Moose and the sparrow"
Helwig, David: "Streetcar, streetcar, wait
for me"
Hood, Hugh: "After the sirens"
Laurence, Margaret: "To set our house in
order"
Metcalf, John: "Early morning rabbits"
Moore, Brian: "Off the track"
Munro, Alice: "Day of the butterfly"

Richler, Mordecai: "Pinky's squealer"
Ross, Sinclair: "One's a heifer"
Stein, David Lewis: "The Huntsman"
Thompson, Kent: "Professor Kingblatt's
prediction"

Klanak Islands. Eight short stories. Henry
Kreisel, Alice McConnell and William C.
McConnell, eds. Vancouver: Klanak Press,
1959. pb $2.50

Illustrated with sketches by Vancouver
artists, this short collection is made up of
contributions from Western and Vancouver writers.

Harlow, Robert: "The Sound of a horn"
Hull, Raymond: "Play, fellow"
Kreisel, Henry: "Homecoming"
McConnell, Alice: "The Apricot story"
McConnell, William: "Love in the park"
Mills, Margaret: "The Present"
Rule, Jane: "A Walk by himself"
Smith, Marion: "The Simple truth"

Modern Canadian Stories. Giose Rimanelli
and Roberto Ruberto, eds. Scarborough,
Ont.: McGraw-Hill Ryerson, 1966. cl $8.95
[0-7700-0129-7] ; 1973 pb $4.95
[0-07-092973-4]

Aiming at "the recognition of a literature
which stands on its own", this anthology
contains thirty-one stories by twenty-three
major twentieth-century Canadian writers
and a critical introduction which establishes
the range and rank of the chosen authors.
Duncan Campbell Scott is presented as the
initiator of an independent Canadian voice,
but the collection is dominated by Malcolm
Lowry's sixty-page piece, "The Forest path
to the spring". Three stories each by Leacock and Callaghan, two each from Sinclair
Ross, Hugh Garner and John Metcalf, make
up the balance of the collection, which
also includes a striking novella by Daphne
Buckle.

Bowering, George: "Time and again"
Buckle, Daphne: "The Sea-haven"
Buckler, Ernest: "The Harness"
Callaghan, Morley: "A Sick call";
"Two fishermen"; "The Cheat's
remorse"
de la Roche, Mazo: "The Celebration"
Garner, Hugh: "One, two, three little
Indians"; "The Yellow sweater"
Grove, F.P.: "Snow"
Hood, Hugh: "Flying a red kite"
Kreisel, Henry: "Two sisters in Geneva"
Laurence, Margaret: "To set our house in
order"
Layton, Irving: "Piety"
Leacock, Stephen: "My remarkable

uncle"; "The Hallucination of Mr.
Butt"; "The Retroactive existence
of Mr. Juggins"
Lowry, Malcolm: "The Forest path to the
spring"
MacLennan, Hugh: "An Orange from Por-
tugal"
Metcalf, John: "The Happiest days";
"A Process of time"
Moore, Brian: "Off the track"
Munro, Alice: "The Time of death"
Nowlan, Alden: "The Guide"
Richler, Mordecai: "The Summer my grand-
mother was supposed to die"
Ross, Sinclair: "The Lamp at noon";
"The Painted door"
Scott, Duncan Campbell: "Labrie's wife"
Wilson, Ethel: "I just love dogs"; "Till
death us do part"
Wiseman, Adele: "A Mouthful of tongue"

**The Narrative voice: short stories and
reflections by Canadian authors.** John
Metcalf, ed. Scarborough, Ont.: McGraw-
Hill Ryerson, 1972. $4.50 [0-07-092791-X]
This strong anthology combines two stories
and an essay by each contributor, except
the last, Harry Bruce, whose three brief
pieces link the short story with personal
journalism. This juxtaposition of practice
and theory illuminates the detail of the
stories and suggests topics for classroom
discussion.
Blaise, Clark: "A North American education"; "Eyes"
Bruce, Harry: "The Courtship of Edith
Long"; "The Bad Samaritan down at
the railroad station"; "The Last
walk"
Faessler, Shirley: "Henye"; "Maybe later
it will come back to my mind"
Helwig, David: "Presences"; "Things that
happened before you were born"
Hood, Hugh: "Socks"; "Boots"
Laurence, Margaret: "The Loons"; "To
set our house in order"
Metcalf, John: "The Children green and
golden"; "Robert, standing"
Munro, Alice: "Images"; "Dance of the
happy shades"
Smith, Ray: "A Cynical tale"; "Peril"
Thompson, Kent: "The Problems of a
truancy"; "Because I am drunk"
Wiebe, Rudy: "Millstone for the sun's
day"; "Where is the voice coming
from?"

72: New Canadian stories. David Helwig
and Joan Harcourt, eds. Ottawa: Oberon,
1972. pb. $2.95 [0-99750-067-6]
This collection of twelve previously unpublished short stories is a mixed bag of
writing ranging from the conventional to
the obscurely experimental. It includes a
high proportion of poets among its authors,
and many of the stories are short, highly
impressionistic pieces.
Atwood, Margaret: "The Grave of the
famous poet"
Bailey, Don: "A Bauble for Bernice"
Fox, Gail: "The Man who killed Hemingway"
Harvor, Beth: "Magicians"
Keeling, Nora: "The Year"
McFadden, David: "Who can avoid a place?"
McWhirter, George: "The Harbinger"
Newlove, John: "The Story of a cat"
Rule, Jane: "Brother and sister"
Sandman, John: "One for the road"
Schroeder, Andreas: "The Mill"
Simpson, Leo: "The Ferris wheel"

73: New Canadian stories. David Helwig and
Joan Harcourt, eds. Ottawa: Oberon, 1973.
pb $3.50 [0-88750-089-7]
These twelve stories vary in setting, situation, and length. Love, marriage and
marital separation tend to be emphasized
and three of the stories concern World
War II. With one or two exceptions these
are skillfully told, conventionally realistic
stories. One of the three less well-known
contributors, Wayland Drew, has written a
haunting portrait of an old immigrant
woman who clings tenaciously to life and
to the memories of her husband's martyr-
dom in the war.
Carrier, Jean-Guy: "A Strangeness of habit,
a twist of mind"
Cohen, Matt: "Amazing grace"
Drew, Wayland: "Homage to Axel Hoeniger"
Garner, Hugh: "Losers weepers"
Harvor, Beth: "Countries"
Hood, Hugh: "Dark glasses"
Horwood, Harold: "The Shell collector"
Marshall, Joyce: "A Private place"
Metcalf, John: "The Strange aberration of
Mr. Ken Smythe"
Simpson, Leo: "The Savages"
Summers, Merna: "The Blizzard"
Zieroth, Dale: "Jeremey, his arrangements"

74: New Canadian stories. David Helwig
and Joan Harcourt, eds. Ottawa: Oberon,
1974. cl $6.95 [0-88750-126-5]; pb $3.50
[0-88750-127-3]
This excellent collection of stories set
primarily in Canada presents a balanced
mixture of humour, the exotic and the

mundane. Many of the characters are verging on insanity although their behaviour appears, on the surface, to be rational. Stories by familiar and new writers are included.

Cohen, Matt: "The Secret"
Drew, Wayland: "Wood"
Euringer, Fred: "The Rat and the goose"
Ferris, Thomas: "The Gun closet"
Findley, Timothy: "The Book of pins"
Gilboord, Margaret Gibson: "Ada"
Horwood, Harold: "Coming to an end"
McFadden, David: "The Pleasures of love"
Munro, Alice: "Home"
Sandman, John: "The Real Mrs. Hunter"
Thomas, Audrey: "Rapunzel"
Valgardson, W.D.: "Hunting"

Sixteen by twelve. John Metcalf, ed. Scarborough, Ont.: McGraw-Hill Ryerson, 1970. pb $3.35 [0-7700-3214-1]

A collection of stories by some of Canada's best writers, this volume does not attempt to provide a common thematic base. It offers instead a variety of subjects and styles allowing the reader to view the breadth of short story writing in Canada. Each selection is followed by a bibliography and by the author's brief comments on short story writing thus enhancing the book's usefulness as a text. A photograph and a short biographical sketch of each writer are also included.

Bowering, George: "Time and again"
Callaghan, Morley: "All the years of her life"; A Sick call"
Faessler, Shirley: "A Basket of apples"
Garner, Hugh: "The Yellow sweater"
Helwig, David: "One evening"
Hood, Hugh: "Getting to Williamstown"
Laurence, Margaret: "A Bird in the house"; "The Tomorrow-tamer"
Metcalf, John: "A Bag of cherries"; "The Estuary"
Munro, Alice: "Boys and girls"; "An Ounce of cure"
Nowlan, Alden: "The Girl who went to Mexico"
Richler, Mordecai: "Bambinger"
Smith, Ray: "Colours"

Stories from Atlantic Canada. Kent Thompson, ed. Toronto: Macmillan, 1973 cl $10.00 [0-7705-0974-6]; pb $2.50 [0-7705-0985-1]

There is nothing exclusively east coast about the nineteen generally excellent stories in this anthology because they reflect the diversity that Thompson sees in the Atlantic provinces. The stories range in time from

the work of T.C. Haliburton to that of Ray Smith.

Bartlett, Brian: "Jay's aviary"
Boston, Stephen: "The Rape of Maysie Weekend"
Brewster, Elizabeth: "It's easy to fall on the ice"
Bruce, Charles: "Young Richard 1864"
Buckler, Ernest: "Another man"
Gibbs, Robert: "I always knew there was a Lord"
Haliburton, Thomas Chandler: "Conversations at the River Philip"; "Mr. Slick's opinion of the British"
Harvor, Beth: "Pain was my portion"
MacLeod, Alistair: "The Boat"
Nowlan, Alden: "A Call in December"; "The Glass roses"
Pittman, Al: "Consommé and Coca Cola"
Porter, Helen: "The Plan"
Raddall, Thomas: "At the tide's turn"
Richards, David Adams: "The Fire"
Roberts, Charles G.D.: "The Winged scourge of the dark"
Smith, Ray: "Cape Breton is the thought-control centre of Canada"
Thompson, Kent: "Window on the revolution"

Stories from Ontario. Germaine Warkentin, ed. Toronto: Macmillan, 1974. cl $10.00 [0-7705-1068-X]; pb $2.95 [0-7705-1069-8]

This solid collection of stories set in Ontario is organized thematically. Bracketed by two stories whose central concern is rescue, the four chapters concentrate on wilderness or immigrant experience, human institutions, human relationships and man's historical sense of himself. The stories represent a variety of Ontario settings and historical periods. The underlying concern with place is often reflected in prominent architectural imagery.

Boissonneau, Alice: "The McCrimmons"
Callaghan, Morley: "Ancient lineage"; "Last spring they came over"
Clark, Gregory: "May your first love be your last"
Clarke, Austin: "They heard a ringing of bells"
Duncan, Sara Jeanette: "The Jordanville meeting"
Elliott, George: "The Way back"
Faessler, Shirley: "A Basket of apples"
Garner, Hugh: "One, two, three little Indians"
Godfrey, Dave: "Out in Chinguacousy"
Helwig, David: "In exile"
Hood, Hugh: "Where the myth touches us"

Knister, Raymond: "The Loading"
Leacock, Stephen. "The Marine excursion of the Knights of Pythias"
Moodie, Susanna: "On a journey to the woods"
Munro, Alice: "The Peace of Utrecht"; "Walker brothers cowboy"
O'Higgins, Harvey: "Sir Watson Tyler"
Reaney, James: "The Box-social"
Scott, Duncan Campbell: "Expiation"
Slater, Patrick: "Adrift"
Thomson, Edward William: "Great Godfrey's lament"

Stories from Pacific and Arctic Canada.
Andreas Schroeder and Rudy Wiebe, eds.
Toronto: Macmillan, 1974. cl $10.00
[0-7705-1144-9]; pb $2.95 [0-7705-1145-7]
These stories range from the humorous to the tragic. All reflect the area from which they come, both in setting and in the variety of experience on which they touch. Biographical notes on all authors are included.

Brunt, R.J.: "The Voice of the north"
Dienheim, Anthony: "Wolf tracks"
Grainger, M. Allerdale: "A Christmas story"
Harlow, Robert: "Carcajou"
Hindmarch, Gladys: "How it feels"
Hodgins, Jack: "After the season"
Horwood, Harold: "Men like summer snow"
Houston, James: "Walrus hunt"
London, Jack: "To build a fire"
Lowry, Malcolm: "The Bravest boat"
McWhirter, George: "The Extinction of 'H'"
Mallet, Thierry: "The Battle of the Drums"
Marriott, Anne: "On a Sunday afternoon"
Mitchell, Beverley: "Letter from Sakaye"
Payerle, George: "The Historian"
Perrault, E.G.: "The Cure"
Rule, Jane: "If there is no gate"
St. Pierre, Paul: "Chief Bill Scow" "A Depressing view from Cardiac Climb"; "Harry Boyle's Volkswagen"
Schroeder, Andreas: "The Roller rink"
Thomas, Audrey: "Kill day on the government wharf"
Virgo, Sean: "Haunt"
Wiebe, Rudy: "The Naming of Albert Johnson"
Wilson, Ethel: "The Window"
Yates, J. Michael: "The Sinking of the Northwest Passage"

Stories from Quebec. Philip Stratford, ed.
Toronto: Van Nostrand Reinhold, 1974.
cl $7.95 [0-442-27910-8]; pb $4.95
[0-442-29910-9].

This is a handsome edition of stories published mainly in the sixties; none has appeared previously in translation. Most of the twenty-eight stories are very short, demonstrating a compression uncommon in English-Canadian short story writing. The collection represents the work of eighteen writers and seventeen translators. Often humorous, the stories range from fantasy to social satire and from the simplicity of folk tale to the sophistication of linguistic experiment. The unfortunately erratic placement of accents is the only obvious flaw in Stratford's otherwise masterful edition.

Aquin, Hubert: "Back on April eleventh"
Bessette, Gérard: "The Mustard plaster"
Blais, Marie-Claire: "The New schoolmistress"
Carrier, Roch: "The Bird"; "The Ink"; "Creation"
Ducharme, Réjean: "The Wedding gown"
Ferron, Jacques: "Animal husbandry"; "Martine, continued"
Ferron, Madeleine: "Sugar heart"; "Be fruitful and multiply"
Fournier, Roger: "Jos-la-fiole"
Hertel, Françoise: "The Shipwreck"
Jasmin, Claude: "Pygmalion"; "Rosaire"
Major, André: "The Thief of Bonsecours Market"
Martin, Claire: "Follow me"; "Springtime"
Renaud, Jacques: "The Coat-rack"
Richard, Jean-Jules: "The 48 hour pass"
Tétreau, Jean: "The Great disappearing act"
Thériault, Yves: "Akua Nuten"
Tremblay, Michel: "The Hanged man"; "Mister Blank"; "The Thimble"
Vigneault, Gilles: "The Bus driver"; "The Buyer"; "The Wall"

Stories from western Canada. Rudy Wiebe, ed. Toronto: Macmillan, 1972. cl $10.00
[0-7705-0872-3]; pb $2.95 [0-7705-0850-6]
This welcome collection of short stories by western Canadian writers about western Canada displays a wide variation in subject; the time format, however, is mainly conventional, a phenomenon explained by Rudy Wiebe in his introduction. The stories are organized thematically and include sections on man and the land, family relationships and the people who inhabit the Prairies. All the best-known writers are represented in the collection which is made up of Wiebe's favourite stories rather than those usually anthologized.

Friesen, Victor Carl: "Old Mrs. Dirks"
Grove, F.P.: "The First day of an immigrant"
Kreisel, Henry: "The Broken Globe"
Kroetsch, Robert: "Earth moving"
Laurence, Margaret: "Horses of the night"
Livesay, Dorothy: "A Week in the country"
McCourt, Edward: "Cranes fly south"
Mitchell, Ken: "The Great electrical revolution"
Mitchell, W.O.: "Hercules salvage"
Niven, Frederick: "Indian woman"
O'Hagan, Howard: "The tepee"
Ross, Sinclair: "A Day with Pegasus"
Roy, Gabrielle: "The Move"
Scobie, Stephen: "Streak mosaic"
Stegner, Wallace: "Carrion spring"
Valgardson, W.D.: "Dominion Day"
Watson, Sheila: "The Black farm"
Watson, Wilfred: "The Lice"
Whyte, Jon: "Peter Pond, his true confession"
Wiebe, Rudy: "Did Jesus ever laugh?"
Wilson, Ethel: "A Visit to the frontier"

The Story so far. George Bowering, ed.
Toronto: Coach House Press, 1971. pb
$3.00 [0-88910-068-3]
This is a collection of twelve stories, chiefly
experimental in form, typography, and
language, published by an avant-garde
Toronto press. An amusing, original, and
often difficult series of explorations into
the potential of story-form, the anthology
contains excerpts from longer, mixed-genre
works, such as *The Collected works of Billy
the Kid*, by Michael Ondaatje, and *The
Book of hours*, by b p Nichol, and includes
plates and drawings by General Idea, an
eclectic group of illustrators.

Blaise, Clark: "Extractions and contractions"
Bowering, George: "Wild grapes and chlorine"
Hindmarch, Gladys: "How it feels"; "Other
men make the"
Kent, Valerie: "Polly wants a cracker"
McFadden, David: "Drapes"
Marlatt, Daphne: "Mokelumne hill"
Nichol, b p: "Story"
Nowlan, Alden: "At the edge of the woods"
Ondaatje, Michael: "The Barn"
Persky, Stan: "The Finger"
Smith, Ray: "The Galoshes"

The Story so far 2. Matt Cohen, ed. Toronto:
Coach House, 1973. pb $3.00 [0-88910-117-5]
These stories have been chosen to demon-
strate editor Cohen's claim that today's
short story "is sprung loose to be more
approximate to whatever realities the
writers perceive". A great variety of settings,
subjects and experimental styles appear,
ranging from the familiar voice and concerns of Margaret Atwood to the mock
Taoist parables of David Berry. One story
"Stolen moments", reflects the recent re-
vival of 1950s pop culture, but its elusive
collaborative narration and photo illustrations lift it into a genre of its own.

Atwood, Margaret: "Encounters with the
element man"
Berry, David: "From the Taoist parables"
Carlson, Chuck: "Petra Goggin's letter"
Charles, Barry: "Egotizm"
Cohen, Matt: "Spadina time"
Coleman, Victor (as Vic d'Or; with David
Young): "Stolen moments"
Collins, David: "Strategies"
Heath, Terrence: "Four Stories"
Kent, Valerie: "PoP PoP"
Lane, William: "The Cookie crumbles"
Nichol, b p:"Twins-a history"
Payerle, George: "The Dying"; "In winter—
in writing"
Rushton, Alfred: "Haynes, the machine,
and Maude"
Smith, Sharon: "Gertrude's ring"
Usukawa, Saeko: "One of a series"
Young, David: "Tom Tom's Sh-sh-shady
Bend's ol' geezer Easter special";
"Stolen moments" (with Victor Cole-
man)

The Story so far 3. David Young, ed.
Toronto: The Coach House Press, 1974.
pb $4.95 [0-88910-150-7]
Neither authors nor subjects of these highly
unconventional stories are necessarily Canadian, since the emphasis is on man's
fragmentary or distorted perception of the
world. The identifiably foreign authors included are: Fielding Dawson, Tom Robbins,
Tom Veitch, M. Vaughn-James, Noddy
McCoy, Keith Abbott, Wade Bell, Hubert
Selby, William S. Burroughs—they are listed here, but not indexed. The stories are
valuable as a counterweight to the themati-
cally-organized and realistic writing
prominent in Canadian fiction. Unfortunately, the indifference to consistent
quality has allowed less successful stories
to be included with the fine experimental
work of Fielding Dawson, George Bowering,
Terrence Heath, Daphne Marlatt, David
McFadden, Matt Cohen and William S.
Burroughs.

Abbott, Keith: "Hero pills"; "Bunting"
Bell, Wade: "Music for a wet afternoon"
Bowering, George: "Ebbe's Roman holiday"

Bronson, A.A.: "A Tale with no women"
Burroughs, William S.: "The Health officer"
Cohen, Matt: "Loose change"
Dawson, Fielding: "Quietly"; "Really";
  "Two stories from a mystery in process"
Gilbert, Gerry: "14 stories"
Harrison, A.S.A.: "A Walk in the park"
Heath, Terrence: "The Psalmist"
Hewko, Kati: "Dimitri"
Holden-Lawrence, Monica: "a biography"
McCaffery, Steve: "The Fall"
McCoy, Noddy: "Diving"
McFadden, David: "The Iroquois Hotel";
  "Free samples"; "Chance meeting in an
  elevator"
Marlatt, Daphne: "Winter moving just in-
  side the door"
Nichol, b p: "GORG"
Robbins, Tom: excerpt from *Another road-
  side attraction*
(R)rose, Barbara: "The Love bug"
Selby, Huber (Jr.): "Double feature"
Smith, Sharon: "A Night in Kap"
Vaughn-James, M.: "The Mole"
Veitch, Tom: "The Nazz"
Watters, Doug: three untitled pieces
Young, David: "Counting combinations";
  "The fact/fiction line"

**The Story-makers: a selection of modern
short stories.** Rudy Wiebe, ed. Toronto:
Macmillan, 1970. pb $1.95 [0-7705-0412-4]

The authors of these stories are of various
nationalities, including Canadian, and be-
long mostly to the twentieth century.
Collected to illustrate the various aspects of
story-making, the stories will be useful for
general English courses and for studies of
short story theory and practice. Wiebe's
introduction presents a thorough and entertaining outline of the different types and
techniques of the genre. Short biographical
notes are included. The following is a list of
the Canadian writers included:

Callaghan, Morley: "Rocking-chair"
Elliott, George: "The Commonplace"
Godfrey, Dave: "The Hard-headed collector"
Hébert, Anne: "The House on the Espla-
  nade"
Lowry, Malcolm: "Gin and goldenrod"
Munro, Alice: "Thanks for the ride"
Ross, Sinclair: "A Field of wheat"
Wiebe, Rudy: "Oolulik"
Wilson, Ethel: "On Nimpish Lake"

Tigers of the snow. James A. MacNeill and
Glen A. Sorestad, eds. Don Mills, Ont.:
Thomas Nelson, 1973. pb $2.75
[0-176-33043-7].

This selection of short stories from well-
known Canadian writers is enhanced by
photographs accompanying each one. The
stories are grouped under two headings:
"Man Alone" and "Man in Community".
MacNeill and Sorestad have attempted to
select pieces that have not been heavily
anthologized.

Bailey, Don: "A Few notes for Orpheus"
Bruce, Michael: "Gentlemen, your verdict"
Callaghan, Morley: "Two Fishermen"
Clutesi, George: "Ko-ishin-mit and Paw-
  qwin-mit"
Duncan, W.T.: "Journey home"
Fontaine, Robert: "Six beauties"
Garner, Hugh: "The Sound of hollyhocks"
Gotlieb, Phyllis: "A Grain of manhood"
Hood, Hugh: "After the sirens"
McCourt, Edward: "Dance for the devil"
McDougall, Colin: "The Firing squad"
Markoosie: "Two sisters"
Mowat, Farley: "The Last husky"
Nowlan, Alden: "The Fall of a city"
Ross, Dan: "Always a motive"
Ross, Sinclair: "The Painted door"
Schroeder, Andreas: "The Late man"
Wilson, Ethel: "We have to sit opposite"

Winnipeg Stories. Joan Parr, ed. Winnipeg:
Queenston House, 1974

These sixteen short stories are by writers
who live in or have lived in Winnipeg and
are mainly set in that city. They vary primarily in subject rather than in style or
theme. Nearly one-third deal with marriage,
often with a plot complicated by the intrusion of in-laws. Ethnicity and poverty are
also prominent. Most interesting in this
collection are the stories, such as those by
Mort Forer, Jim Burke and W.D. Valgardson,
that have unpredictable endings.

Burke, Jim: "Willie"
Duncan, Chester: "Up and down in the
  Depression"
Forer, Mort: "My uncle's black-iron arm"
Haas, Maara: "A Way out of the forest"
Kleiman, Edward: "Westward O pioneers!"
McRae, Garfield: "Millie, 'Ears', and the
  supreme test"
Maynard, Fredelle Bruser: "That sensual
  music"
Paluk, William: "Back door"
Parr, John: "White land, blue toe"
Robinson, C.R.: "Off the prairie"
Ryan, Patricia: "The Cardinal's levee"
Valgardson, W.D.: "The Baseball game"
Waddington, Miriam: "Summer at Lonely
  Beach"
Williams, David: "The Supper guest"
Williamson, David: "Courting in 1957"
Williamson, Rossa: "The Pink hat"

Short Story Author Index

Short Story Title Index

"Acceptance of their ways" Mavis Gallant
GCSS

"Ada". Margaret Gibson Gilboord 74NCS

"Adrift". Patrick Slater SFO

"After the season". Jack Hodgins SFPAC

"After the sirens". Hugh Hood K CV TS

"Agathe". Nora Keeling FSH

"Akua Nuten". Yves Thériault SFQ

"All the years of her life". Morley Callaghan
SBT

"Always a motive". Dan Ross TS

"Amaryllis". Marian Engel FSH

"Amazing grace". Matt Cohen 73NCS

"The American eagle". Thomas C. Haliburton BCP TCE

"The Amulet". Thomas Raddall ABCS

"Ancient lineage". Morley Callaghan SFO
TCC TCE CSS2

"Anguish of God". Yves Thériault GCSS

"Animal husbandry". Jacques Ferron SFQ

"Another man". Ernest Buckler SFAC

"Antigone". Sheila Watson TCC

"Apples". George Bowering FSH

"The Apricot story". Alice McConnell KI

"Aquarius". Audrey Thomas CV

"At the edge of the woods". Alden Nowlan
TSSF

"At the tide's turn". Thomas Raddall SFAC

"Back door". William Paluk WS

"Back on April eleventh". Hubert Aquin
SFQ

"The Bad Samaritan down at the railroad
station". Harry Bruce NV

"A Bag of cherries". John Metcalf SBT

"Bald eagle". Thomas Raddall TCC TCE

"Bambinger". Mordecai Richler SBT

"The Barn". Michael Ondaatje TSSF

"The Baseball game". W.D. Valgardson WS

"A Basket of apples". Shirley Faessler
SBT SFO

"Bass fishing on Lake Simcoe". Stephen
Leacock CL

"The Battle of the drums". Thierry Mallet
SFPAC

"A Bauble for Bernice". Don Bailey
72NCS

"Be fruitful and multiply". Madeleine
Ferron SFQ

"Because I am drunk". Kent Thompson NV

"Benny". Mordecai Richler ABCS

"Benny, the war in Europe and Myerson's
daughter Bella". Mordecai Richler CSS

"Bernadette" Mavis Gallant CSS2

"A Biography". Monica Holden-Lawrence
TSSF3

"The Bird". Roch Carrier SFQ

"A Bird in the house". Margaret Laurence
SBT CWT

"The Black farm". Sheila Watson SFWC

"Blind MacNair". Thomas Raddall CSS

"The Blizzard". Merna Summers 73NCS

"The Blue kimono". Morley Callaghan
ABCS

"The Boat". Alistair MacLeod SFAC

"The Boat". Desmond Pacey ABCS

"The Book of pins". Timothy Findley
74NCS

"Boots". Hugh Hood NV

"The Box social". James Reaney SFO

"Boys and girls". Alice Munro SBT

"The Bravest boat". Malcolm Lowry
SFPAC CSS

"A British Tory on the Canadians the
Americans and the savages". Frances
Brooke BCP

"The Broken globe". Henry Kreisel SFWC

"Brother and sister". Jane Rule 72NCS

"The Bully". James Reaney CSS

"The Bus driver" Gilles Vigneault SFQ

"The Buyer". Gilles Vigneault SFQ

"A Call in December". Alden Nowlan SFAC

"Canadian politics". Thomas C. Haliburton
BCP

"The Candidacy of Mr. Smith". Stephen
Leacock TCC TCE

"Cape Breton is the thought control centre
of Canada". Ray Smith SFAC

"Carcajou". Robert Harlow SFPAC

"The Cardinal's levee". Patricia Ryan WS

"Carrion spring". Wallace Stegner SFWC

"The Celebration". Mazo de la Roche MCS

"Chance meeting in an elevator". David
McFadden TSSF3

"The Cheat's remorse". Morley Callaghan
MCS

"Chief Bill Scow". Paul St. Pierre SFPAC

"The Children green and golden". John
Metcalf NV

"A Christmas story". M. Allerdale Grainger
SFPAC